Art & Reality

Art & Reality

John Anderson on Literature and Aesthetics

Edited by Janet Anderson, Graham Cullum and Kimon Lycos

This edition published in 2017 by Sydney University Press
First published in 1982 by Hale & Iremonger
© Sydney University Press 2017

Reproduction and Communication for other purposes
Except as permitted under the Act, no part of this edition may be reprodced, stored in a retrieval system, or communicated in any form or by any means without prior written permission. All requests for reproduction or communication should be made to Sydney University Press at the address below.

Sydney University Press
Fisher Library F03
The University of Sydney NSW 2006
AUSTRALIA
sup.info@sydney.edu.au
sydney.edu.au/sup

National Library of Australia Cataloguing-in-Publication Data

Creator:	Anderson, John, 1893–1962, author.
Title:	Art and reality : John Anderson on literature and aesthetics / John Anderson ; edited by Janet Anderson, Graham Cullum, Kimon Lycos.
ISBNs:	9781743325094 (paperback) 9781743325100 (ebook: epub)
	9781743325124 (ebook: PDF) 9781743325117 (ebook: Kindle)
Notes:	Includes bibliographical references and index.
Subjects:	Literature—Aesthetics.
	Literature—Philosophy.
	Art—Philosophy.
	Aesthetics.
Other Creators/ Contributors:	Anderson, Janet, editor.
	Cullum, Graham, editor.
	Lycos, Kimon, editor.
Dewey Number:	801.93

Cover images are public domain, sourced from Wikimedia Commons
Cover design by Miguel Yamin

Contents

Foreword		vii
Introduction		xi
1	Some Questions in Aesthetics	1
2	Biography	31
3	Classicism versus Romanticism	37
4	Romanticism and Classicism	43
5	Psycho-Analysis and Romanticism	51
6	The Comic	59
7	The Nature of Poetry	67
8	Poetry and Society	71
9	Art and Morality	77
10	*Ulysses*	91
11	The Banning of *Ulysses*	101
12	James Joyce	105
13	James Joyce: *Finnegans Wake*	115
14	*Exiles*	121

15	*The Applecart*	129
16	George Bernard Shaw	135
17	*The Perfect Wagnerite*	145
18	*Emperor and Galilean*	159
19	Kenneth Grahame	171
20	Kipling	179
21	George Meredith	189
22	*The Enormous Room*	201
23	H. G. Wells	209
24	Thomas Love Peacock	219
25	Herman Melville	231
26	Feodor Dostoevsky	241
27	R. H. Benson	257
28	The Detective Story	265
29	Orage and the *New Age* Circle	275
30	Music and Emotion	283
31	Art and Morals	289
32	Australian Culture	293
33	Literature and Life	297
34	Literary Criticism	301
35	Further Questions in Aesthetics: Beauty	307
Notes		315
Index		324

Foreword

People who read with any degree of thoughtfulness are concerned with the problem of how to evaluate the books that come into their hands; in particular, how to recognise when a book is really great and belongs to the great literature of the world. In these studies, Professor Anderson puts forward a theory of aesthetics, covering all art, but dealing especially with the art of literature. The theory is not fully worked out, as he himself acknowledges, and he mentions instances where he but points the way to further studies. Had he lived longer, he would doubtless have developed this theory more fully; as it is, the present work is mainly a breaking of the ground for the construction of a positive theory of aesthetics.

The studies fall into two groups: those that deal with various aspects of the theory, and those that are criticisms, in the light of that theory, of certain well-known authors. Each can be read quite independently of the others, for most were addresses given at widely different times: but they throw light on each other, and together make a consistent whole.

One other division can be made in the matter of the studies. Some are reprinted from various addresses and articles that Professor Anderson himself prepared for publication, but others have been constructed from his notes. Those who knew him know that he was of the opinion that an address given for the purpose of discussion was necessarily of a form different from that of an article prepared for publication. It seemed too formidable a task to achieve Professor Anderson's concentrated thought and terse prose; consequently, the studies have taken more the form of the addresses as they were given, and reports in the University of Sydney *Union Recorder* in particular have been heavily drawn upon. The given dates of the various addresses and articles are important, not only because they help the reader to understand references in the studies, but because they illustrate the consistency of Professor Anderson's aesthetics as he passed through various political phases. Needless to say, his philosophy provided a background for his aesthetics, and while the connection is interesting and informative, a lack of knowledge of his philosophy does not prevent readers from understanding his aesthetic theories.

It has been contended that a scientific, logical attitude to aesthetics makes for coldness — for lack of emotional understanding. Readers of his critical estimations of the work of Dostoevsky, Joyce, Melville and Kenneth Grahame will find no want of feeling in them, in spite of the logical approach. Nor does Professor Anderson insist that one can find interest in nothing but the best, although it must be admitted that since reading the work of Joyce, he found little in contemporary writing to hold his attention. In this connection, his own teaching and practice would contradict such an idealist position. He would have said, and did in fact say, that we like books for many different reasons. We may like them for the information they sometimes give us: we may like them because of certain characters portrayed in them: we may like them for the unfinished themes that intrigue us: we may even like them because we learn something from their very weaknesses. But these are personal or subjective judgements — not objective or aesthetic ones. In all art he would demand structure, and the important thing in literature, he has said, is the artistic presentation of states of mind.

Many people give a subjective interpretation to every work of art — to painting, to music, to sculpture, to architecture, as well as to literature. One of the most difficult of the arts to assess aesthetically is the art of portraiture. A dialogue from one of the short stories of Dorothy Sayers ('The Unsolved Puzzle of the Man with No Face') brings out something of the difficulty of an objective estimation of this type of work. The artist in the case is unwilling to sell a portrait (that Lord

Peter Wimsey wants to buy) on the grounds that it is not finished, that he himself is dissatisfied with it, that it is 'not altogether satisfactory as a likeness'. Lord Peter replies, 'What the devil does the likeness matter? I don't know what the late Plant looked like, and I don't care. As I look at the thing it's a damn fine bit of brushwork, and if you tinker about with it, you'll spoil it. You know that as well as I do. What's biting you?'

It seems here a question of technique — of a good use of the materials with which an artist has to work. But even so, in what way does a good use of the materials constitute a work of art — a portrait with such qualities as would induce an admirer of it to want to purchase it, though he has never seen the living subject that the artist has portrayed? Questions such as this are what any aesthetic theory has to answer, and though Professor Anderson does not deal with painting or music, sculpture or architecture as extensively as he does with literature in these studies, he supplies pointers to indicate along which lines a critic — or an appreciator — of art of any kind would be well advised to proceed.

He has been criticised and sometimes decried because he has left no 'magnum opus', only articles and lectures and addresses and notes — the latter often in pencil and now difficult to decipher. It is so even as regards philosophy with which literature shared so much of his mind. He once remarked that there was a time when he felt a great urge to answer Arnold Bennett's call (through the *New Age*, I think) to come to London and devote his life to literary criticism: but he chose philosophy. Yet he had time and taste to gain a wide knowledge and appreciation of music and painting, Mozart being his favourite composer and Cézanne his favourite painter. And he was very interested in politics. That he has produced no magnum opus of any kind may be due to the multiplicity of his interests, but I think it is due more to a kind of intellectual impatience. He did not wish to retrace his steps — he wanted to press on and on till his intellectual curiosity was satisfied. This trait was most evident at the time of his renunciation of Stalinism. When Eugene Lyons (*Assignment in Utopia*) and others were busy writing books to explain their apostasy, he was delving into Trotskyism and whatever books he could lay hands on to probe further into the theories of Communism. He worked his way through Trotskyism, always quite publicly, so that anyone might see, if he cared to look, thought (or criticism) in action. His final political position is somewhat hard to define, but I have often thought of him as one who had gone full circle and ended up (now consciously and politically) as he began — one of Gilbert's 'little Liberals'.

But even that may not be the full explanation. In her *Letters of Ruth Draper*, well-known monologuist Neilla Warren says that Ruth Draper did not write her sketches down till quite late in her career, 'refining them, tightening them, adding bits, discarding bits', and quotes Ruth Draper herself as saying: 'They change all the time. I should never be satisfied with a final written form.' And it is the case in the various courses Professor Anderson gave on any philosopher: no two were ever quite the same, and arguments arose among his students as to which was the best, or which was better than another. His work was never stereotyped.

Janet C. Anderson

Introduction

John Anderson's published views on aesthetics, on art and literature, are found in a few scattered articles and pamphlets in various publications not easily accessible to the general public. In addition to these, during the 1930s and 1940s he regularly addressed various societies at the University of Sydney and elsewhere on literary topics and themes. In bringing together in one volume Anderson's published and unpublished papers on these topics, we make accessible to a young generation of readers — those unacquainted with Anderson's views or to whom Anderson is only a legendary figure hovering over the intellectual history of the university — the views of a philosopher who exercised, from his acceptance of the Challis Chair in Philosophy in 1927 until his retirement in 1958, a remarkable influence over colleagues and students alike. More importantly, perhaps, the collection shows Anderson working through, in the case of novelists, dramatists and poets, the implications and ramifications of a realist position in aesthetics and literary criticism.

This collection of general theoretical papers and particular critical studies reveals Anderson's belief in the importance of art, aesthetics and criticism as essential parts of the intellectual life. At the same time it suggests how philosophy finds a challenge and an ally in great works of creative literature: how creative and analytic impulses interweave and inhabit a common world. Further, the essays in this collection provide an important example of Anderson's unique way of exploring a philosophical position in areas usually regarded by academic philosophers as falling outside their professional concern.

In this latter respect, readers who are not familiar with Anderson's general philosophical views and his characteristic method of argument may miss the overall temper and dialectic governing his intellectual endeavour. Each of the essays stands on its own and makes its own points as, indeed, do the philosophical essays in *Studies in Empirical Philosophy* (Angus & Robertson, Sydney, 1962). Yet Anderson had conceived of them becoming a book and they can be seen as a sustained and coherent contribution to his more general intellectual task.

This task was the exploration and defence of 'realism' in all areas of intellectual inquiry — in the central philosophical concerns of logic, metaphysics and epistemology as well as in the fields of social and ethical theory, aesthetics, and educational theory.

It is not our purpose in this introduction to give a detailed and comprehensive account of Anderson's philosophy as a whole. To do so would be out of place and, in any case, there are two excellent introductory essays which address this admirably.[1] Nevertheless, the systematic nature of Anderson's thought requires that some explanation be given of the connection between his essays on literature and art and his general position in aesthetics, as well as of the relation between these and his general philosophy.

What distinguishes Anderson from other philosophers, even from those who engage in system building, is his realisation that the conflict between realism and rival positions, as well as that between objectivism and subjectivism, is not confined to various recurring conflicts in the history of philosophy. Realism, and the forms of opposition to it, Anderson thought, are evident in the whole spectrum of intellectual endeavour: in philosophy as well as in politics, education, art and science.[2] As a realist and a philosopher Anderson clearly saw that to defend realism meant engaging critically the arguments and theories of its opponents. It also meant examining the spirit of various ways of thinking outside philosophy to reveal anti-realist tendencies.

This unifying concern to work out the implications of realism as an intellectual position gave Anderson a unique way of combining philosophy with other general intellectual concerns. This aspect of his thought brings him closer to some continental European philosophers than to many academic philosophers in the Anglo-Saxon tradition. The views and attitudes he exposed and criticised, though philosophers might articulate them more esoterically, are to be found embedded in ordinary ways of thinking and talking, in the utterances of political leaders and influential public figures, in the pronouncements of popular moralists, in the popularising ventures of scientists, educationalists and psychologists, in the comments of literary critics and artists, as well as in the creations of writers and artists.

In Anderson's hands philosophy became relevant to all intellectual issues. His pervasive influence on Sydney intellectual life of the 1930s and 1940s[3] was in no small measure due to the intensely passionate yet systematically relentless way he criticised opponents of realism in all spheres of inquiry. His critical commitment to realism prompted those who came into contact with him to recognise that their beliefs and attitudes were inescapably caught in an intellectual struggle between realism and its rivals. Faced with the power and range of Anderson's critical methods, many intellectual interests, whether they were in politics, art or education, were at once philosophised. Contact with his critical methods led to an intelligent and theoretical suspiciousness — a determination to enquire into the philosophical underpinning of popular views and traditional beliefs on a whole range of issues.

As well as acquainting readers with Anderson's critical and aesthetic views, these essays illustrate his unique way of exploring this general philosophical conflict in art and literature. The essays are not merely ancillary to *Studies in Empirical Philosophy*, and they are of more than historical interest. For one thing, subjectivist and relativistic tendencies in criticism and in attitudes towards literature and art (to go no further) are in the ascendant, and Anderson's uncompromising critique seems timely. Of particular relevance to our time is his exposure of the philistine element in much literary and artistic criticism. Further, the view that discourse about literature and art has its own 'practical' rules and procedures — that it is cut off from other more 'objective' discourse — still receives wide, unthinking acceptance. Anderson offers a powerful criticism of this view, and shows how genuine criticism requires both the application of general aesthetic principles and an awareness of relationships and discontinuities between literature and life: between art and nature.

It was one of his central contentions that a criticism divorced from general aesthetic principles was in danger either of becoming a collection of 'particular observations on particular works', or of promoting the confused doctrine that criticism is the art of aesthetic judgement rather than the investigation of aesthetic facts. Commenting on J. A. Passmore's deflationary view of aesthetics (in 'The Dreariness of Aesthetics', *Mind*, Vol. 60, 1951, and widely reprinted), Anderson points out that:

> To deny that there is a common subject-matter of the arts is not to deny that there are common aesthetic principles (principles of beauty), and, failing such a basis, there would be no ground for speaking of principles of literary *criticism* — there would only be particular observations on particular works, observations little if at all removed from the 'that reminds me' procedure. ['Literary Criticism']

This emphasis on common principles as a *sine qua non* of objective inquiry in any field is a strong feature of Anderson's philosophy as a whole. A brief account of the key tenets of Anderson's philosophy and of his method of argument might aid an understanding of some features of his views to be found in these essays. J. L. Mackie observes that it is a difficult task to abstract Anderson's doctrines from the intricate and subtle dialectic of his realist philosophy. Yet it is easy to sum up the salient features of that philosophy. For Anderson, as Mackie puts it,

> there is only one way of being, that of ordinary things in space and time, and ... every question is a simple issue of truth of falsity ... there are no different degrees or kinds of truth. His propositional view of reality implies that things are irreducibly complex, that we can never arrive at simple elements in any field. Anderson rejects systematically the notion of entities that are constituted, wholly or partly, by their relations: there can be no ideas or sensa whose nature it is to be known or perceived, no consciousness whose nature it is to know, no values whose nature it is to be ends or to direct action. Knowledge is a matter of finding what is objectively the case; all knowledge depends on observation and is fallible; we do not build up the knowledge of facts or laws out of any more immediate or more reliable items. Ethics is a study of the

qualities of human activities; there can be no science of what is right or obligatory, and the study of moral judgements would belong to sociology, not to ethics. Similarly aesthetics can only be a study of the characteristics of beautiful things, not a study of feelings or judgements and not a source of directives for artists. [See note 1, op. cit., p.265]

This indicates the philosophical background behind the characteristic moves Anderson makes when attacking anti-realist doctrines. Two such moves recur in his discussion of aesthetics and art. The first consists of detecting and revealing *relativism* — by which Anderson means the confusion of *things* (or qualities) with the *relations* such things or qualities enter into. The second move, which he often combines with the first, is to insist on objectivity — on attending to *what is the case.*

Insistence on objectivity is not merely Anderson's way of maintaining that there are objective facts to be discovered, or of pressing us to direct our attention to what is the case in the field of inquiry under discussion; his aim is to expose confused and misleading ways of talking and thinking, which he regarded as obstacles to the development of positive knowledge. For example, Anderson holds that in aesthetics there is no possibility of establishing a definite and coherent body of knowledge unless attention is directed to the actual objects of the discipline: beauty or the characteristics of beautiful things ('Some Questions in Aesthetics'). But, he argues, there are a number of ways of thinking about art objects — implicit in common ways of talking about painting, music and literature — that deflect our attention from the characteristics of beautiful things and direct it towards our attitudes to, or our judgement about, such things. To talk, for instance, about a work of art in terms of the feelings of pleasure or displeasure that it arouses in us, or to talk of a work in terms of its 'purpose' or 'meaning' — whether we have in mind the author's purpose or intention, or whether we refer to a 'purpose' or 'meaning' somehow inhering in the work itself — is to talk in a confused and misleading way. It is confused, Anderson claims, because it fails to distinguish between aesthetic facts and the appreciation of these facts. The feelings of aesthetic pleasure or displeasure are directed towards something; and we need to distinguish between a theory of such *feelings* and a theory of the *things* towards which such feelings are directed, the things that 'please'.

Anderson's insistence on objectivity here alerts us to the error of supposing that we have defined the qualities of a thing if we say it is aesthetically pleasing. In fact, all we have asserted is that the thing stands in a certain relation to us, namely, that of arousing feelings of pleasure. The crude yet widespread view that the beauty or excellence of a work of art is a 'matter of taste', or that it is a 'question of individual response', and the more sophisticated version of this view, that it is 'what expert critics and judges agree upon', betray this error. For one thing, consensus among critics cannot establish the truth of their judgements. For another, the claim that certain things please gives us no indication of their real natures. The questions 'Does work x please?' or 'Does x have aesthetic value?', and many common answers to them, misleadingly suggest that the real differences between what does and does not please are established by the mere assertion that certain things are pleasant or have aesthetic value.

It is at this stage of Anderson's dialectic that he reveals the confusion of relativism. He points out the danger of treating mere reflections of our attitudes or habits of judgement and responses as if they were features of the things themselves; the features in terms of which we differentiate aesthetically between things. Anderson views the error involved here as both deep and endemic in the history of thought; in metaphysics and epistemology, as well as — and perhaps more powerfully — in ethics and aesthetics. It is one thing to believe that there are real objects available for study. It is another thing altogether to suppose that our responses to or feelings about these objects constitute their natures. While our desires, feelings or aspirations might shape our perception — for Anderson a question in psychology — it is hardly the case that they govern the nature of things. However we may want things to be, and whether or not we can make them so, the fact remains that things are so or not. The question of whether they are so or not is obfuscated if it is not clearly separated from our desires and from utilitarian considerations.

Anderson's fundamental objection to what he calls 'relativism' is that if we specify something only by the relations it has to us or to other things, we know nothing about the thing itself. The fact that something is attractive to me does not logically imply anything intrinsic to that thing. To be able to use the fact of its attractiveness to me as an indication of something about it we would need independent

Introduction

information about the sorts of things that enter into this relation. Things that attract me and things that repel me or leave me indifferent must differ in their own character. But my being attracted, repelled or indifferent cannot be a criterion of what this character is, since, in order to explain the fact that something attracts me and repels you, we need to refer to the object's characteristics that enter into both these relations and, of course, we also need to refer to the characteristics of you and me. In this case, what leads to the error of relativism — to treating attractiveness or repulsion as a criterion of a thing's beauty or excellence — is the confusion of two distinct interests: the interest in discovering the real qualities of something is confused with the impulse to secure agreement or social uniformity of judgement on the matter.

Not only may this desire for agreement obstruct the discovery of what is the case, it may also lead to the conflation of how things are in themselves with how they affect us, or of how we might be impelled to commend or condemn them. It is such a confusion, Anderson thinks, that underlies the search for criteria of aesthetic goodness. The search for ways of telling whether a work of art or literature is good assumes that over and above the objective qualities of the work there is some mark or feature — its attractiveness, its aesthetic appeal, its 'significance' and so on — the apprehension of which constitutes the aesthetic experience of the work or its 'goodness'.

Though views differ widely as to what this mark of aesthetic excellence is, Anderson believes that they all involve the same misunderstanding of the subject-matter of aesthetics: they impede an inquiry into the characteristics of beautiful things by asking the confused question, 'What *makes* something beautiful?' The question seems to allow such answers as 'The fact that it pleases me', or 'It expresses aesthetic (spiritual, moral, political) values', or 'It secures the consensus of the critics'. But even though such answers might satisfy a questioner, little has been made clear. There are two distinct questions: both are factual, but Anderson contends that only one belongs to the science of aesthetics. The first question is 'What are the characteristics of beautiful things?'; and it is in terms of answers to this question, answers dealing with aesthetic facts, that the truth or falsehood of critical judgements about 'goodness' or 'badness' is to be assessed. The other question is 'Why do people make the critical judgements they do?

What determines the judgements critics make?' This is also a factual question, though not, he thinks, about aesthetic facts but about social or psychological facts. The objects of inquiry are different in the two cases, though in both cases we are dealing with issues of fact.

We see, then, how Anderson combines his insistence on objectivity with his exposure of relativism in attacking aesthetic views that perpetuate confusions. An important point of Anderson's dialectic should be noted here. He employs it against a whole variety of aesthetic views, not merely because, as a philosopher, he is concerned to expose inconsistencies and confusions of thought; he employs it primarily because he wanted to *free* a positive study of aesthetic facts from errors that arrest its development.

Nevertheless, the scope of his argument, as distinct from the spirit in which Anderson employed it, is such that it leaves open the possible reply that there are no real aesthetic facts and therefore there can be no genuine aesthetic inquiry; all we know, in this field, are objective facts about how people in general and critics in particular respond to works of art or nature. Of the two factual issues Anderson disentangles from the confusions of relativism, it might be claimed that only one, namely the one relating to the complex responses of appreciators of works of art and nature, is open to genuine inquiry. It might be said that there are no beautiful characteristics of things; there are only people valuing things in certain ways; and this is all there is to study in the field.

Anderson disagrees with this view, though he allows that one who maintained it could not be accused of inconsistency.[4] The dispute is possible because his attack on relativism can be seen as involving two theses, only *one* of which need be accepted. One might grant that if we could specify a thing only by its relations we would not know anything about the thing itself. But Anderson also wanted to argue that we do recognise and speak of beauty or goodness, and, therefore, that we must already have recognised aesthetic or ethical qualities. Now, there are no logically compelling reasons why we should accept this second thesis. Nevertheless, his view was that the removal of relativistic errors from such fields as ethics and aesthetics would *liberate* these fields and make possible a positive study of these qualities. In aesthetics this amounted to the investigation of the characteristics of beautiful things, and the development of a coherent set of principles of beauty.

Introduction

Anderson's insistence on objectivity forms part of his view of beauty; of his conception of a work of art; of the way he proceeds to characterise what is good or bad in art and literature; and of what he regards as sound or unsound criticism. Now, many readers on first encountering Anderson's use of such terms as 'beauty' and 'beautiful', of 'presentation' and 'representation', of 'classic' and 'romantic', may be disconcerted by the way his usage differs from usage currently prevailing among philosophers, critics and laymen alike. Again, a little explication might be useful.

Anderson treats beauty as an objective character of things, directly recognised in the way, say, that the redness of things is recognised. As in the parallel case of 'goodness' in ethics, the science of aesthetics is concerned with the investigation of the characteristics actually belonging to things recognised as beautiful. Although Anderson admits that the statement 'x is beautiful' has a usage expressing some form of commendation, he does not regard that particular usage as relevant to aesthetics. If there is such a science as aesthetics it can only be concerned with the characteristics of things recognised as beautiful, whether or not such things are also the subject of commendation or other attitudes. To say that something is in fact beautiful, according to Anderson, is to say something about what x is in itself, quite independently of our attitudes to x, and also independently of whether we recognise x to be beautiful.

To say that beauty is a quality like redness is to say that we directly recognise it, and that no question can arise about what is required for beauty. We can no more ask for *criteria* of beauty than we can ask for criteria of redness. The important point Anderson makes here is that there cannot be conditions of beauty. The parallel with redness is instructive. A physicist may investigate the conditions for the occurrence of things being red, but it would be a mistake, and a relativist one according to Anderson, to say what the physicist discovers are the conditions for redness. Doing so would be to treat 'that which produces the perception of redness' as if it were the same as redness. But, unless people directly recognise redness as a distinct character of things, the physicist's investigations into what accounted for things being red could not even begin.

The word 'red', according to Anderson, simply refers or directs us to the colour. To ask how we know that it does so, implies that there is something — an 'idea', an 'impression', an 'experience' — that tells us whether we are applying the word properly or not. Anderson's point here is that either the same problem arises with this 'intermediary' entity (how do we know we have recognised it correctly?) or our use of the word 'red' does indicate a colour, a quality of things that we directly recognise.

As with redness so with beauty: it is something we recognise directly in our interaction with things. And although we can ask what the conditions are for a work of art, a craft work, or something in nature being beautiful or not beautiful — a question in the science of aesthetics — we must not take this to be a question about the conditions of beauty itself.

What, then, are for Anderson the features of a beautiful thing? His answer in part echoes Stephen's view of aesthetic appreciation in Joyce's *A Portrait of the Artist as a Young Man*. Appreciation consists in the recognition of the wholeness, harmony and radiance of a thing; when it is apprehended as one thing, as a thing, and as the thing that it is.[5]

For Anderson, structuring is necessary if, for example, a work of art is going to present us with a thing as it is in itself and if it is to be a beautiful presentation of it. A subject must be 'seized', shaped and structured (for example, criminality in *Crime and Punishment*, loneliness in *Moby Dick*, exile in *Ulysses*, wrath in *The Iliad*), consciously or unconsciously, and everything in the work built up around it so that it hangs together. 'In all art, then,' he says:

> we find some kind of arrangement; in literature, an arrangement of situations among human beings; in music an arrangement of sounds in time; in painting and sculpture an arrangement of masses in space. But all these arrangements must go to make a single work if it is to be beautiful; it must not be simply a collection of bits and pieces. It must be built round some *theme* forming what I have called the structure of the work. ['Further Questions in Aesthetics']

Anderson is not saying that structure, that 'wholeness', 'harmony' and 'radiance', are what *constitute* a thing's beauty. That would lead to the unwelcome conclusion that everything is beautiful since everything has a structure. It would also, and more seriously, reduce his position to a relativist one by denying that beauty is a quality we directly recognise. For, if structure constituted a thing's beauty, then, logically, Anderson's position would be no different from the view that a thing's beauty consisted in its being pleasing, or in its expressing a feeling or an ideal. As we saw, for a realist aesthetics there can be no question of what a thing's beauty consists in, of 'criteria' or of guarantees of beauty. We simply discover or recognise that something is beautiful.

It is a further and distinct question — a question to which Anderson devotes much of his attention — of how to characterise what it is about a thing (work of art or a natural object) that permits or obstructs the apprehension of that thing's beauty, the aesthetic appreciation of that thing. Anderson's notion of a structure, like Joyce's marks of aesthetic appreciation, is meant to answer the question, 'What is it about something that permits, or does not permit, as the case may be, the aesthetic appreciation of it, the recognition of its beauty?' Quite clearly, this question can be asked of a work of art just as it can be asked of a craft work or a natural object such as a sunset or, even, an ulcer.

If we now ask 'And what is it about the presentation of a thing which makes *it* beautiful?', the answer, Anderson contends, will be in terms of the degree to which the presentation allows the appreciator to separate what is essential from what is inessential about the thing. For example, Dostoevsky's treatment of criminality allows us to see that, though there may be all sorts of social conditions for criminality, it is as a state of mind that we best understand its nature. Anderson says:

> We have, for instance, the presentation of A who is a man. A is exhibited *qua* man, and the more the 'whatness' (X or manhood) is brought out, the more beautiful aesthetically is the presentation of A. For A is many things besides a man; A falling on one's head, for example, is appreciated not as a man but as a mass; but the more we are impelled to say 'That's a man' (and not to say anything else) the more we are appreciating *manhood* in him — the more we find him to be *beautifully* human. ... Thus aesthetic contemplation might be considered as the finding in the instance A what is involved in xness (whatness) where A is also Y and Z, etc. ['Further Questions in Aesthetics']

Anderson, here, is evidently working out Joyce's three conditions for aesthetic appreciation — wholeness, harmony and radiance — emphasising that the third is the more important; that, indeed, it implies the other two. On this view, the artist will always be faced with the problem of revealing the 'essence' of something, the typical or characteristic, while dealing with particular situations and things.⁶ The good artist will have to avoid the twin pitfalls of extreme 'individuality' and of presenting 'ideal types' or 'natural kinds', while still permitting the appreciator to grasp the essential among the inessentials. And in order to avoid these pitfalls the artist will have to present A as having the wholeness and harmony of a certain sort of thing; as having the phases, order or structures involved in xness; even though A will be presented as having a number of other characteristics. Anderson points out, for example, that because we know such things as criminality, loneliness, estrangement and various features they may have in common,

> we can even recognise a thing of that sort without having the group of common characters presented *in their interrelation and balance* (in which case we have 'that sort of thing' incompletely presented). ... [Meredith's] *The Egoist*, was thrown out of balance by the fact that Meredith seemed to be concerned to make him the 'perfect egoist', the model of an egoist, and had not introduced the necessary 'repetition with variation' ... by presenting egoism as it would appear in Laetitia Dale and Clara Middleton, both of whom lay claim to being egoists. ['Further Questions in Aesthetics'; cf. also 'George Meredith']

In this case, thought Anderson, *The Egoist* compared unfavourably with the various aspects, or 'moments', of loneliness revealed in *Moby Dick*; of exile in the *Odyssey*; or of wrath in *The Iliad*.

It follows from Anderson's view that even though beauty is a quality we directly recognise, the full appreciation of the arts requires much learning and study. Equally, however,

> ... artists who are 'not for an age but for all time' have nothing to fear from an increase of knowledge. This is particularly obvious in the case of literature, since all the latest discoveries of psychoanalysis have but served to show how truly the great writers built their structures, and how the Greek dramatists take their place with Shakespeare,

Introduction

> Dostoevsky, Melville and Joyce in the examination and understanding of the human mind. ['Further Questions in Aesthetics']

Great art, it appears, presents knowledge in its own special way; yet that knowledge cannot be of a special or privileged kind. But the bad work of art — a work that is not beautiful — will be a work in which the enunciated theme is not set forth with clarity and distinctness. It may also be a work which, by subordinating the presentation of a theme to other purposes (such as to please, to titillate, to elevate, to morally instruct, to politically persuade), obstructs appreciation of that theme, whether the treatment of it in the work is genuine or merely pretended.

Anderson's opposition to what he regards as romanticism, his insistence that classicism informs the finest art, is based on the same general principles as his 'epistemology' of a bad or unrealised work of art. To the extent that a work confuses or muddies our appreciation of the thing it deals with, it is not beautiful: the various forms of romanticism in art are among the many ways in which such confusion is generated. Anderson does not have a historical definition of romanticism — he is not concerned to give a particular account of Romantic Poetry, although he does dismiss Wordsworth and Shelley without sustained argument. Rather, he uses the word 'romantic' to suggest a work that is incompletely formed and expressive of error. His sense of 'romantic', then, will bear comparison with that of another defender of the 'classic', Matthew Arnold, whose works Anderson often quotes, both here and in *Studies in Empirical Philosophy*.

Still, a question remains. Why does Anderson link the excellence of a work of art to beauty? If Anderson believes that when we talk of beauty we are indicating an objective character of things, either in works of art, craft works, or works of nature, it may appear odd to treat what is required for a good work of art as identical to that required for something being beautiful.

Anderson's analysis of weaknesses or kinds of badness in works of art is central to his aesthetics. It not only throws light on his attitude to the opposition between the classic and romantic approaches to art and criticism, it also underlies his critical method in discussing particular authors and literary works. Further, his analysis of a 'failed' or bad work of art has important links with his general philosophy, particularly his views on falsehood, and with the opposition he saw between an aesthetic attitude towards the world and the various practical, 'utilitarian' impulses that foster confusion and lead to a wrong understanding of art, science and philosophy.

Anderson's sense of the difference between artistic successes and failures is similar to his sense of what makes for true or false propositions. The good work of literature, while itself not asserting, is like a true assertion in that it presents directly the order and development of particular occurrences such as criminality, loneliness, wrath, alienation and so on. What distinguishes such works as good literature is their presentation of structures of psychological or human material as they actually are: affording the appreciator insights into their natures. In contrast, a bad work of literature, like a false assertion, necessitates reference to the mental state of an author.

It was Anderson's view that in asserting a proposition we asserted the facts, and not something — 'the proposition' — that was somehow between us and the facts. In asserting 'All men are mortal' we assert the actual mortality of men, rather than something that 'represents' the mortality of men (see 'Empiricism and Logic', *Studies in Empirical Philosophy*, p. 169). Consequently, Anderson thought, when we judge an assertion to be false we are claiming that something has occurred which has the character of a mistake.

The point needs some elaboration if its relevance to Anderson's view of artistic failure is to become clear. We may take Anderson's view of a true proposition to be that in asserting such a proposition the predicate (for example, 'being mortal') indicates what the structure of the subject (for example, 'being human') actually is. In contrast, when what we assert is false, the predicate indicates the structure of a subject other than the one it ostensibly deals with. This is so because all predicates indicate structures, and with a false assertion we are led to ask the question, 'of *which* subject does the predicate indicate the structure?' Anderson's answer is that since the subject as it really is (humanity or whatever) does not have the structure attributed to it, the structure indicated by the predicate characterises the subject *as conceived by some mind.*

Thus, if the false assertion is, for example, that 'All men are immortal', then, given that no man is immortal, the predicate 'immortal' indicates how someone *thinks* of men; it indicates the structure of a mental occurrence or fabrication. The analogy with a work of art lies in this. The work is a development of a theme and such development, like the predicate in an assertion, indicates the structure of the theme (the analogue of the subject in a proposition). When the work is a success, it presents us with the various phases of the development of a theme in its true nature. A failed work, however, presents us with a development that distorts or falsifies the actual phases of a theme. Like the predicate of a false assertion, therefore, a bad work of art presents us with the development of a theme not as it *is* in itself but as it is *conceived* or fabricated in the author's mind; it presents us with the phases of a fabrication.

Anderson's rejection of the treatment of works of art as 'representations' or 'imitations' of life or reality — which parallels his objection to regarding propositions as 'pictures' of facts — follows upon his view that a work presents us with the phases of a theme as it is structured. A work cannot be a passive image of what actually is; it cannot merely mirror a further thing or a 'significance' (see 'Some Questions in Aesthetics'). Rather, the great artist 'seizes' and shapes his structures and knowledge. Given this, the work is not to be regarded as an articulation of what an aspect of reality or life 'means', nor as an expression of the 'significance' or 'value' an author invests in his subjects. Anderson's sharp contrast between the literary character of a work and questions of representational effectiveness emerges clearly in his discussion of works where issues of verisimilitude or representation naturally arise, such as works of biography and historical novels. He points out that the accuracy of the factual or historical material contained in such works is quite independent of their qualities as works of literature. When we speak of a good biography we are making an aesthetic judgement because it is a 'presentation of the life as a structure — as a sequence of phases, such as we find in any drama or novel' ['Biography']. Similarly, a good historical novel is such apart from the fact that all its incidents actually happened and apart from the fact that it relates to a certain epoch. Its goodness depends on how well it works out a human theme. He says, whatever connection there may be between the two, good history is a treatment of a certain *social* complex, while a good novel or play deals with a *psychological* complex. ['Biography'; see also 'Literature and Life', and 'Emperor and Galilean']

Anderson's rejection of the 'representational' view of art, of the idea that there is something 'outside' or 'behind' a work which accounts for its aesthetic merit, again informs his attack on romantic literature and on a romantic approach to literature. Anderson often uses 'romantic' to refer to the view that literature has a single theme, 'life', or 'the meaning of life': the view that life has a single significance.

Correspondingly, although he grants that a literary critic is concerned with the meanings of words, he castigates as romantics those critics who take their task to be to 'interpret' or characterise *the* meaning of a work. His objection is that, given the diversity of human situations,

> the single theme of the romantics could not be presented but only symbolised ... the romantic 'meaning' [is] something we [are] unacquainted with apart from the 'slices of life' which [are] said to symbolise it, so that there is no standard by which the adequacy of the representation [can] be determined. ['Literature and Life']

Not having any standards by which to determine what is symbolised, the romantic critic has to fall back on the feelings of satisfaction or exaltation the work induces in him. From the classicist point of view, however, a romantic work is not a work of literature at all, or at least, is *bad* literature, since there are in it elements that interfere with its working out of a human theme in its own terms (cf. his account of Kipling and Chesterton).

Anderson's attack on romantic doctrines in aesthetics and literary criticism is closely bound up with his view that romantic elements in works of art are responsible for their badness. While he does not maintain that all bad works of art are 'romantic', he finds a close connection between the impulses leading to romantic interpretations of art and the features of some artistic failures. A bad work of art presents us with gaps and omissions, with disproportions and alien material, which detract from the presentation of a theme. What we find in a bad work of art, Anderson holds, is that

> the missing connections are to be found in the artist's associations, that, as in dreams, the superficial incoherence and incongruity are overcome if we discover what the various elements (including the relations and even the incongruity itself) 'mean' for the mind that has given them forth. And since this analysis reveals the artist's yearnings as of the same stuff as the romantic interpretation of art, we may, by a natural extension of the use of the term (though the distinction should always be kept clear), call the works themselves 'romantic'. ['Romanticism and Classicism']

In calling a work 'romantic', then, Anderson is engaged in reconstructing the phases of an artistic failure. In contrast, the romantic critic believes that by exhibiting the struggles and aspirations operating in the artist's mind he is accounting for artistic success. But we cannot remove the incoherence in a work, thinks Anderson, by invoking and 'reapplying' the artist's mind in this way. In referring to the artist's mind when he presents us with a bad work, the

> subject of our analysis is really a different one from that which [the artist] attempted. What we have done is to find 'in nature' a coherent structure of mental operation on available material; we have observed the phases of an artistic failure. ['Romanticism and Classicism']

To characterise a work as 'romantic' is to say more than that it is a failure; it is to say that the phases of a *particular* failure have been observed. In contrast, though to call a work 'classical' is to say that it is an artistic success, it is not to say anything about the phases of the construction of that success. The success of a work of art *is* its presenting us with the structure of a thing. Romantic art, in contrast, is more concerned with constructing, building up, a theme as it goes along, the end being more important than the beginning and the process of creation more important still.

Even if the artist's striving may appeal to our own romantic aspirations, Anderson held, it is no merit in an artist that his *effort* is seen when we look at or read his work. Indeed, to the extent that this occurs we are confronted with something analogous to Freudian dream interpretation — the structure of the 'dream-work' — where we observe the phases of the *struggle* of a wish or an impulse to gain access to consciousness, rather than being presented with the wished-for object as it is in itself.

> It is, indeed, only from the point of view of classicism that appreciation of nature can be put on the same footing as appreciation of art, since, in the latter case, the work of art is distinguished from the operations of the artist and judged on its own merits. In like manner, we consider the truth of a scientific theory in terms of the propositions put forward, and independently of who has proposed them or how he came to do so; and thus we erect no barrier between actual truth and 'theoretical' truths. But error is another matter, one in which a mind is involved. The recognition of error presents us with the problem of determining *truly* how certain mental processes have interacted with their surroundings so as to be mistaken about them. So aesthetic disproportion, a bad work of art, raises the problem of its maker, of the person who 'dreamed' it and how he came to do so, of the structure of his valuations. But aesthetic harmony in itself raises no such problem, even when it is a person that has produced it. It could be held to do so only at the cost of a romanticising of all nature and the denial of all real distinctions. ['Romanticism and Classicism']

Anderson's defence of what he regards as classicism in art and literature has close ties with Joyce's work in general and, more particularly, the latter's aesthetic theory as it emerges in *A Portrait of the Artist as a Young Man*. Joyce has Stephen Dedalus say,

> Aristotle has not defined pity and terror; I have. ... Pity is the feeling which arrests the mind in the presence of whatsoever is grave and constant in human sufferings and unites it with the human sufferer. Terror is the feeling which arrests the mind in the presence of whatsoever is grave and constant in human sufferings and unites it with the secret cause. ... The tragic emotion, in fact, is a face looking two ways, towards terror and towards pity, both of which are phases of it. You see I use the word *arrest*. I mean that the tragic emotion is static. Or rather the dramatic emotion is. The feelings excited by improper

art are kinetic, desire or loathing. Desire urges us to possess, to go to something; loathing urges us to abandon, to go from something. The arts which excite them, pornographical or didactic, are therefore improper arts. The esthetic emotion (I used the general term) is therefore static. The mind is arrested and raised above desire and loathing.[7]

The classical attitude regards the work of literature as something that presents us with a theme in its order and development, and judges it in accordance with what we already know about the theme. The romantic critic, in contrast, regards the work as part of the author's spiritual striving or as the realisation of 'ideals'; he is not satisfied with what is presented and is always trying to see something beyond, some meaning or purpose or significance which the work intimates or expresses. So while classicism judges a work according to its structure — that is, according to whether it succeeds or fails in working out a theme, independently of the author's or the appreciator's feelings or values — the romantic looks at the work as part of an adventure into the realm of values in which the work, the author and the appreciator are fused.

The prevalence of romanticism in our literary schools leads to the blurring of all aesthetic distinctions; not only is the substance of the literary work itself presented in the guise of adventure in the realm of values, but it is merged with the artist's spiritual adventure in creating it, and the task of the appreciator in his turn is to let himself become charged with the same values. ['Romanticism and Classicism']

Anderson admires Joyce not only because the latter exhibits a thorough classicism in his works, but also because he sees Joyce's large works as essays in the theory of art as well as being art themselves.[8] Joyce's work 'not merely does what art does but shows what art does' ('Art and Morality'). Although rejecting the doctrine of 'art for art's sake', Anderson finds in Joyce the theme that genuine art promotes an aesthetic outlook on life in contrast to the practical and 'utilitarian' concerns which infect our ordinary lives.

Utility insists on conditions and consequences; its sharp distinction of means and ends is bound up with hierarchy, with the master-servant relationship. But for art all things are on an equality; they are all alike aesthetic material; in any of them *character* can be discovered. Art, in other words, is concerned not with what things are 'for' or what they are 'by means of but with what they are. And this is hard to find just because of utility, because in human life things become cluttered up with meanings and purposes. It is this which gives point to the description of the painter as restoring 'the innocence of the eye', breaking up conventional associations; and in the same way the literary artist can be described as restoring the innocence of our sense of humanity, as against adventitious commendations and condemnations. On this basis, too, we can see that the artist is supremely productive or creative — in fundamental opposition to the 'consumer's view'. That is to say, the good artist; for all arts can degenerate, and the bad artist is the supreme purveyor of consolation, the most efficient caterer to the consumptive or servile mentality. ['Art and Morality'; see also 'Further Questions in Aesthetics']

Anderson also finds in Joyce the related theme — a theme prominent in Anderson's social and ethical theory — of genuine art as a liberator from illusions. Anderson's view of freedom and the conditions of its existence and emergence is closely linked to the artist's predicament as presented by Joyce. This emerges clearly in the essays collected here. It is by recognising the binding character of imposed values, by seeing through the various illusions that *are* the bonds, that one comes to understand the task of liberation, the release from servitude, as one of learning to recognise what is the case about the world, society, and minds; learning, therefore, both that liberation will be opposed and also why and how that opposition takes place.

Here we can glimpse Anderson's belief that freedom and the commitment to the world as aesthetic phenomenon go along with, 'cooperate' with, the commitment to inquiry as independent of purposes, higher aims, and unifying ends or meanings. The recognition of the complexity and multiform character of minds, society and nature, and the concern to confront things as they are — this is the Homeric vision, the foundation of the spirit of classical thought and culture. That is the ideal of a classicism which 'stands for the unity of culture against all forms of subjectivism and interestedness, and for the unity, the common principles, of criticism against specialism and *ad hoc* devices ...' (*Studies in Empirical Philosophy*, p. 202). It is a vision that has been attained by few philosophers or literary critics.

At the beginning of the collection we have brought together those papers that address general aesthetic questions (1–9). These are followed by the papers on Joyce and Shaw (10–17), throughout which Anderson pursues and considers related questions in aesthetics and criticism. Papers 18 to 29 are simply arranged in chronological order. Items 30 to 34 are summaries of addresses taken from the University of Sydney *Union Recorder*. Anderson usually wrote, or vetted, these summaries for publication to guarantee their accuracy. Unfortunately, no further or fuller notes for these items appear to have survived in his literary papers. The addresses were, perhaps, given extempore, but the reports are cogent and extend our knowledge of Anderson's thinking about art and aesthetics. The final item (35) is a set of undated notes from various lectures and discussions which Anderson clearly meant to work into an article.

In a footnote on the first page of each paper we indicate its source, date of delivery (where appropriate) or provenance. Ten of the pieces (1, 4, 5, 6, 9, 10, 11, 12, 17, 29) were published by Anderson. The rest (excluding items 8 and 30 to 34) are reconstructions from, and edited versions of, drafts, suggestions and proposals, notes and marginalia from his literary papers. Mrs J. C. Anderson contributed the bulk of the labour here. Without her patience, skill and determination the collection would not have seen the light of day. As well, we are grateful to A. J. Anderson for his encouragement and generous advice concerning aspects of his father's work; T. A. Rose for comments on an early draft of this Introduction; Catriona McKenzie for invaluable research assistance; and Chris Falzon for help with the reading of proofs.

Where necessary, we have provided editorial notes. These are numbered by chapter, and placed at the end of the book. We have tried to keep them to a minimum. Anderson's own footnotes have been retained as footnotes, and are indicated in the text by symbols (* and †).

Graham Cullum
Kimon Lycos

John Anderson, c. 1960, upon his retirement from the Challis Chair of Philosophy at the University of Sydney.

– 1 –
Some Questions in Aesthetics

It is a condition of progress in aesthetics, of the establishment of a definite and coherent body of aesthetic knowledge, that attention should be directed to the actual subject of the science — beauty, or the characteristics of beautiful things. But professedly aesthetic discussions have been so taken up with other questions (even though these have a certain connection with the subject-matter of aesthetics) that it becomes necessary to approach the subject by clearing away the confusions thus fostered, and by showing that prevailing views imply the possibility of a theory of beauty, but do not provide it.

This is clearly the case with appeals to 'aesthetic feeling' or 'the aesthetic judgement', and with other forms of confusion between aesthetic facts and appreciation of these facts. Now, with regard to the aesthetic judgement (as in the allied case of the moral judgement), the point to be noted is that something is judged to be a fact, some proposition is asserted to be true, and it is this proposition, and not the fact that someone believes it, that is the matter for discussion. And whether such aesthetic assertions are true or false, they indicate a region of fact in which discoveries may be made. Similarly, the 'feeling of aesthetic pleasure' is directed towards something; and, though there might be a theory of such feelings, it would be distinct from the theory

Published by the University of Sydney Literary Society, 1932.

of the things which 'please'. It is, indeed, the commonest error in aesthetics to say that we are discussing these things when we say that they are 'pleasing', i.e., that they stimulate some feeling in us. These errors are summed up in the view that beauty is a 'matter of taste', which implies that there can be no aesthetic science at all.

The theory of the aesthetic as the pleasing can, however, be easily refuted. Things which please us and things which do not please us must differ qualitatively or in their own character; and that our pleasure is not a criterion of their quality is further indicated by the fact that things which please some people displease others. Attempts are made to meet this difficulty (as with the corresponding difficulty in 'subjectivist' ethics) by setting up as a standard the consensus of opinion or the opinion of 'good judges'. But, as regards the former, there can be consensus of opinion only if each person holds that opinion, and that means that he finds something to be the case, not that he finds a consensus. In fact, consensus could be an argument only to someone who held the opposite opinion, and in that case there would not be consensus; and, no matter how many people did agree with him, he would require them to show him the facts which proved him wrong.

In the same way, the opinion of 'good judges' provides no criterion. To say that a man judges well is to say that what he asserts is true; and it is this truth, and not his asserting it, that is the 'standard'.[1] Again, to recognise anyone as a good judge we ourselves must know some of the facts; we must see that what he says turns out to be true, i.e., we also must judge correctly. And, even if we profess to follow his judgement, that means that we now pass the same judgement, i.e., find the same proposition to be true. Thus, any sort of reference to opinions involves the raising of issues of fact. If, then, there are aesthetic opinions, it is the facts in question that form the field of aesthetic science.

A further objection to the treatment of the aesthetic as the pleasing is that pleasing is an ambiguous term. People like things for many different reasons, and in many different ways. A man can like a picture, he can wish to possess or continue contemplating it, because of a sentimental attachment — because, for example, it portrays or reminds him of scenes of his childhood. The admiration for and saleability of *le nu*, like the discovery of 'beauty' in the opposite sex, are based for the most part on likings of a quite unaesthetic character. In fact, if

1 Some Questions in Aesthetics

aesthetics is to be distinguished from economics, if the pleasing is to be other than the desired or demanded, it has to be qualified as the *aesthetically* pleasing, i.e., that which, having found it to have a certain aesthetic character, we want to own or to look at. But the assertion of *its having this character* is distinct from our wants in the matter, and is clearly the thing to be discussed in aesthetic science.

The characters of aesthetic objects, then, are quite distinct from our attitudes to them, including our recognition of them. It may, incidentally, be the case that a certain training is required for aesthetic knowledge, and that some persons are specially fitted for critical work on the subject. But this training and this work will take the form of a direct consideration of beautiful things, and not of our attitudes to them. It is just through the confusion of these different matters that it is possible to hold that mental attitudes are the actual objects of appreciation. A notable example of this position is the theory of *expressionism*, according to which the work of art expresses or embodies its creator's mentality when he created it; the psychic configuration of the creative state is supposed to be put into the material, and, in order to appreciate what the artist has done, we, in turn, it is contended, have to get into the same frame of mind. Thus, according to the expressionist, the same complex of feelings is to be found in the artist, in the work of art, and in the appreciator. In point of fact, however, we do not find feelings actually present in a picture or a piece of music; and since the expressionists have to admit the distinction between the artist's activity and the thing produced, as well as the fact that we attribute aesthetic characters to the latter, their doctrine is seen to be untenable.

Expressionism also fails to account for the recognition of beauty in nature as well as in art. An attempt may be made to evade this difficulty by considering 'works of nature' as God's handiwork, as in the conception of science as 'thinking God's thoughts after him'; or the more general idealistic position may be adopted of regarding all things as spiritual, so that appreciation will consist in finding their 'spiritual meaning', whether this has already been meant by a creative artist or not. But, just as science is misconceived in the above way, since the question for the scientist is to discover what is true, no matter who else has thought it, so the question for the aesthetician is the character of certain things and not how they have been produced or what underlies them. Undoubtedly, mental activity may itself be the thing considered; a certain 'spirit' may be the aesthetic *material*, but, still, its characters and anyone's appreciating its characters will be different things. On the idealist view, however, there would be no such thing as a work of art, but only a certain spirit appreciating or 'enjoying' itself; there would be no aesthetic propositions and no such thing as the 'displeasing' — but there are. Thus, while feelings may be the materials of a work of art, and while it may always be feelings that appreciate art or beauty in general, the doctrine of expressionism cannot even account for these facts and must be rejected.

We see, then, that the two questions, what happens when a person admires a work of art or regards it as 'good' and what happens when an artist produces a work of art, are, however interesting they may be in themselves, quite distinct from the aesthetic question of when a work *is* 'good' or, more generally, when a thing is beautiful. The conception of the artist's activity as characterising the product is an instance of the common confusion between origin and character, between what a thing is and what it arose from. In this connection we find such unaesthetic descriptions of a work as that it is 'well done', the point being that, if it is 'well', the fact that it is 'done' is irrelevant; or that it is 'original', i.e., that it differs from other things through having a different origin, the real question being in what respects it does differ and not how that came about. The demand that a work should be original, that it should 'bear the marks of its origin' in an originative mind, is thus quite off the track of aesthetic criticism. Everything is originated somehow, and nothing bears the marks of its origin; the marks themselves, that is to say, cannot tell us how it was originated, but only separate experience can do so; yet it is with these marks, with the character of the works themselves, that we are concerned. Nevertheless, supposedly aesthetic discussions are largely taken up with the origin of works as well as with their effects (e.g., in giving us 'pleasure').

One good example of this is the interpretation of works of art (and particularly of literature, where this method of estimation would be easiest, if it were possible at all) in terms of their social origin and effects. It is maintained, because art is a social product and a social agent, that aesthetic judgements have a social content; but clearly the

1 Some Questions in Aesthetics

fact that the things judged have social conditions does not in the least prove that they themselves are social in character. Thus the statement of Panferov (quoted in an article on 'Soviet Literature' by Z. Lvovsky; translated by Isabel Renfree; *Stream*, Sept., 1931) on the attitude of the Soviet writers may indicate how they come to write and what they expect their works to accomplish, but it gives no characterisation of the works themselves.

> Unlike bourgeois authors, we are not concerned with an impassive contemplation of life; we enter into the game, we devote ourselves to the construction and organisation of the new world. ... What is a Soviet writer? We must define him once and for all. He is primarily a practitioner. But he is at the same time a theorist who, before commencing his work of art, makes a long and careful study of economics and Marxism, the indispensable bulwark of all proletarian creative art.

We may consider it possible that such works as Panferov's *Brousski*, the theme of which, he tells us, is that 'incalculable natural wealth is lost because of an unpardonable ignorance', should assist the carrying out of the Soviet Government's policy; we can readily believe that they are devised by people who think that they are acting as practitioners and Marxists. But even if these books did 'help on the good work', this would not enable us to judge them good. Recognising that a work of art has effects, we may recommend it because it advances a certain form of social organisation; but this recommendation is not a description of the work itself, and is not to be confused with a recommendation of the work because it is good. The desire to increase the circulation of good literature is, of course, also a social attitude; but the judgement of a book and the recommendation of it on the basis of that judgement are different things. Literary theory consists, in fact, not of recommendations and condemnations, these being social attitudes which have many different sources, but of a consideration of certain characters of the books themselves.

The same may be said of the study of any art. Artistic production is a social activity, affecting and affected by other social activities, and possibly forming part of a social movement, but it is not on that account the case that the works have a social character and are to be estimated in terms of that character. If it were, the study of all the arts would coalesce in social study. And, in exactly the same way, since scientific investigation is a social activity, the study of any science would be study of society. This is simply false. The study of mathematics for example, develops under social conditions, and has social consequences; but the question for the mathematical student is not what has caused or what will result from the formulation of a mathematical proposition, but whether the proposition is true. So the question for the student of aesthetics is whether a book or a picture is good; and how the artist came to produce his work or what he hopes to achieve by doing so (as Panferov says he produced the third volume of *Brousski* from a consideration of the problem of 'how to utilise our peat-bogs'), has nothing to do with its aesthetic character, though it may be quite an interesting question for the student of society.

A similar position arises in connection with the fact that artistic production and scientific investigation are *mental* activities. It would be clearly fallacious to argue on this ground that study of any art and of any science is psychological study, though, again, interesting questions for the psychologist could be raised in the consideration of how the artist or the scientist came to produce his works or his theory. Thus Ernest Jones, in his *Essays in Applied Psycho-Analysis*, endeavours to show that certain of the characteristics of the painting of Andrea del Sarto were due to his attitude to his wife and particularly to his taking up a *feminine* attitude in love. But this psychological view depends on a *prior* recognition of outstanding characters of the paintings themselves (as Jones, indeed, appears to admit), and the statement, 'This is the kind of painting a man dominated by his wife would produce' is not an aesthetic proposition.

In the work of many psycho-analysts, however, it seems to be assumed that an account of the psychical origin of art, of what makes artists produce, is an account of the works themselves. Thus Otto Rank remarks (*The Trauma of Birth*, p. 166), 'The highest idealisation of the birth trauma attained in plastic art is, in compassion-arousing tragedy, resolved once again into the malleable primal element of the anxiety affect, capable of outlet, whereas in epic and satiric poetry the too highly strung idealisation breaks out as boastful untruthfulness.'

1 Some Questions in Aesthetics

This is expressionism, the treatment of art as what it means to its creator, what it is in his soul, with some reference to what it arouses in other souls. But no theory of this kind can stand up to the fact that much that we recognise as beautiful in art or in nature is not in any soul, and that the sort of thing which is said to enable us to be untruthful or to feel compassion differs *in itself* from that of which this cannot be said.

When the theory of the social interpretation of art is worked out in any detail, it also is seen to be expressionist. Trotsky (*Literature and Revolution*, p. 169)[2] considers that controversy about 'pure art' and art with a tendency is unbecoming to Marxists.

> Keeping on the plane of scientific investigation, Marxism seeks with the same assurance the social roots of the 'pure' as well as of the tendencious art. It does not at all 'incriminate' a poet with the thoughts and feelings which he expresses, but raises questions of a much more profound significance, namely, to which order of feelings does a given artistic work correspond in all its peculiarities? What are the social conditions of these thoughts and feelings? What place do they occupy in the historic development of a society and of a class? And, further, what literary heritage has entered into the elaboration of the new form? Under the influence of what historic impulse have the new complexes of feelings and thoughts broken through the shell which divides them from the sphere of poetic consciousness? The investigation may become complicated, detailed or individual, but its fundamental idea will be that of the subsidiary role which art plays in the social process.

But, whatever historical influences have affected the development of art, this has nothing at all to do with the doctrine of 'pure art', if this means the assertion of an independent science of aesthetics. And Trotsky's argument indicates not merely that the social interpretation of aesthetics is open to the same logical objections as the psychological interpretation, but that it has to use the latter as an intermediate link, arguing from art to feelings and from feelings to classes, as if psychological as well as aesthetic questions could not be discussed in entire independence of social movements.

Trotsky does admit (p. 178) that

> it is unquestionably true that the need for art is not created by economic conditions. But neither is the need for food created by economic conditions. On the contrary, the need for food and warmth creates economics. It is very true that one cannot always go by the principles of Marxism in deciding whether to reject or to accept a work of art. A work of art should, in the first place, be judged by its own law, that is, by the law of art. But Marxism alone can explain why or how a given tendency in art has originated in a given period of history; in other words, who it was who made a demand for such an artistic form and not for another, and why.

Now it may be that the social forces dominant in a given period will occasion the appearance of certain artistic tendencies; it is clear, at least, that they affect the development of such tendencies, once they have been originated. But when it is admitted that there can be judgement of works of art independently of social history (and otherwise, as Trotsky himself indicates, what we call 'art' would be merely a branch of commerce), it is implied not merely that there are works good and bad in themselves, but that there is an independent *interest* in good work — an interest which, however slight its social effects may be and however it may be affected by other interests and social conditions, is not 'subsidiary' to anything.

The view that 'art is always a social servant and historically utilitarian' is thus simply false. As we have noted, artistic production may advance a certain form of social organisation, but it is not this fact that makes it 'artistic'. If we are primarily interested in society, then we may consider artistic tendencies as they affect or enter into social movements. But we may just as well, in discussing social movements, consider whether they encourage or oppose artistic production and enjoyment, and it may actually be considerations of this kind that lead in particular cases to the taking up of an attitude of support or opposition to a certain social movement. If, for example, we take the view of Sorel that the working-class movement is a movement of *producers* and conclude that it will advance artistic production and aesthetic appreciation, and if at the same time we consider that these

1 Some Questions in Aesthetics

things are hampered by the existing commercial civilisation, then these will be important social conclusions and may also be incentives to action. This line of approach will, at least, give us a clearer view of society and of art than is possible along the lines suggested by Panferov. But it depends on the possibility of an independent aesthetic, a theory of beauty apart from any consideration of its 'utility'.

The theory of art as exhibiting beauty, then, has nothing to do with its origin and effects; and it is in this sense that the formula, 'Art for Art's sake', should be understood. It is misunderstood as an account of the motives of the artist — though, even so, it has been shown that, unless there is an interest in beauty itself, there cannot be aesthetic views or intentions, whatever commerce there may be in *objets d'art*. This misunderstanding is shown in the question put to Aldous Huxley ('An Hour with Aldous Huxley', by F. Lefevre; translated by F. Quaine; *Stream*, July, 1931), whether, in face of existing social dangers, 'English writers remain at the phase of Art for Art's sake, or, on the contrary, do they think they have something to say? For yourself, what is your position? In *Point Counter Point* you seem to give a sympathetic presentation of Illidge, the red-headed forerunner' — and in Huxley's answer, 'Art for Art's sake is difficult to practise today. Many write to say something about the world. Spandrell, one of my heroes, is in some degree a rendering of the story of Baudelaire.' It would certainly be difficult to find an artist who was devoted wholly to art, who had nothing but an aesthetic purpose. An artist may be stimulated by an interest in Baudelaire or by an interest in horse-racing. He has to choose some theme, and this is not an aesthetic choice, since no theme is more aesthetic than any other. But the criticism of the work when it is done is in terms of its own character and not of the artist's interests or intentions.

'Art for Art's sake', then, is not a doctrine to be 'practised', a demand that the artist should do his work *for artistic purposes*; he might do it to make a living or simply because he 'felt like it', without its artistic 'purity' being in any way affected. The demand is for a clearing of the aesthetic ground, for the recognition of goodness in a work because of its structure and not 'because it advances social organisation' or 'because it says something about the world' — even if the artist wanted to say something about the world. It is not necessary that an artist should appreciate his own work. A certain appreciation is involved in his stopping when he does; he would appear to be saying that his theme is now worked out. But, of course, artists are sometimes mistaken about this; we find them failing to develop a theme completely, or, again, introducing matter which does not belong to the subject — not knowing, in fact, when to stop and when to go on. And, apart from such criticisms, an artist may be unable to indicate the leading characteristics and stages of his own work. We should be surprised, indeed, to find an artist to be as good a judge even of his own work as a man who devotes himself to criticism; it is perhaps especially his own work that the artist would be attached to for unaesthetic reasons (because he had 'put so much into it', and so forth), reasons which he could easily confuse with aesthetic reasons — a position exemplified in Ibsen's preference of *Emperor and Galilean* to his other works. In the same way, we do not expect a critic to be a good artist — at least, in the art he is criticising; his merit should be in the art of criticism, for, of course, a good criticism, like any good work of art, must have construction.

The point is illustrated by Henry James in *The Middle Years*, when he contrasts Tennyson's failure in appreciation or, at any rate, in appreciative *rendering* of 'Locksley Hall' with Browning's presentation of some of his own poems. Tennyson

> lowered the whole pitch, that of expression, that of interpretation above all; I heard him, in cool surprise, take even more out of his verse than he had put in, and so bring me back to the point I had immediately and privately made, the point that he wasn't Tennysonian. ... My critical reaction hadn't in the least invalidated our great man's being a Bard — it had in fact made him and left him more a Bard than ever; it had only settled to my perception as not before what a Bard might and mightn't be. ... On two or three occasions of the aftertime I was to hear Browning read out certain of his finest pages, and this exactly with all the exhibition of point and authority, the expressive particularisation so to speak, that I had missed on the part of the Laureate; an observation through which the author of *Men and Women* appeared, in spite of the beauty and force of his demonstration, as little as possible a Bard. He particularised if ever

1 Some Questions in Aesthetics

a man did, was heterogeneous and profane, composed of pieces and patches that betrayed some creak of joints, and addicted to the excursions from which these were brought home; so that he had to *prove* himself a poet, almost against all presumptions, and with all the assurance and all the character he could use.

To grasp this contrast, we need not accept James's conception of a 'Bard'; we need not suppose that a great artist cannot be a great appreciator or expositor, any more than we need accept Arnold Bennett's contention (in *Books and Persons*) that creative artists are the best appreciators. The main point is that the two activities are distinct, and that a certain 'blind creativeness' is possible. Thus, an artist's mentality is not in question in a judgement of his work, and what slogans he may adopt, what movements he belongs to, are matters of no aesthetic importance.

The aesthetic irrelevance of considerations of effect, as of origin, can be illustrated from Huxley's remarks (in the same interview) on Joyce.

> I greatly admire his talent, but his researches are barren — they end in a cul-de-sac: very interesting, but a cul-de-sac, just the same. This meticulous labour, this unheard-of torture of language, in which each word has four or five meanings, is nothing short of fantastic. It all touches on black magic. The objections that can be made to *surrealisme* apply to *Ulysses*. To attack art fired with the determination to cut every bridge with the public seems truly paradoxical. It is an untenable position: so much so that, if the surrealists begin to write in earnest, they abandon their theories.

There are two serious confusions here. First, Huxley implies that the value of a work of art is connected with its ability to reach the public. But appreciation requires training, and we find that the best work is not widely appreciated, and that the most popular work is utterly bad. The question of public appeal, then, is a purely commercial one, and to say that *Ulysses* does not reach many people is in no way an 'objection' to it. Secondly, the statement that Joyce's researches are 'barren' is also unaesthetic, if it means that, to do valuable work, he would have to lead the way somewhere. The possibility of his having followers does not affect our judgement of *Ulysses* itself. If, on the other hand, Huxley merely means that Joyce's preliminary work does not lead to the construction of a good novel, he should refer directly to the defects of his writings (presumably the reference is mainly to the published fragments of the 'Work in Progress') and not talk in a roundabout way of their being produced by methods which do not produce good work. In either case, the notion of 'fruitfulness' merely confuses the aesthetic issues.

The two sets of considerations, then, the motives and mode of working of the artist and the effects and appeal of the finished work, are irrelevant to the discussion of its character. The formula, 'Art for Art's sake', would be absurd if it demanded that an artist should work simply for art's sake and that people should like works simply for art's sake. These things do not commonly happen; and all that can be demanded is that a consideration of the works as art should be a consideration of their aesthetic character. This is a condition of there being a science of aesthetics; relativism, the confusion of a thing with its relations or things related to it (causes, effects, and the like), is an obstacle to any science. For aesthetics, then, we must find a thing beautiful 'for its own sake', i.e., *as it is*.

Rejecting in this way all forms of expressionism and relativism, we must refuse to take as the basis of judgement of a work the feelings or intentions or reactions of either producer or 'consumer'; we must deny that either 'puts feelings into it' and that it expresses a social or a spiritual purpose or outlook. But, while denying that feelings and, in particular, the artist's feelings are the substance or 'content' of a work of art, we can still admit that a study of the mental operations of the artist is worth undertaking for itself, and that it may even direct our attention to characters of the work, and also that certain works of art do have feelings as their subject-matter.

The last point is particularly important for the clearing up of confusions in aesthetics. If, in fact, aesthetic material may be either human or non-human, the aesthetic question will simply be whether the material is developed properly; an analysis of the subject, a presentation of its structure, will be what we look for in a work of art. Thus, in the case of a human subject, we shall be concerned with an emotional structure, and, in the case of a non-human subject, with a structure into which feelings do not enter at all. According to Croce, however, all art is of a *lyric* character,[3] because it is always 'the epic and drama of the feelings'; thus there is only one aesthetic material, which, incidentally, is identified with the artistic attitude. But the very existence of the term 'lyric' shows that a distinction is made between works whose substance is personal feelings and works in other material; and we cannot at once make that distinction and pass it over.

In fact, if we take the arts seriously, we cannot say that they are simply different forms of expression of the one material, because this difference would be entirely irrelevant to the *really* artistic material; and, of course, we should be quite unable to show how the same thing could be 'expressed' in many ways, the supposed distinction of form being actually a distinction of *content*. Thus the distinction between music and painting is a distinction of materials, and if we say that they both 'mean' feelings because they can stimulate and arise from emotional processes, we shall have to say that everything means feelings — that feelings, in fact, are the only aesthetic subject because they are the only existing subject, and there will simply be no such thing as music or painting or any other alleged externalisation. The doctrine of meaning not only leads logically to the denial of all forms of art but, as it stands, is opposed to aesthetic theory, since theory must deal with what things are and not with what they 'mean' — and we could as well ask what feelings mean in terms of something else (say, triangles) as ask what musical sounds mean in terms of feelings.

The refutation of the theory of aesthetic meaning is made at once more complicated and more necessary by the special way in which considerations of *representation* enter into certain of the arts, viz., painting and literature. In the case of a painting we are confronted with a coloured surface, and this surface makes us think of a three-dimensional structure (a landscape, e.g.) with which we are not in the same sense confronted. Hence the surface is said to represent the solid structure, and appreciation of painting is taken to be appreciation of success or skill in this sort of representation. But, besides this, the painter commonly does his work in the presence of a three-dimensional scene, the flat projection of which he utilises in his picture, and thus the goodness of the work comes to be regarded as lying in the *likeness* of the scene it makes us imagine to the scene with which the painter was confronted. So literature, in which by means of words we are made to think of certain events (human actions, e.g., in plays and novels), is said to be good in so far as it is *like life*, though not, as in the case of painting, any particular bit of life, the verbal portrayal of which would commonly be regarded as history and not as aesthetic.

Now, in the first place, we see that in connection with painting two quite different notions of representation arise, viz., representation of a solid by a surface, and representation by this solid of another solid, the scene 'portrayed'. As regards the former, we may certainly take as a mark of skill in painting, success in achieving solidity, in actually making us see a solid which is to be appreciated; but our 'appreciation' of the skill of the painter is not appreciation in the same sense and has nothing to do with aesthetic consideration of the picture. If he fails to present us with a solid, or if we know that the solid he presents us with is other than the one he intended to present, we say he is an unskilful painter; but the question of the aesthetic character of his work has still to be raised. A writer may be similarly unskilful in the use of words, but criticism of his skill is not the same as criticism of the work of art, viz., *what the words mean*. There is, of course, also a possibility in such cases of failure on our part, either in that we do not recognise beauty when it is put before us, or in that *we* are unskilled in passing from surfaces or words to solids or events described. In either case, a certain training or aptitude is required, but the two questions are distinct — the former is an aesthetic question, the latter is not. Aesthetically, then, we are brought back to the consideration of certain presented or imagined material, the solid scene or the actions meant.

If we now try to introduce representation in the second sense, we are faced with a fundamental inconsistency in our aesthetics. We cannot consistently say that in music or sculpture we appreciate a certain arrangement of sounds or shapes, representing nothing, and that in painting or literature we appreciate the *likeness* of an arrangement of coloured solids or of actions to a certain 'real' landscape or to a general subject, 'life' — so that the question is of the reproduction of 'a bit of real life'. What we appreciate cannot in the one case be a character of the structures themselves and in the other case a relation of likeness between different structures, or, again, the ease with which presented material leads us to imagine other material. If we insist on representational

1 Some Questions in Aesthetics

appreciation, then we shall have to find out also what music and sculpture 'represent', and so with all the arts.

Sculptors, it must be admitted, commonly work with the human form, but 'non-representational' sculpture also meets with appreciation. Moreover, certain pieces of sculpture are praised as giving 'idealisations' of the human form, which can only mean as presenting us with something better, something the merit of which lies in the fact that it does not 'reproduce life'. Again, we have 'artificial' *groupings* of figures (as in the *Laocoon*), even if each is 'lifelike', and the artificiality is not taken as a defect. It is still more obvious that in architecture we are presented with structures, the appreciation of which has nothing to do with their resemblance to anything else. Elements in the structure are, no doubt, suggested to the architect by other things, but, in asking whether it is good architecture, we do not concern ourselves with the question of what suggested it. Musical sounds, again, may be like sounds the composer has heard 'in nature', but there is no more question of the beauty in the music residing in this likeness than of the beauty (if we find any) in the 'natural' sounds residing in their likeness to further sounds. The admitted fact of resemblance between works of art and other things, and the fact that artists introduce in their work various things of which they have had experience, are quite insufficient to enable us to attach any meaning to the question, regarding any aesthetic object, 'What is represented here?'

The only way, then, in which representational appreciation could be maintained, since it would have to apply to the whole field of aesthetics, would be by reverting to expressionism and making the appreciated object stand for certain feelings. But this would mean that it was *not* the appreciated object, that it was a mere means to the reinstatement, or simply to the installation, of certain emotional structures which were 'enjoyed' in and by themselves. Even then, however, the aesthetic question, the question of distinguishing (as we do distinguish) between the aesthetically good and bad, would still have to be raised. Thus we find Croce remarking (in *Breviario di Estetica*; quoted by E. F. Carritt, *Philosophies of Beauty*, p. 242) that

> what we admire in genuine works of art is the perfect imaginative form in which a state of mind clothes itself; that is what we call the life, the

unity, the fulness, the consistency of a work of art. What offends us in false and faulty work is the unresolved discord of different moods, their mere superimposition or confusion or their alternation, which gets but a superficial unity forced upon it by the author, who for this purpose makes use of some abstract idea or plan or of some unaesthetic passion. ...

Leaving aside the question of 'unaesthetic' passions, we see that Croce, in admitting that we may be offended by faulty work, is admitting the distinction between appreciator and appreciated, and the fact that the former finds certain characters (of 'discord' or of 'consistency') in the latter.

It is thus implied that the aesthetic question is whether the things *have* these characters, that beauty resides in the structure of such things and not in skilful evocation of feeling or in enjoyment of feeling. And we shall certainly not suppose that such characters are found only in feeling or in mentality, unless we take the idealist view (which is itself founded on a relativism similar to that which we have considered) that all things are mental; and even the idealists have to distinguish phases or levels of mentality and to recognise structure *at all levels*. We note, moreover, as a minor point in the argument, that, in terms of representation of the expressionist variety, the question of 'likeness to life' in certain of the arts no longer arises. But the main point is that the treatment of aesthetic objects in terms of their relations, resembling, expressing, or what not, is a mere obstacle to aesthetic science.

Representationism in art, the judgement of the work by its likeness to 'life' or the attempt of the artist to secure such likeness, is sometimes called 'realism', but the realist position has nothing to do with likeness. The realist aesthetician demands that a work of art should have a real theme and that the theme should be properly worked out, i.e., in its real stages or phases. A bad work, on this view, exhibits heterogeneity or absence of a single theme (as is suggested by Croce) and disconnection. Gaps in the structure have to be bridged over or concealed, and this is frequently done (notably in some of Kipling's stories) by the introduction of the occult or supernatural, in other words, by saying that the thing is done, without doing it. Failure in construction can, of course, be recognised just as we recognise a gap or fallacious transition

1 Some Questions in Aesthetics

in an argument. Material is inserted which does not belong to the theme, and instead of having a structure we have a fabrication. This incongruity appears also on the side of appreciation, in the notion, e.g., of *einfühlung* (allied to expressionism), of reading feelings into the presented material. Thus we have both romantic or sentimental criticism and romantic or sentimental works, where the author has produced a patchwork by what he has 'felt into' his material.

The realist position, in opposition to romanticism or idealism, is forcibly stated by Shaw (in the Preface to *Plays Pleasant*).

> Idealism, which is only a flattering name for romance in politics and morals, is as obnoxious to me as romance in ethics or religion. In spite of a Liberal Revolution or two, I can no longer be satisfied with fictitious morals and fictitious good conduct, shedding fictitious glory on robbery, starvation, disease, crime, drink, war, cruelty, cupidity, and all the other commonplaces of civilisation which drive men to the theatre in order to make foolish pretences that such things are progress, science, morals, religion, patriotism, imperial supremacy, national greatness, and all the other names the newspapers call them. ... To me the tragedy and comedy of life lie in the consequences, sometimes terrible, sometimes ludicrous, of our persistent attempts to found our institutions on the ideals suggested to our imaginations by our half-satisfied passions, instead of on a genuinely scientific natural history. And with that hint as to what I am driving at, I withdraw and ring up the curtain.

Shaw, that is, demands that drama (and the same will apply to any other art) should be natural and historical, that it should present real themes in their actual order. This position is not weakened by Shaw's own lapses into romanticism; and it is not opposed to the presentation of *human beings labouring under illusions*, as drama constantly does. Rather, as Shaw indicates, it supports presentation of such natural conditions. But to present the illusory or 'idealised' itself, to make out that there is a 'stuff of fancy' which can be the content of a fanciful art, that there can be appropriately fantastic presentation of a fantastic theme, is to say that we can appreciate the building up of something which has no recognisable structure, or the concatenation of elements, the order of which can be varied as we fancy, and which can, therefore, never make a finished work. Aesthetic realism, then, is not a form of representationism; it merely asserts that to have definite order a thing must be definite — so that we can never say that in a certain work 'the supernatural' is artistically or consecutively presented, for there is *no* supernatural, whatever feelings of awe and eeriness people may have. We can, therefore, aesthetically condemn the fanciful or fabricated, even though, like a dream, it may reveal something as to its author, and, in any case, 'means' something to him or satisfies certain of his urges. So, whatever analysis or translation is possible in the case of dreams, there is fabrication in criticism of works of art, when they are found to symbolise some spiritual entity or ideal, and especially the spiritual state or strivings of the artist.

The conditions of the study of the mentality of the artist and of his work of production should now be clearer; and, in particular, it should be clear that this is not a part of aesthetics, however it may be connected with aesthetic matters. Expressionist and similar confusions, then, have to be removed from current views of the nature of the artist's procedure. Joyce's formula (*Ulysses*) of 'the eternal affirmation of the spirit of man in literature' may be taken to refer to that main part of literature which deals with human material, and in that case there is at least a suggestion of the false view that the theme presented, or 'affirmed', in works with human material is always the same, viz., humanity or the human spirit — a view akin to the romanticist assumption that the theme of all art is 'Life' or spirit in general. The formula may mean, however, that the literary artist *affirms his (human) spirit* in producing his work — and here no distinction should be made among the arts, for, even when what is affirmed and what affirms are both human activities, they are distinct, and the literary artist, though he may quite properly get his material, or some of it, out of himself, is not thereby 'expressing' himself or his spirit.

If the formula is not to be taken as expressionist, then, it must be that the artist, in producing his work, is asserting himself against obstacles, and, in view of the theme (dissociation or sundering from self) of *Ulysses*, these might be taken to be inner obstacles. It is suggested, that is to say, that conflict is a condition of artistic work, and that the work enables the conflict to be overcome. This is not, of course, an aesthetic characterisation of the work. But it may be held that the building up of the work out of diverse materials, the bringing into a single structure of apparently conflicting phases, *corresponds* to the overcoming of the artist's inner conflict; i.e., not that it 'represents' the latter, but that it takes place *when* the latter takes place, and that, as the latter is a solution of the artist's problem, so the work is a solution of the problem presented by its theme. Thus the artist would solve his own mental problem, or disentangle a certain complication in his mind, in solving the aesthetic problem, i.e., in finding the structure of the subject. This would give a certain aesthetic characterisation of the work, viz., that it is a solution or is articulated. But how far a connection could be established between the stages in an artist's work and the phases in the product is another matter, and one with which we should not, as appreciators, be concerned, since we are confronted with the work of art and not with the proceedings of the artist.

To say, then, that a work is produced by the overcoming of a conflict in the author's mind and, if we take that view, that the conflict is strongest when he is dealing with human material, is not to say that we can discuss the work in terms of the author's personality — not even if the material is taken from his personality. For example, Joyce may present his emotions in his poems, but we appreciate them as emotions, not as belonging to Joyce more than to anyone else, and not as matters in which we 'sympathise' with Joyce. It may be contended that when he writes, in 'I hear an army', of the heart's despair, he could not have done so unless he had despaired, and that we could not appreciate the work unless we also had done so — though this suggests an idealistic confusion between *knowing* feelings and *having* them, and might at least be questioned. But in any case the subject is despair, and, whatever the writer or a reader may feel, it is not his despair but despair as such that is in question. If the opposite view be taken, there can be no aesthetic discussion. Nevertheless, it is still possible that appreciation as well as creation solves inner conflicts.

The conception of art as overcoming conflicts is also put forward by Shaw. In *Candida* he presents Eugene Marchbanks as possessing the poetic temperament — as when, in making a bid for Candida, he offers 'my weakness, my desolation, my heart's need'. And this, it is suggested (when Candida turns to her husband as 'the weaker of the two'), is really his strength; he is creative because he does not demand 'happiness', i.e., the spurious solution of a problem by covering it up, or consolation which is really defeat (the notion of art as a solace, as lifting us out of the hurly-burly and enabling us to forget, is touched on by Shaw in *Misalliance*), but tries to work things out in their own terms. He brings out the characters (the hidden conflicts) of persons and things, and thus creates the drama, because he is not afraid to expose himself. As Norwood puts it (*Euripides and Shaw*, pp. 103-4), Eugene's power is

> that of a naked soul, whose weapon is an indifference to the ready grin of the crowd at the man who does not hide his feelings. Through this power he reveals the real woman behind Miss Garnett's brassy respectability, the inmost soul of the superficially benevolent Candida, the unsuspected weakness of Morell the clergyman.

The description of the function of the artist as *exposure* may be taken as simply a way of stating the aesthetic fact of exposition or presentation of a theme, though there is a certain romantic suggestion of bringing out the underlying essence of things. Romanticism appears more definitely in the theory of art propounded in *The Dark Lady of the Sonnets* — where Shaw, however, may be merely indicating what he takes to be the romanticism of Shakespeare.

> *The Man:* ... But though you spake with the tongues of angels, as indeed you do, yet know that I am the king of words —
>
> *The Lady:* A king, ha!
>
> *The Man:* No less. We are poor things, we men and women —
>
> *The Lady:* Dare you call me woman?
>
> *The Man:* What nobler name can I tender you? How else can I love you? Yet you may well shrink from the name; have I not said we are but poor things? Yet there is a power that can redeem us.
>
> *The Lady:* Gramercy for your sermon, sir. I hope I know my duty.
>
> *The Man:* This is no sermon, but the living truth. The power I speak of is the power of immortal poesy. For know that vile

> as this world is, and worms as we are, you have but to invest all this vileness with a magical garment of words to transfigure us and uplift our souls till earth flowers into a million heavens.

In the theory of the artist overcoming his inner conflict by producing works of art, there is nothing to affect their aesthetic independence. But in this conception of art as spiritually uplifting, as overcoming what is vile in life, there is definite aesthetic confusion. Vileness is not presented as vileness, but is poetically transfigured; art gives *redemption* from vileness. In other words, art is conceived functionally or representationally, just as in the conception of it as a solace. The point is further illustrated in a later passage in the play.

> *The Dark Lady:* Ay, I am as like to be saved as thou that believest naught save some black magic of words and verses — I say, madam, as I am a living woman I came here to break with him for ever. Oh, madam, if you would know what misery is, listen to this man that is more than man and less at the same time. He will tie you down to anatomise your very soul: he will wring tears of blood from your humiliation; and then he will heal the wound with flatteries that no woman can resist.

Indeed, art, on this showing, would be an 'art of flattery'; a consolation by magic, by rising above sordidness instead of compromising with it and seeking comfort, but on the same logical footing as the latter as a form of 'salvation'. It is implied not merely that, in solving aesthetic problems, we solve our inner conflicts, but that the two are the same; and thus in the attempt to discover 'the function of art in life', the aesthetic issues are confused. Nevertheless, there is a psychical conflict between the attitudes of seizing and evading, and a social conflict between art and comfort. And not only is a certain kind of mentality required for the seizing (not 'transfiguring') of things, but this fact may be brought out in the structure of a work itself, as it is notably in Joyce's 'I hear an army'.

Joyce's poems, in fact, serve admirably to illustrate the question of works whose content is feelings. We see at once that the theory of the lyrical character of art, as involving the identity of creative urge and artistic product, is not true even of the lyric. In his poems generally Joyce may be said to adopt the attitude of the young lover, but this is really to say that he presents it, and whether or not he is a young lover is not relevant to our appreciation, e.g., of the poem 'Alone' (*Pomes Penyeach*):

> The moon's greygolden meshes make
> All night a veil,
> The shorelamps in the sleeping lake
> Laburnum tendrils trail.
>
> The sly reeds whisper to the night
> A name — her name —
> And all my soul is a delight,
> A swoon of shame.

What is here presented is the mingled shame and delight, the veiled intensity of feeling, of the young lover — his joy breaking through his false calm, as 'her name' breaks through the verse. So in the two poems which follow, 'A Memory of the Players in a Mirror at Midnight' and 'Bahnhofstrasse', we are presented with loss of love or of youthful love — or, at least, with certain aspects of that theme, which may be said to be the general theme of *Pomes Penyeach* — and, again, our appreciation is not of whether the author has lost love or youthfulness, or whether we have, but solely of the presented subject. In the earlier volume, *Chamber Music*, likewise, the poems form a series, treating of successive phases of the theme, young love — though each phase may itself be considered a theme and the poems separately appreciated — and culminating in the loss of love ('My love, my love, my love, why have you left me alone?') which becomes the theme of the later volume. It is as they work out their themes that the poems are to be appreciated, and not in respect of how Joyce came to compose them or of what they reveal about his personality.

1 Some Questions in Aesthetics

H.S Gorman's criticism of *Chamber Music* (in *James Joyce: His First Forty Years*) is of this unaesthetic kind.

> A.E., when he first read Joyce's poetry remarked (according to Padraic Colum), 'I don't know whether you are a fountain or a cistern.' The reason for his remark is patent when one goes through *Chamber Music*. They are frankly Elizabethan lyrics, composed in a Herrick-like fashion, and following a long-established tradition in the most deliberate manner. As far as these poems are concerned Joyce was a cistern. He held beautifully what he had imbibed but he brought little that was new to it. An occasional turn of thought, a brief flare, an unusual moment or two toward the end of the small volume, is all that we find of Joyce's personality in these verses.

And again,

> Joyce, it is rumoured, took his poetry seriously, speaking of it in an arrogant manner and comparing himself to the Elizabethans. No more indelible proof of his careful refusal to be swallowed up in the vast pool of the Celtic Renascence is needed. ... Such an attitude ... suggested a mental freedom, at any rate, that might not be guessed if we note but the bare fact that Joyce was imitating the Elizabethan song-birds.

This criticism by reference to periods and movements comes very close to the style of the 'that reminds me' school, critics who will talk about anything except the matter in hand — a point which comes out still more clearly in Gorman's reference to the Celtic character of the last two poems, particularly when 'we are reminded for an instant of Yeats' "Hosting of the Sidhe" with "Niamh tossing her burning hair"'; apparently by the line 'They come shaking in triumph their long, green hair' — and does not at all bring out the character of the work. We can hardly say that there are Elizabethan themes, and, if we say that there is an Elizabethan manner of treatment, we are falling back on the theory of fancy, of an arbitrary though 'pleasing' order. Joyce may quite well have been influenced by the Elizabethans, but a consideration of the poet's education still leaves the poetry to be considered.

The same applies to the question of Joyce's personality, which, Gorman says, is rarely evident in the book, but of which certain manifestations are present. 'A certain meticulous finish, a rare and restrained impulse that betrays Joyce as the solitary resident of his own Ivory Tower, a slightly arrogant aloofness, these are the things that suggest the poet as being (at least intellectually) haughtily self-concerned.' If this means that arrogant aloofness is part of the subject-matter, we have to consider how it is worked out, and not whether Joyce was arrogantly aloof. If he was, he might still have failed to present that theme. And if the poet is one who is able to present his solitariness or his haughty self-concern, it still has to be appreciated in its own character and not as his.

Gorman is right in finding in the last two poems a change in the kind of mood presented, though, as has been suggested, they are the culmination of the general theme. In the earlier poems we are presented with phases of youthful love, but it is hard to observe anything 'Elizabethan' in such an example as the fifth of the series.

> Lean out of the window,
>   Goldenhair,
> I heard you singing
>   A merry air.
>
> My book is closed;
>   I read no more,
> Watching the fire dance
>   On the floor.
>
> I have left my book,
>   I have left my room,
> For I heard you singing
>   Through the gloom.
>
> Singing and singing
>   A merry air.
> Lean out of the window,
>   Goldenhair.

1 Some Questions in Aesthetics

In the last poems of the series there is a transition to loss of love, the second last, treating not directly of love but of a mood of the lover, being preliminary to the last, in which this final phase of the theme comes out definitely.

> All day I hear the noise of waters
>   Making moan,
> Sad as the sea-bird is, when going
>   Forth alone,
> He hears the winds cry to the waters'
>   Monotone.
>
> The grey winds, the cold winds are blowing
>   Where I go.
> I hear the noise of many waters
>   Far below.
> All day, all night, I hear them flowing
>   To and fro.

The preliminary character of this poem is shown in the repetition of the words 'I hear', with which the next and final poem opens. This last, though it completes the development of the general theme, is itself a work of art, a great and terrible poem.

> I hear an army charging upon the land,
>   And the thunder of horses plunging, foam about their knees.
> Arrogant, in black armour, behind them stand,
>   Disdaining the reins, with fluttering whips, the charioteers.
>
> They cry unto the night their battlename:
>   I moan in sleep when I hear afar their whirling laughter.
> They cleave the gloom of dreams, a blinding flame,
>   Clanging, clanging upon the heart as upon an anvil.

They come shaking in triumph their long, green hair:
They come out of the sea and run shouting by the shore.
My heart, have you no wisdom thus to despair?
My love, my love, my love, why have you left me alone?

There is in this poem a notable divergence between two lines of thought. This is not a failure to achieve singleness of theme, because a certain conflict *is* the theme. But there is a strongly marked contrast between description (in the form of personification) of 'nature' and the lover's reaction to it, a contrast which comes out most strikingly in the transition to the last two lines (which give the clue to the poem), where the person hearing and personifying the advancing tide suddenly calls on his heart not to despair. And even in these lines the divergence remains, between the wisdom appealed to and the despair presented in the heart-cry of the last line. We find from this ending that despair is the subject of the earlier lines; the waves beat on the shore as waves of despair beat on the heart — despair in love, the despair of the overwrought and abandoned lover.

Now, if the metaphorical description of the waves had been given, without the contrast with the feelings of the person speaking, we should have had the ordinary 'imaginative' poem, the representational description of nature as 'expressing' the feelings. But Joyce is concerned with the objective material, not with 'the metaphorical' but with the *use* of metaphor, just as there can be presentation of illusions of the supernatural as actual mental attitudes, though not of the actual supernatural. Thus Joyce presents, on the one hand, personifications as imagined by despair or other deluded feelings, as still wanted by despairing love, and, as against this, bringing out its illusory character, the recognition of objectivity by wisdom. But the conflict between subjectivism and objectivism is characteristic of despair itself, which swings between the recognition of loss and the desire to retain or regain the illusion.

And this is connected with its being *despair in love*. For love is one of the chief forces leading to personification and thus to the ordinary 'lyric' attitude. We find in the loved one everything we want; we find a friendly world, one which is akin to us, which denies us nothing, because it has given us all in the person of the loved one. It is thus, at

1 Some Questions in Aesthetics

the height of love, that our heart beats with the heart of things, that romantically we find all things to be tending our love. And this, love and the search for love or for 'union', is the main root of an expressionist aesthetic, of the treatment of things as making up a dream-world, full of 'meanings' and satisfactions for us. But in loss of love (while still straining after it), we find that the world, like the loved one, has grown unfriendly; we find the forces of nature still having a personal relation to us, but one of hostility — attacking us, mocking us, beating on our hearts, triumphing in our loss. Our wisdom (recognition of the fact that things, and the loved one, do not after all answer to our wishes but act objectively, in their own way) serves only to reinforce our despair, our sense of loss, and our vain struggle to regain.

Here, then, the poet's wisdom presents the conflict, the root of personification and the illusion of kinship with nature, and the basis of the feeling of loss and unfriendliness. This conflict, emphasised, as we noted, by the swing from personification or the 'expression' of feelings to the feelings themselves, is further brought out by the contrast between the rhyming of the first and third lines of each verse and the assonance of the second and fourth lines; and also by the contrast, in the seventh and eighth lines of the poem, between a mainly visual presentation, suggesting the (illusory) 'vision' of the happy lover, his lover's 'insight' — though here linked with pain and loss in the notion of 'blinding' — and a mainly tactual one, suggesting the force, the *blow*, of hostility and disillusionment. The whole poem is, then, a structural presentation of the lover's despair at the loss of his friendly and harmonious world, a world 'created' by his harmony with the loved one.

The question arises here which is of importance for literature in general, viz., if we take the material of the poem, that which is presented or built up, and the construction of which is appreciated, to be feelings, what we are to make of the words. The view has been taken that the aesthetic material is the *meaning* of the words (what the words make us think of). Clearly, the material is not simply the words themselves; something is *said* in the poem. And if we take the subject-matter not as what the words mean but as the complex, 'the words meaning the things', we shall be unable to say what the theme of the poem is. This is not to say that the words are of no artistic importance. For example, in the line, 'Clanging, clanging upon the heart as upon an anvil', the beat and clang of the words bring out more sharply the beating of despair on the heart, which is what we are to think of. But while we can thus, as in painting, recognise the artist's skill in using the immediately presented material to make us think of the real subject, we must not confuse 'appreciation' of this skill with appreciation of the aesthetic character of the work as built up.

We find in this poem, then, illustrations and confirmations of the main points made — the independence of the work as an aesthetic object, i.e., its independence of the author and the reader alike; the unsoundness of representationism, of appreciation in terms of likeness or successful reproduction, though the possibility of indirect presentation, as in painting and literature, is admitted; and the need for a *real* theme, a recognisable complication whose working out has an objective order, if there is to be any appreciation of structure, any recognition of the goodness and badness of works, and thus any aesthetic theory and discussion. For we can discuss Joyce's poem (remembering that the earlier members of the series have presented phases of youthful love) only in terms of this real theme, the heart's despair. But the poem is the more notable because the clash of forces in the heart's despair is a clash between realism and expressionism, and because it thus shows that the rejection of expressionism, the establishment of a positive aesthetic, heightens creativeness and extends appreciation.

1 Some Questions in Aesthetics

Family group. Left to right: John Anderson's paternal grandmother, brother Willie, father Alexander, John, sister Catherine (Katie), mother Elizabeth (née Brown), and sister Helen (Nellie).

– 2 –
Biography

When we speak of a good biography, are we making an aesthetic judgement? Biography is certainly a work in human material — it is the presentation of an actual person's life. But is this a theme, and, if so, what are the problems involved in the working-out of it?

While it is obvious that a certain historical judgement is involved, and while we expect a biography to be true to the facts (whatever else we may say about it), a purely factual account of a person's life, cataloguing in temporal sequence his thoughts and his activities, would be certainly uninspired and as certainly very boring. But granted that it is true to the facts, then the further condition of goodness in a biography might be said to be an aesthetic one — the presentation of the life as a structure — as a sequence of phases, such as we find in any drama or novel.

Would, then, a biography of Socrates have Socrates as its theme? And would this be a theme that could be worked out? It is to be remembered that we know Socrates as a certain sort of thing; and this sort of thing must have its phases — its regular ways of working. There is also the question of accident in his history — the kind of people who happened to cross his path; the situations, not of his making, into which he was plunged. But we immediately recognise that such accidental

---

Notes dated 1 March 1932.

features are inseparable from *any* artistic literary presentation, for it is by means of the interaction of characters with other characters and with situations (problems) that an author can proceed to give those psychological analyses that are the stuff of literature. Obviously in the case of a biography, the writer cannot know everything about his subject, and even if he did, he could not use it all. So the life of Socrates cannot be presented 'in all its details', and the biographer, like the novelist and the dramatist, has in fact to *select*. He has to choose what he finds most important or most significant from the data at his disposal, and this means that he has some theme, some *kind* of human character (or human material) in mind. This would also suggest that we could have different good biographies of Socrates, all of them true to life, and all of them showing a particular structure, according to the way the artist seized his subject (e.g., Socrates as x; Socrates as y, etc.). If we chose to deal with Socrates as a philosopher, we should not attempt to present his life as we should try to do in the study of Socrates as an Athenian; we should present only his philosophic history. But just as we would never be able to present his whole life 'in all its details' in one work, in the same way we would not be able to present his whole *philosophic* life in one work, and we would again have to choose the significant features, which again means that we would have some particular theme in mind.

These considerations are closely connected with the notion of history as an art and with the question of the historical novel; and similar questions arise also in the case of the novelists who think they have created a work of art when they have presented 'the whole life' of the hero from the cradle to the grave; or who begin with the birth and deal exhaustively with the early years and then give in a final chapter 'what happened afterwards', as Scott sometimes does. Such biographical novels would be bad as biography and bad also as art, because the authors had failed to *seize* a theme, had in the one case thought of the work vaguely as 'A life of x', dragged in all sorts of superfluities and had neglected any kind of significant structure. In the second case, the early years might conceivably have a theme which could be worked out, but the addition of the chapter to tell what happened after suggests that the theme was not thoroughly worked out, and that the author felt the need of some additional 'alien' material to complete the work — much as Shaw did with the prefaces to his plays and with his addition to *Pygmalion*.

In the historical novel, the main theme may not be concerned with actual historical characters, but in utilising historical material to provoke 'interest' the author may give the reader insight into certain historical conditions and connections. This, however, will remain fragmentary as history, and mainly irrelevant artistically as far as the main theme is concerned. A multiplicity of interests, again, distracts attention from the theme, and weakens the critical approach. Peacock has a few words to say on the historical novel in *Crotchet Castle*, where Lady Clarinda asserts that the 'Wizard of the North' has made her learn many things that she would never have dreamed of studying, by his amusing admixture of romance and history. 'Very amusing, very amusing', retorts Dr Folliott, and in further reply to Mr Chainmail, who asserts that Scott has grossly misrepresented the twelfth century, he remarks, 'He has misrepresented everything, or he would not have been very amusing. Sober truth is but dull matter to the reading rabble.' Despite Dr Folliott's judgement, however, there can be good historical novels (Scott's *Old Mortality* is one of his best), and a good historical novel will be good apart from its connection with a certain epoch, and apart from the fact that some or all of its incidents actually happened; or it will be good mainly as *history* (as a structural presentation of a certain social complication); though even here its artistic goodness will not depend on the fact that all the incidents actually happened, but on its working-out of a human theme.

It should, of course, be pointed out that, whatever connection there may be between the two, good history is a treatment of a certain *social* complex, while a good novel or play deals with a *psychological* complex. A good biography would have a psychological subject though, as with all psychological subjects, there will be social connections and circumstances. Biography, then, with the additional question of fidelity to actual facts, is on the same footing aesthetically as that part of literature (novels and plays), which works with human material.

This being so, the question of representation does not arise. We may be able to say that the presented structure is very like, or quite like, a particular historical sequence, or that the subject of the biography is very like the person we have imagined, because of our knowledge from other sources; or, again, that certain historical events made the author think of his theme (indeed we might always be able to say this, even if the events themselves did not appear in the work); but this would not affect our aesthetic judgement — our judgement of the structure as such.

2 Biography

Students of Hamilton Academy: John Anderson is third from left and Janet Anderson (née Baillie) sitting, second from left — the winners of the Bursary Competition for all Scotland, 1911.

– 3 –
Classicism versus Romanticism

Classicism is ordinarily considered cold and formal in comparison with the warm 'living' atmosphere of romance; it is taken to give a *static* conception of things in contrast to the *dynamic* one that characterises the latter. This point of view could not be better exemplified than by the statement of Mr William Archer that 'Shakespeare had no conception of the idea of progress'.[1] Whether or not this was so is unimportant. Shakespeare might never have thought of such a thing, but if the idea had been brought to his notice he would have rejected it, as all great artists must reject it. For the idea involves the belief that all processes are summed up in one process and that this process is in the direction of the better; or it involves the idea of unity and finality. This is not to be understood as meaning that progress is to be regarded as inevitable or at least as unhindered; rather it is to be regarded as consisting in the onward movement of a principle or power (e.g., 'Life') by the overcoming of obstacles. Hence we have the notion of a struggle wherein we may be on the side of the angels or against them. To be on their side is to be filled with the principle of life and to be thus at one with all who have been so. As against this view stands that attributed to Shakespeare in saying that he did not believe in progress — a view which belongs to all classicists, viz., that all things do *not* work

---

Constructed from a draft dated 1932, and from connected notes.

together and that there is no finality, no victory in a life-struggle; that, on the contrary, there are many independent processes, each of which in occurring is achieved.

When a certain kind of process recurs under other conditions, the later process is not thereby 'in touch with' the previous one — as though the kind or universal were a whole 'containing' its particulars; and even when a process does fall within a 'wider' or longer one, the latter is not to be treated as its purpose, as something better or higher than it, because it is more inclusive. Allowing, for example, that there may be a national occurrence (or course of history) within which the actions of individuals operate, the individual's action is not *summed up* in this 'wider' movement; he is himself, and even those of his actions which are of importance in the national movement are, as his, independent of that movement. If we take the actions common to his history and to the nation's, we treat them in a different perspective according as we are considering him or it; and, whichever we deal with, we deal with as independent of, even if continuous with, the other. The romantic and the classic, then, each deal with a process, but while the romantic deals with it as a progress and as a union with a certain spirit, the classic deals with it simply as itself with a beginning and an end within certain limits of time. The classic writer considers the matter 'beyond good and evil'; he presents a certain theme which has occurred under certain conditions, and says, 'Here is x.' This thing (x) in its own nature, apart from any union or purpose, is what the classic writer sets out to present. And in doing so, he follows the only line of art.

The classic principle is, then, that each work has a theme, that it presents one thing and no other. By this it is not meant that things do not interpenetrate and complicate one another, but simply that they are nevertheless distinct. A person may live in a certain society, but he is one occurrence and the society is another. In order to present him we require to present his social relations but not therefore to present in its completeness every association of which he is a member. Again, to take an example from the plastic arts, a nose occurs in a face and a face in a body, but a nose in a picture of a nose will be different from a nose in a picture of a face, and a face in a picture of a face will be different from a face in a picture of a body. If the romantic (as he will) lets the nose develop into the face and the face into the body, he will lose the

3 Classicism versus Romanticism

nose and the face and not achieve the body. Things interpenetrate, then, but in the complexity with which we are faced we turn our attention from one specific thing to another, and we are continually discovering new things. Now a work of art consists simply in setting forth such a discovery, in making visible the thing discovered. Its importance as a work of art depends on the clearness and distinctness with which the thing is set forth, and aesthetic appreciation consists simply in the recognition of the thing set forth. The aesthetic emotion is discovery, the recognition of a thing in its distinctness, as itself and no other. This does not mean that two works of art cannot have the same theme. The same character or quality may appear under different conditions or with different materials, but it is the recognition of the character that constitutes appreciation, as it is the working of it out of the materials that constitutes creation.

We appreciate a work of art when we say, 'This is x'; e.g., taking the theme of the *Iliad* to be the wrath of Achilles, we appreciate the work when we say to ourselves, 'This is wrath'. (We may appreciate a work, recognise the distinctness of its theme, without being able to name that theme, but appreciation is greater when we can do so.) In this work the siege of Troy is important only as background, as providing materials out of which is wrought the distinct thing *wrath*. It is of no importance how or when the war began or will end. The whole epic is summed up in 'This is wrath', and the whole criticism turns on whether it is so or not; whether anything is lacking in the delineation of wrath or anything superfluous is brought in. It is in fact from such considerations that certain portions are held to have been added by later hands; the justification of such revision is in the end aesthetic. The siege of Troy does temporally include the wrath of Achilles, but it does not epically include it; and it is not better or nobler because it is more inclusive. It is the theme that determines the structure of a work of art; the materials are used in its service and there is failure in artistic achievement when authors wind up by telling us what happened 'afterwards', i.e., outside the story, to all the characters as Scott and Dickens sometimes do. Similarly, if the *Aeneid* is a serial of 'what happened to Aeneas', it is a lesser work than the *Odyssey* with its theme of the home-seeking of Odysseus; it would only be valuable in so far as it approached a theme or a group of themes.

It is sometimes remarked of Millais' painting, *The Cardplayers*, that the scene is so real that the players seem to be about to play their next cards; but this does not indicate a virtue in the work. A work of art is to be appreciated 'as a whole', not in respect of some part of itself nor in respect of something beyond itself. Thus Arnold Bennett simply fails in appreciation of *Ulysses* when he finds it unintelligible while admiring various passages (*Things That Have Interested Me*). He wants a book to tell him what it is all about, not realising that *Ulysses* is not *about* anything. It speaks for itself; it *is* Hell and the unintelligibility he complains of is precisely a characteristic of the thing, Hell or Damnation. There is no question, apart from what arises in envisaging the process itself, of what happens before or after. Hell is *there*, presented to us, and the person who, having read the book, says, recognises or has discovered that it represents Hell, has appreciated the work. It may be said that the theme of Dante's *Inferno* is also Hell; the critical question will then be which of the two works is more truly hellish (and nothing else). Whatever may be the answer to that, the fact remains that Joyce has, out of the material he had, discovered Hell.

Romanticism, however, is always trying to see something beyond, as when John Middleton Murry talks of 'the voice of God', the 'individual in his wholeness', and the 'hidden principle of life itself', in connection with the stories of Katherine Mansfield.[2] In the volume called *Bliss* especially, Katherine Mansfield appears as a classic, not a romantic. She has seized some definite thing or process and to appreciate her work is to appreciate the thing she has seized. Thus, in reading 'Je Ne Parle Pas Francais' we can say, 'This is agony' — and there is nothing more to be said. But the romantic critic wants to say more in each case, e.g., to find Katherine Mansfield continually 'affirming the human spirit'. Actually she affirms many things, but one at a time as the themes of different stories, and we may affirm or know them after her. If a story like 'Je Ne Parle Pas Francais' arouses our pity, that might tell us something about ourselves and our attitude to art. If, on the other hand, the work appealed to pity, made a bid for it, that might enable us to discover something about the author; for a direct appeal to pity would be a weakness in the work — it would be an endeavour to move us, and the perfect work of art neither urges us towards anything nor turns us away from anything; it is simply there. Even a work with Pity

3 Classicism versus Romanticism

as its theme would not be expected to arouse our pity, any more than the *Iliad* with its theme of Wrath is expected to arouse our wrath. They are both psychological studies in the realm of literature, presented to us for our appreciation.

In maintaining that the classic work of art has form and structure, one is not saying that classicism is imitation, adherence to certain forms as models. That would mean taking the form or structure of one thing and applying it to another, and the 'classical' eighteenth century was largely imitative in that way. The classic work gives us the structure of a thing — not its construction, its building, as romantic art does. Here the artist tries to build up his theme as he goes along, and the end is always more important than the beginning, while in place of the objectivity of the classicist, the tendency is to emphasise the individuality of the artist — which is of psychological, but of no artistic, importance. Hence we are more likely to think of the production of the romantic artist as 'the work of so and so', in contrast with the appreciation of the impersonal austerity of form of the classical work. For it is no merit in an artist that his *effort* is seen when we contemplate his work, however much this striving may appeal to our own romantic aspirations.

– 4 –
Romanticism and Classicism

The romantic view of art and especially of literature is closely connected with the romantic view of life, i.e., with the conception of it as a field of spiritual striving or the realisation of 'ideals'. To approach art or life in a matter-of-fact way is, for the partisans of the uplift, to divest it of its 'significance' and to exhibit one's own poverty of spirit. It is thus that the prevalence of romanticism in our literary schools leads to the blurring of all aesthetic distinctions; not only is the substance of the literary work itself presented in the guise of adventure in the realm of values, but it is merged with the artist's spiritual adventure in creating it, and the task of the appreciator in his turn is to let himself become charged with the same values. On this view the distinctions between the arts disappear, since all are alike adventures of the artist; and thus in literature, music, painting and the rest there are not different themes but only different treatments of the one theme, 'Life' — different heights of spiritual expression — the material in which the work is done being merely incidental, a mere means whereby the spiritual exaltation can be shared.

The adverse effect which this romantic attitude has on literary and aesthetic theory needs little demonstrating. In the first place, the vagueness which it engenders is the death of exact criticism; a clear

---

First published in *Hermes*, XL, Michaelmas Term, 1934.

line is not drawn between good works and bad, and the way is left open for anti-theoretical notions of 'good taste' and the authority of 'sound judges'. True, as has been indicated, an attempt is made to retain differences of *degree*; some works are more fully expressive of Life, more highly spiritual, than others. But exact demonstration of how highly each work is charged with spirit is naturally not forthcoming; and the distinction is a relative one at best, since the 'appreciator' is free to cram all the significance he can into the work before him. On this view, indeed, condemnation of a work — refusal to read wonderful meanings into the drivellings of Wordsworth, for instance — is taken as a sign of the inadequacy of the critic's spiritual resources. Works of art, then, merely serve as texts for vague and arbitrary moralising, and strict analysis is frowned upon as calculated to 'spoil' appreciation of the work — just as explanation of a joke is supposed to spoil it, and inquiry into the mechanism of humour is taken to indicate a lack of humour in the inquirer.

The further consequence of this unscientific attitude is that the field of literary studies becomes cluttered up with all manner of irrelevancies. In the absence of concentration on the works themselves, consideration is given not merely to their origins and their effects, to their authors' 'view of life' (high or not so high) and their influence ('uplifting' or depressing) on their readers, but to whatever can be associated with them. And since there is nothing that cannot be associated with anything else, nothing that a work cannot 'mean' for someone, literary discussion comes to embrace everything — except literature. Or, more accurately, literature comes to be discussed in anything but its own aesthetic character.

This in itself, of course, is not romanticism. Associative appreciation tends to be sentimental rather than romantic, to be more concerned with the personal interests and reminiscences of the appreciator than with 'the ultimate significance' of the work. But since there is nothing which is *the* meaning of the work (apart from the work itself), since what a person regards as the ideal, in terms of which other things are to be interpreted and evaluated, is always something that he personally demands, the two attitudes are not readily distinguishable — in fact, it might be said that our sentimental attachments serve as partial outlets for the more deep-seated impulses which lie at the

4 Romanticism and Classicism

root of romanticism in general. On this view, sentimental appreciation will be a particular mode of operation of romanticism; it will always accompany, though it will never quite displace, the ineffable longings which romantic poets have hymned. In any case, the mechanism of the two forms of evaluation is the same, and there is a ready passage from either to the other.

Expressionism, again, i.e., the interpretation of works in terms of the soul-states of the *artist*, may be regarded as a particular form of romanticism. If the spiritual content of the work is not to be entirely incommunicable, the appreciator must be able at least to approach the same height of spirituality; and, while he may always doubt whether he has quite fathomed the artist's meaning, it will be spirituality as such, or spirit raised to that particular power, that is the object of appreciation. It may be important to observe that the spirit had first to be focused in the artistic consciousness, but what gathered there will still be an expression of the ultimate significance of life in general. Minor forms of romanticism will be as various as the conceptions of what is important in life, e.g., the (allegedly) 'proletarian' theory which interprets art in terms of the class struggle, and the 'modernist' view which judges works according as they tell the time of day, i.e., according to their place in a fanciful scheme of human progress. All such views may be called *extrinsic*, in the sense that they estimate works by something outside the works themselves, and all of them have the defect already noted of breaking down the distinctions between the arts, confusing the aesthetic issues by supposing it possible to translate music, e.g., into plastic or into literary terms, instead of recognising that each has its own materials, its own range of themes.[1]

In this connection, the main tendency is to give a *literary* interpretation of the other arts by finding, in each case, the 'spiritual equivalent' of the presented material. Romanticism attaches itself especially to literature for two reasons. One is that traditionally (and apart from the special case of 'scientific literature') literature has been concerned with human material; and the other is that literature is work in words. The former condition facilitates the confusion between the subject-matter (the mental processes presented) and the mental processes of the artist or of the appreciator, and this, as we have seen, opens the way to a similar confusion in the case of other arts where it is not, on the face of it, mental processes that are presented. The confusion is further strengthened by the fact that any aesthetic subject can be discussed, i.e., can be dealt with in words. But the more important point here is that in work with words we really have to distinguish the words themselves from their meaning, and thus a loophole is given to an aesthetic of meanings — and also to a humanistic aesthetic, since it is only for human beings that words mean.

Nevertheless, it is not at all difficult to make the distinctions necessary to extricate aesthetic science from this romanticist web. Without dwelling on the extravagances of the literary or spiritual interpretation of such arts as music and architecture, we may observe that it is no more possible to lump all literary themes together than to amalgamate the arts. *Hamlet* and *Othello*, whatever common features they may possess, are not variants of a single theme, and we should resent the intrusion of Othello into the court of Denmark or of Hamlet into Othello's campaigns. In other words, we have a conception of what does and what does not belong to each of these developing situations, and it is only so, and not by reference to mentality in general or to Shakespeare's mentality in particular, that we can estimate the plays. If connections that are essential to a work are to be sought for in the artist's mind, that is a question of *where* the complete working out is to be found (assuming that it is accessible to us at all) and not of *whether* the working out has taken place. But at least, if it has not taken place in the work, we should say that the work is bad. The main point that emerges from these considerations is that appreciation is of the subject or theme; and, with an irreducible diversity of subjects, the doctrine of degrees in a single scale and the whole attempt at spiritualising the arts must be abandoned.

Here, then, we have the position of classicism, replacing a vague appreciativeness or sensitivity to 'values' by definite judgements of particular works and recognition of them as good or bad according as they succeed or fail in working out the theme, i.e., according to their *structure*. It is on this account that classicism is accused of being 'formalistic'; the vicious disjunction of form and content is called in to bolster up the romanticist case. But clearly the form of a work (the order or, in general, the relations of its constituents) is just as much a part of its content (what it contains) as is any constituent we care to select; clearly also what the work is said to 'signify' is not part of what it contains but is something outside it. Even if there were something signified by a work, it would have a form of its own, differing from the form of the work, and in distinguishing the two forms we should be distinguishing *what was formed* in each case. Thus any spiritual content would have its own structure, and the aesthetic question would only be raised, not settled, by saying that this formed content was signified by a particular work; to confine form to the side of the thing signifying and content to the side of the thing signified is as unaesthetic as it is illogical.

Only a classical aesthetic, then, will enable us to come to grips with the fact that in literature the aesthetic object is not the words but what the words mean; that the determination of whether the work is coherent or disjointed must be made in terms of the mental operations presented, of the emotional sequence unrolled. Divagations on 'style' are only another example of the elaboration of associative material at the expense of the subject itself whose structure awaits examination. Questions of technique in the arts have, of course, an interest of their own, but they cannot be gone into until the main question has been settled. It must be admitted that in what has passed for classicism at various times, the same sort of confusion has been operative; that arbitrary forms have been laid down for imposition on any material, with a consequent intrusion of what is alien to the theme and omission of what is essential. The doctrine of the 'unities' of time and place is a case in point, and the treatment of certain metrical forms as 'classical' is another; for, though one is concerned with subject-matter and the other with verbal apparatus, both are fetters on the development of the theme. But it will never be possible to get a guarantee against confusion in thinking and the attachment of irrelevant meanings to terms; the main issue is nevertheless clear, and the distinction between insistence on consecutive working out and concern for 'higher things' is well enough conveyed by the antithesis of classicism and romanticism.

The above suggestions of linguistic difficulties might be taken as weighing against the treatment of the work of art as having a structure independent of the artist's mind, but they do not really do so. The question of the understanding of literature in its verbal presentation is the same as the general question of understanding a language;

misunderstandings occur, there are variant usages, but still the attainment of a common understanding is possible or the language could not be learned at all.[2] It is attained, as is the case with learning in general, in the course of joint activities. Such activities, then, are a condition of the understanding of literature, but it is *what is understood* that then becomes the subject of aesthetic judgement. So, if the artist alone understood a certain work, he alone could judge it aesthetically, but the rightness or otherwise of his judgement would depend not on his authorship but on whether the structure meant by his words had or had not the characters he attributed to it.

In the preceding discussion, romanticism and classicism have been treated as forms of aesthetic theory; but the terms are just as commonly applied to actual works. If it is asked, then, what we should mean by calling a work *classical*, the only possible answer is that we should be attributing goodness to it, that the aesthetic object (which in the case of literature, as we have seen, would be what the words meant) is presented in its proper order, that the development of its phases or arrangement of its forces is coherent and complete. But it would be harder to maintain that every bad work is *romantic*, for even if the disproportions, alien material or gaps in a work were due to the artist's striving to make it signify some ultimate reality, that significance would not belong to the work itself. A romantic outlook might be the cause of bad work, but we should be falling into romantic confusions ourselves if we took the outlook to characterise the work (or to be its 'spiritual equivalent').

The fact remains, however, that the missing connections are to be found in the artist's associations, that, as in dreams, the superficial incoherence and incongruity are overcome if we discover what the various elements (including the relations and even the incongruity itself) 'mean' for the mind that has given them forth. And since this analysis reveals the artist's yearnings as of the same stuff as the romantic interpretation of art, we may, by a natural extension of the use of the term (though the distinction should always be kept clear), call the works themselves 'romantic'. Even what we should regard as grossly incompetent work will have the same dream-structure; it will be expressive of the author's 'values'. But this is not to say that behind the defective work we find a sound one, that we fill out the defects

4 Romanticism and Classicism

by further application to the author's mind; the incoherence is not overcome in that sense. The subject of our analysis is really a different one from that which he attempted. What we have done is to find 'in nature' a coherent structure of mental operation on available material; we have observed the phases of an artistic failure.

It is, indeed, only from the point of view of classicism that appreciation of nature can be put on the same footing as appreciation of art, since, in the latter case, the work of art is distinguished from the operations of the artist and judged on its own merits. In like manner, we consider the truth of a scientific theory in terms of the propositions put forward, and independently of who has proposed them or how he came to do so; and thus we erect no barrier between actual truths and 'theoretical' truths. But error is another matter, one in which a mind is involved. The recognition of error presents us with the problem of determining *truly* how certain mental processes have interacted with their surroundings so as to be mistaken about them. So aesthetic disproportion, a bad work of art raises the problem of its maker, of the person who 'dreamed' it and how he came to do so, of the structure of his valuations. But aesthetic harmony in itself raises no such problem, even when it is a person that has produced it. It could be held to do so only at the cost of a romanticising of all nature and the denial of all real distinctions.

– 5 –
Psycho-Analysis and Romanticism

As was pointed out by J. A. Passmore in his article on 'Psycho-Analysis and Aesthetics' in the last issue of the *Journal*, psycho-analytic findings may be of assistance to the literary critic in two different sets of cases — where phantasy (someone having phantasies) is the actual subject-matter of the work, and where phantasy operates as a distorting influence on the work — but the general body of psycho-analysts fail to make this distinction, and, in treating all literature and indeed all art as romantic or phantastic, hinder the development of the science of aesthetics. Nevertheless, the exposure of the roots of romanticism should in the end be more of a help than a hindrance; it lays the foundation, at least, of a fruitful co-operation between psycho-analysts and positive aestheticians.

The most important point in this exposure is the demonstration of the *backward-looking* character of phantasy, the longing for the restoration of an original condition of bliss, whether this 'golden age' is that of infancy or (as shown by Passmore in connection with 'Kubla Khan') of the pre-natal state. In any case, the blissful period is one of inarticulateness, before our present problems and difficulties had arisen, and this accounts for the sense of the 'ineffable', and the use of

---

First published in *Australasian Journal of Psychology and Philosophy*, XIV, 3, September 1936.

symbols, in the products of romanticism. But if it could be established that *all* symbolism (and mysticism) is of this backward-looking character and that the ultimate object of the search for restoration is always the pre-natal state, this would be of immense importance not merely for psycho-analysis but for the criticism of romanticism in all fields.

This is substantially the view of Otto Rank, who maintains (*The Trauma of Birth*, p. 5) that the analysis itself 'finally turns out to be a belated accomplishment of the incomplete mastery of the birth trauma'. Thus it may be true of *romantic* art, though not, as Rank would have us suppose, of art in general, that its constructions are a partial overcoming of the trauma, 'a representation and at the same time denial of reality' (p. 166), a compromise between what we long for and what we are confronted with — this compromise frequently taking the form of the projection of the ideal state into the future.

Such constructions are by no means confined to literature in the narrow sense — their very occurrence, indeed, indicates the intrusion of a non-literary element into literary work — but appear in social* and philosophical theory; though again, in the latter case, the intrusion of mysticism is at the expense of strictly philosophical inquiry. Thus Socrates in the *Phaedo* characteristically links his hopes for immortality with a doctrine of *reminiscence*. It is, however, in literature, or what passes for such, that phantasy has its freest scope and that, the disguise of sober theory being removed, the true connections come out most clearly; and Wordsworth's 'Ode on Intimations of Immortality' is an outstanding example of the weakness of the attempt to give a prospective turn to an avowedly backward-looking attitude. The child still has memories of 'Heaven', and the man has memories of these memories —

---

* In *Reflections on Violence* (Hulme's translation, p. 150), commenting on Marx's opposition to Utopianism and with special reference to his statement, in a letter written in 1869, that 'the man who draws up a programme for the future is a reactionary', Sorel remarks: 'Of what can Utopias be composed? Of the past and often of a very far-off past; it is probably for this reason that Marx called Beesley [E. S. Beesley (1831–1915); Professor of Ancient History at London University] a *reactionary*, while everybody else was astonished at his revolutionary boldness.'

5 Psycho-Analysis and Romanticism

> O joy! that in our embers
> Is something that doth live,
> That Nature yet remembers
> What was so fugitive!

— but the forcing of a conception of *immortality* on these recollections, the suggestion that the child, because he has a greater sense of the past, has also a greater sense of the future, is so obviously arbitrary that even Wordsworth hardly presses it. The effect of the poem is to expose the alleged 'future' of the metaphysical theories as a past.

Hugh Walpole's book, *The Golden Scarecrow*, is characterised by the same backward-looking attitude, with perhaps a greater effort to amalgamate it with a forward-looking one. The book is a series of stories about children who in their adjustment to the world's demands and in setting out to have adventures of their own (or, as Walpole puts it, on their 'pilgrimage from this world to the next') progressively, though in differing degrees, lose touch with a certain Friend who, to begin with, had been their closest intimate and in comparison with whom even their parents had been strangers — and who, 'at the end of it all', when the pilgrimage is over, receives them again.

The similarity to Wordsworth's of this account of the sense of things unseen is obvious enough; indeed, we get a rather feeble *echo* of Wordsworth in the passage, 'Every baby knows about it; then, as they grow older it fades and, with many people, goes altogether.' And the whole book strengthens the supposition that reminiscence of the pre-natal state is the origin of romanticism and symbolism in general. What is distinctive about Walpole's presentation of the matter is not merely the personification of that which is remembered; the representation of the Friend as a dark man with a beard might seem merely to indicate the symbolic use of present material, though, in the working out, as protector, comforter, voice in the darkness, he clearly personifies the pre-natal environment with its darkness, warmth and security. The striking feature of Walpole's account is the identification of the Friend with St Christopher.

It is St Christopher, we are informed specifically in the 'Prologue' to the book, who watches over the child's early years and tells him things which, if he will only listen, will keep him from growing up a matter-of-fact person with no sense of what is 'beyond' the things he sees. The speaker explains that he himself has too little sense of what is in front of him. 'Of course, the ideal thing is somewhere between the two; recognise St Christopher and see the real world as well.' This is on the line of compromise already referred to, and its importance lies in the fact that it is only by combining our present experiences with our longings, only by amalgamating forward-looking with backward-looking, that we can take restoration to bliss as still possible. That is the formula which roughly sums up the romantic outlook; we have to go on to get back. But always there has to be some disguising of the inversion whereby that which is actually preparatory to our present life is turned into that for which our life is a preparation.

The St Christopher legend is not peculiar to Christianity,* but it is all the more important for this discussion in being present in various mythologies. In its Christian form, in which the saint carries the child across the water and finds the burden growing heavier and heavier until he almost sinks under it, it is obviously a myth of gestation and birth; the symbolism of water, carrying, etc., will be familiar to anyone who has paid more than casual attention to psycho-analytic literature. It is particularly interesting, therefore, that Walpole should identify this 'carrying' figure with the Friend of infancy, who, in most cases at least, is rapidly forgotten as the tasks of life are faced. The identification, however Walpole arrived at it, strikingly confirms the interpretation of his work in pre-natal terms.

The function of the Friend as watcher and protector, and of the saint as preserver, suggests another aspect of the question — not brought out by Walpole — that which is described by analysts as the 'Oedipus saving phantasy'. In the chapter entitled 'A Forgotten Dream' in his *Papers on Psycho-Analysis*, Ernest Jones remarks on it as a peculiarity of the dream he is interpreting that the dreamer *saves himself*; in the 'more typical form of the saving phantasy' the dreamer saves his mother.

> The portrayal of the act of birth by a deed of saving life is a theme to which much attention has been paid of late (1912) by Freud and

---

* Cf. J. M. Robertson, *Christianity and Mythology*, pp. 205–15.

5 Psycho-Analysis and Romanticism

others. It originates in the gratitude felt by the child to his mother on hearing that his life was a gift made by her at the risk of her own. The phantasy of saving her life, or someone's in her presence, represents the grateful desire to repay her *by doing for her what she did for him* — i.e., by making her a gift of a life. (p. 233, 2nd Edition; my italics)

It appears to me that what she did for him was to generate or create him, and that this is the meaning of 'saving' in the phantasy. If so, the reference to 'gratitude' is somewhat misleading, and the saving of oneself is much more 'typical' than might appear at first sight. For if the dreamer represents himself as having generated those who actually generated him* — a point reinforced by the fact that some dreams of this type are of saving the father or both parents — he is, in effect, claiming to have created himself. There must, in phantasy, be some compromise with the facts, but as the various forms of this type of dream, apart from other phantasies, suffice to show, there is no fixed point at which compromise must be made. The Christopher legend is one particular compromise, one version of creation, and it may possibly be linked with the conception of a carrying by the father prior to a carrying by the mother. The notion of *self*-creation is not prominent in it; but it is at least interesting that, in spite of the strength required for his work as 'ferryman', the saint is almost borne down by his burden, and, in some versions of the legend, having picked up a child, he sets down on the other side a grown man — points which suggest the possibility of that reversal of roles which is characteristic of the 'Oedipus saving phantasy'.

---

* The typical repayment (*quid pro quo*) would not take the form of showing 'affection and gratitude to the mother for begetting him, by begetting a child by her in return', but rather of begetting *her* in return. J. C. Flugel (*The Psycho-Analytic Study of the Family*, p. 109) speaks of 'an obscure notion of self-begetting' which is sometimes to be found in the rescue phantasy, but makes it a question merely of 'the creation of oneself without the co-operation of the parent of one's own sex'. Jones again, in his paper on 'The God Complex' (*Essays in Applied Psycho-Analysis*, p. 206) regards the aspect of God as the Creator as 'far from being either the most prominent or the most typical to be represented amongst the phantasies belonging to a God-complex' — i.e., one in which the patient identifies himself with God.

I would suggest, in conclusion, that theories of creation are invariably a compromise between the facts and the idea of self-creation, and that this idea (along with the desire for reversal) is closely connected with the mystic depreciation of *time*, the treatment of it as 'appearance', as subordinate to 'eternity'. And all this is closely connected again with romanticism in art and life. The thorough establishing of these connections would, of course, require a very lengthy discussion, though, as regards the treatment of the intra-uterine life as the symbolised *par excellence*, Rank may be said to have covered a good deal of the ground. The above discussion may at least have indicated along what lines certain positions in philosophy, aesthetics and psychology can be linked.

5 Psycho-Analysis and Romanticism

John Anderson

– 6 –

The Comic

At the end of Plato's *Symposium*, it is recorded that Aristodemus, having been awakened towards daybreak by a crowing of cocks, found that

> the others were either asleep, or had gone away; there remained only Socrates, Aristophanes and Agathon, who were drinking out of a large goblet which they passed round, and Socrates was discoursing to them. Aristodemus was only half awake, and he did not hear the beginning of the discourse; the chief thing which he remembered was Socrates compelling the other two to acknowledge that the genius of comedy was the same with that of tragedy, and that the true artist in tragedy was an artist in comedy also. To this they were constrained to assent, being drowsy, and not quite following the argument. And first of all Aristophanes dropped off, then, when the day was already dawning, Agathon. Socrates, having laid them to sleep, rose to depart; Aristodemus, as his manner was, following him.

We may consider it unfortunate that Socrates did not repeat his discourse to more sober company, or that Plato did not invent it; it might have prevented the talking of a great deal of nonsense on the distinction between tragedy and comedy. It may be, of course, that

---

First published in *Hermes*, XLII, Lent Term, 1936.

the clarity of mind which enables Socrates to resist the fumes of the cup, was connected with a complete ignorance of the subject under discussion — a subject which Socrates elsewhere treats in a very unaesthetic manner. It may certainly be conjectured that Socrates is here, in his usual manner, treating an art as a 'capacity of opposites', so that, just as the best doctor is the best poisoner, the man who is best able to devise a tragic outcome of a human complication would also be best able to devise a comic outcome. There may well have been as many people then as now who classified drama by the character of its upshot (as if one were to classify men by the length of their toe-nails), and it is just against such 'external' criteria that the Socratic criticism is commonly and deservedly directed.

Equally though not so obviously external is the criterion adopted by Gilbert Norwood in his essay on 'The Nature and Methods of Drama' (in the volume entitled *Euripides and Shaw*). 'The dramatist,' he says,

> has always ... to deal with some tangle in human life, but his treatment will vary according to his philosophy of life and according to his temperament. The first factor will determine whether he shall portray life as serious or as absurd, there being of course arguments on both sides.

Whatever these arguments may be, we can hardly regard a tragedy as a taking of sides by its author, a declaration of the seriousness as against the absurdity of 'life'. The unsatisfactoriness of the position is so far realised by Norwood himself that on the next page he adopts quite a different view. 'Comedy is drama that studies universal interests and depicts their meaning or influence, quite as certainly as does the tragic method, but it enlightens us through our sense of laughter, not of tears of horror.' Presumably we could be enlightened in either way, and we should not, in our laughter, feel bound to declare that the tragedian had a false 'philosophy of life' — as, on Norwood's first view, we should be bound to do. It is the mark of the romantic to treat all works as having the single theme, Life, instead of recognising the variety of themes and considering the working out of each in its own terms.

So far, then, if we adopt the classical point of view, it may quite well appear that there will be no distinction between the tragedian and the comedian, that the man who is expert in the working out of human

6 The Comic

entanglements can turn his attention equally to tragic and to comic themes. It might happen indeed that a particular dramatist had a preference for the tragic and another for the comic, but this would not be an aesthetic distinction, any more than the distinction between an 'animal painter' and a painter of landscape or of the human figure is an aesthetic distinction. Clearly, also, the question of our reactions is not an aesthetic question; we might laugh at tragedy and be horrified by comedy, but this would be quite irrelevant to the working out in either instance.

Nevertheless, it may be questioned whether there are actually tragic and comic themes, whether the difference is not in the working out, and whether in consequence, since there cannot be two workings out of the same entanglement, one of the two types is not definitely inferior as drama. The elucidation of these points demands some reflection on the nature of drama. According to Norwood, 'one element, and no other, is invariably present: a difficulty appropriately solved. Drama is the presentation by living persons of a complication in life and of the unravelling as effected by their interplay.' There must, it is contended, be some entanglement, some intertwining of demands. Mere mechanical opposition, the pushing of forces in opposite directions, is not drama. Nor is there drama in physical upheaval; an earthquake may have results of the sort we call 'tragic' and of the sort we call 'comic' but it is not dramatic. The peculiar *human* clash involves satisfactions and dissatisfactions; it involves, therefore, some element of illusion, some clash of 'ideals' with reality, and the working out of the complication is the *showing up* of the ideals, the exposure of illusions and pretences. Where it is a question of mere exposition and not exposure, where, for instance, a man is simply going on with his job, there is not drama.

From this it appears that romanticism is the very subject-matter of drama, and that a romantic 'treatment' of a theme, being a failure in exposure, is a dramatic failure. But now, if it can be maintained that tragedy is romantic, it will appear that drama and comedy are the same thing. In the first instance, it might be argued that the difference between tragedy and comedy is expressible in terms of the reaction of the 'hero' or leading figure. Where he clings to his 'ideals', where he would rather lose life than lose his illusions, we have tragedy; but, it may be argued, the exposure may be quite complete *for the spectator*. In the same way, however, the falsity of a theory, and thus the truth of the case, may be quite apparent to a hearer or reader; we do not on that account say that the theorist has expounded the truth. So we may not be under the illusions which determine the dramatic entanglement, but we expect to see the illusions shown up in the play — and, if there is a leading figure, in the play of his sentiments. On this view, we are free to admit that there are 'tragic facts' in real life; there are ideals that remain unexposed, illusions that are persisted in, complications that are not worked out. There remains the dramatic, the comic fact, the showing up of illusions. And if, as Meredith has it,

... In tragic life, God wot,
No villain need be! Passions spin the plot;
We are betrayed by what is false within

drama is precisely the unravelling, the exposure of what is false within — its exposure *within*, since exposure without would be a different drama.

Tragedy, then, is unfinished drama, an incomplete working out of the theme. This explains why such a play as *Hamlet* remains unsatisfactory. The illusions under which Hamlet is labouring have not been thoroughly exposed; for all that the play does, we should be left sharing some of his illusions. It is not merely that the ghost engenders an illusory complication to begin with. But the upshot of the play is actually to *enable* Hamlet to take a 'righteous revenge', and thus his main illusion goes unexposed. Malvolio, on the contrary, while he is left smarting and threatening revenge, has been forced to see through his pretensions — even though his exposure is only incidental to the play, which, it may be contended, has not a main theme at all. And if Alceste, again, retains some of his illusions to the last, it cannot be said that he goes quite unilluminated. It is not perhaps required that the hero should be as thoroughly illuminated as the spectators; at any rate, if the theme were not fully worked out till *all* his pretensions were exploded, no theme would be worked out. Alceste is finally confronted with the fact that his 'honesty' is incompatible with any social relation whatever — that was the main thing to be exposed, and we can scarcely think of him as failing to accommodate himself to the fact.

Meredith, in his 'Essay on Comedy', connects comedy closely with social conditions. In this he is concerned especially with the conditions

6 The Comic

of the *appreciation* of comedy; but these must also be, to a large extent, the conditions of its production and, more broadly, of the *occurrence* of comedy in society. We can readily agree to the view that there are periods and classes in which comedy particularly flourishes, if we admit that there are periods and classes in which pretences are more fully exposed than in others. It may be argued, indeed, that each class has its own special illusions, but it will scarcely be disputed that some classes are peculiarly free-thinking — and the same applies to periods. This is connected with the question of the 'dating' of comedy, with the passing away of the illusions exposed. But, while, in this connection, we may consider that the greatest comedy deals with the most abiding human illusions, we may still appreciate the worked-out exposure of an illusion which we do not share.

It is interesting also that Meredith considers the supreme condition alike of comic perception and of comedy presented to be the meeting of men and women on terms of intellectual equality. Clearly, the relations of the sexes constitute one of the main fields of operation of the sentimentalism which Meredith finds to be a foe to comedy even among the cultivated, and of the brutality which sentimentalism often imperfectly conceals. All the more, then, it is in this field, however many stages of cultivation have to be passed through in the process, that salutary exposure can take place. Such stages are exhibited in the various ways in which ridicule may be administered and received, as illustrated by Meredith in the relations of lovers. The main point is that illusions are not removed all in a piece, that, as Meredith says, 'to love Comedy you must know the real world, and know men and women well enough not to expect too much of them' — but still, in loving it, you have the strongest weapon to combat sentimentalism, Puritanism and Bacchanalianism — the unaesthetic, in all its forms.

The inferior forms of the comic, like the inferior forms of laughter, are those in which the barb is projected, in which we do not recognise the exposure of our own illusions. Freud, in his book on Wit, takes laughter to be the release of previously dammed up energy, and thus to have a cathartic effect. But, insofar as it has a cathartic and not a reconstructive character, it signifies that we have got round, not got over, our inhibitions. We are, as the phrase goes, 'laughing off' exposure; we are relieved at the showing up of the illusion or pretence in someone else. There are two types of persons who do not laugh at a witticism — those who are quite free from the illusion pilloried, and those who cling to it and resent its being attacked. And the man who laughs loudly comes nearest to the latter class; his laugh is his escape from being offended, his declaration that he is not the guilty party and thus is not called upon to make correction. The comic laugh is otherwise: it is a *sharing* in correction. And this is the basis of the enlivening of the wits, which, Meredith holds, is the benefit to men 'in taking the lessons of Comedy in congregations'.

6 The Comic

The University of Glasgow, where Anderson matriculated, and where he later lectured (1919–20).

−7−
The Nature of Poetry

In the field of literature there is no aesthetic difference between poetry and prose. Both deal with the same material and the aesthetic judgement of both is based on the quality of the theme and the way in which it is worked out. Word-painting and word-music, which are thought to be the special domain of poetry, occur quite frequently in prose literature also; but whether they appear in poetry or prose the criterion of judgement is the same for both. Unless the description of the scene or the sound of the words and their rhythms are part of the emotional complex of the characters involved (or of the author as character, or narrator as he is in the case of lyric poetry) and so are really human material, the work of which they form the whole or the part is of an inferior kind.

Poetry presents its material more vividly than prose, with a more marked rhythm and with, in many cases, the use of rhyme. It is essentially more dramatic than prose, being the presentation of a more sharply defined mood, and having a theme which is even more definitely cut off from surrounding circumstances than is the theme of a play. It is likewise a difference in the manner of presentation which distinguishes a literary work of art from scientific literature, even when the latter is dealing with human material, as is the case

---

Address to the Literary Society, 1939.

with psychological and psycho-analytic writing.[1] The literary artist is not concerned, for example, with demonstration or the finding and presentation of evidence; and there is a further difference of presentation in scientific literature according to whether we have an exposition of the theories of a scientist or the demonstration (proof) that these theories are true.

Nevertheless there could be said to be a connection between poetry and science though the presentation of each differs so widely. Vico's theory of the nature of poetry is of considerable interest here, for he holds that it is man's primitive speech and would therefore be most appropriate for presenting the first dim gropings after truth in an unfamiliar field.[2] Thus we might say that the inspiration of the poet and that of the scientist which leads them both to set up hypotheses are prior, but not superior, to the careful examination and verification which mark the work of science. Hence good poetry might be such as suggests a solution (or a way towards a solution) of problems that affect man at a particular time — inspired 'groping' we might call it; while bad poetry would be groping after, or presenting, what has been scientifically dealt with or is, at the time, generally known. This view might help to explain why some poems, which were considered interesting or 'poetical' in the past, in the present seem so trite and uninspired. But it would also imply that the aesthetic value of poetry is relative to the age in which it is written (as contrasted with the 'eternal' truths of science), for subjects once suitable for it are now no longer so.

While that may be true of certain poems and their subject-matter, it cannot be denied that there are poems which have retained the qualities of poetry throughout the years: they have not become dead nor do they seem mechanical. We can still appreciate the sonnets and blank verse of Shakespeare, the *Canterbury Tales* of Chaucer and the poets of ancient Greece and Rome. There *are* subjects of perennial interest to mankind, and while it may be said that since so much has already been written on almost all of them it is very difficult to write anything fresh on any one of them, the fact remains that the most familiar thing can be treated poetically if the artist approaches it with sufficient 'innocence of eye' — if he can separate it from utilitarian associations and desires and rid it of its usual connotations by the words and rhythms and rhymes that he uses. We have only to think of the lyrics of James Joyce to see what can be done poetically with subjects that have been often dealt with, and themes that are ever recurring — and this, too, in a 'scientific' age. The poet here might be said to be making discoveries for himself (whatever men may know), breaking the crust of custom, bringing out a fresh aspect of the subject and showing it as a particular thing, uncluttered by considerations we are inclined to take for granted — as something 'standing out' from its prosaic surroundings.

The poet, then, in one of his aspects, is an innovator, a part which has often led him to assume a didactic role, showing the world its faults and pointing the way to better things. A good deal of Meredith's poetry is of this kind, but his best poem, 'Hymn to Colour', has as its subject 'Creation' — the appreciation of new beauties that emerge to the 'seeing' eye. The poet plays, or has played, other parts as well, for with rhyme and rhythm the old bards told their stories and kept the legends of the race in the minds of the living. Connected with this function of the poet is the use of poetry in incantations, rites and ceremonies, and in traditional and patriotic verse. But this function is one which brings thinking and investigation to a stop. There is no 'groping', inspired or otherwise — only a heavy certainty, marked by heavy rhythms and the crystallisation of ways of thought and ways of living. In place of the new perceptions, the new expressions, which are the mark of poetry more than of any other kind of literature, we have something in the way of a tranquilliser, for the ubiquitous rhymes and rhythms are merely ways of 'putting it across' — of saving the reader from the necessity of thinking; in fact, they can sometimes lull him to sleep.

The realist conception of poetry — of good verse — and of literature in general, links it aesthetically with music and the plastic arts. In all of them there is structure — the building up of something that is itself and no other. In all of them, man recovers innocence of eye or ear, and learns to appreciate structures of shapes and of sounds and of human emotions freed from any ulterior connections they may have with his personal attitudes and desires; and poetry requires this fresh perception to a greater degree than any of the other arts.

Janet Baillie at graduation, November 1917.

– 8 –
Poetry and Society

The view of art, and similarly of theory, as having a social content or expressing a social tendency is one of the commonest of present-day positions; and those of us who reject it are still constrained to admit that artistic production is a social phenomenon, having important relations to other social phenomena. It is especially easy to give a social interpretation to literature, since it deals with human beings who have social relations; but strenuous efforts are also made to read social meanings into arrangements of shapes and tones in plastic and musical art. And the examination of such views may lead to important social as well as aesthetic conclusions.

The attitude in question is exemplified in condemnations of 'modernism' in music, painting and literature. Thus Mr A. J. Tout, president of the New South Wales Public Service Association, has recently taken it upon himself to attack surrealist paintings and their 'decadent daubers', poems written by 'debased cads', pornographic books produced by 'dirty-minded' present-day authors, 'discordant clashing sounds' broadcast in the name of music — all as examples of a debased art, embodying a false approach to life. But the debasement in question is no more than a rejection of *popular* standards, and it is above all against popular standards that the arts as social activities are directed.

From the *Union Recorder*, 7 June 1945.[1]

This will be particularly so of poetry, in so far as the mark of the poetic, as against the prosaic, is the arrival of 'new perceptions' — the bringing out of characteristics which the conventional and utilitarian associations of the subject-matter commonly conceal. Such new perceptions must, of course, be distinguished from fanciful accretions to the subject; in fact, it is the business of the critic to distinguish phantasy from insight, as 'modern' poetry gives him much occasion for doing. But the ordinary run of criticism is not of this character but rather is an appeal to popular prejudice — as in the condemnation of painting which requires study, which cannot be immediately grasped by the untrained observer. The principal medium of this type of criticism is the Press, which daily forces its vulgarity on us and, while professing to uphold moral standards, succeeds in lowering aesthetic standards. There have recently been several Press sensations connected with painting, and, for poetry, there was the 'Ern Malley' case.

The 'Ern Malley' poems were, of course, a hoax perpetrated on Max Harris by McAuley and Stewart, with the object of showing up his critical judgement.[2] It is easy to be wise after the event, but I would say that the success of the hoax does demonstrate a certain weakness of judgement in Harris — particularly in his being prepared to believe that work of such sophistication could be produced by a person without higher education, as Malley was supposed to be. (Some of Harris's associates are apparently still taken in by the 'Preface and Statement' which is balderdash. But no doubt many good poets say just as silly things when they try to theorise.)

However, the hoaxers themselves do not come too well out of the affair. As Harris has pointed out in his reply to their criticism, they associated themselves with Simpson of the *Sunday Sun* in making the populace the judge in aesthetic matters. The arguments they put forward had to be such as could be assimilated by readers of 'Fact', and thus the level of discussion was necessarily low. In particular, they put themselves in a weak position by stressing their *intentions* in writing the poems. They implied that because they intended to hoax, and used various tricks to get their effects, the work was bound to be poor. Actually, the matter can be settled only by reference to the poems themselves; and Harris's contention (based on such material as he could get hold of) that they are better than the poetry published by the authors over their own names seems to me to be a sound one.

Assuming that this is so, we have to inquire into the reason for it. And one point worth noting is that McAuley and Stewart underestimate their own effort of creation of the person Ern Malley and the poems appropriate to his character. It is true, of course, that there is much nonsense in these poems and, indeed, in the work of the schools ('apocalyptic' and what not) that the hoaxers wished to satirise. But there is also much merit in them; and the source of that merit is the element of *protest* which is absent from the ordinary work of these two writers. This is connected with the question of new perceptions. The poetic mind, taking things in new ways, is departing from and (as far as the process is conscious) protesting against traditional views. In other words, the poet is a heretic; he has had to force himself free from customary associations, to see the arbitrariness of orthodox beliefs and attitudes. The point is illustrated in the accusation of 'indecency' brought against so many of the great poets. Again, what has been called Shakespeare's ' pessimism' is just his rejection of the customary consolations.

In fact, the art of consolation is spurious art, a mere playing up to current illusions. But it is such art that is made a part of education; the poetry included in the school curriculum is poetry safe for children. And that is why it is found deadening and dull, since problems of which even the child has some conception are not properly dealt with. It is only bad poetry that can form a part of 'peaceful education'. This whole idea of education is a false one; education is not a peaceful process, it is a tackling of problems, a questioning of orthodox assumptions, not a mere presentation of material — and until this is realised we have not reached the highest level of culture.[3]

If we say that poetry is heretical, we are not thereby interpreting it socially, attributing to it a social content. The view that art has a social content is especially associated with Marxism, but the conception of it as consolation also gives it a social meaning — or at least makes it subservient to social demands. At present, the attempt to make art the servant of social tendencies is most clearly seen in Russia. It was the mid-nineteenth century that was the period of great literature in Russia — when literature was the vehicle of protest against the assumptions embodied in Absolutism. Now that it is State-controlled it has lost its force. It is remarkable that this control should go along with the 'theory' that art follows, or reflects, the state of society — a theory for which the evidence is manufactured by the forcing of art to follow the party line. Max Eastman's *Artists in Uniform* gives a good picture of the anti-aesthetic and anti-theoretical character of this party dictation.

An artist is not a person who can be put into a uniform; it is a condition of his work that he should reject the ordinary adherences and avoidances, that he should not be subject to the common standards. Indeed, the extent to which customary 'sanctions' are applied to artists is a test of the cultural level of a people. There will, of course, in any society be a populace (or mob) demanding such sanctions and resenting the artist's independent judgement. This opposition to independence is illustrated in the indicting of Ezra Pound as a 'traitor' because of his broadcasts from Rome. Pound is not a poet of the first rank, but he has produced some powerful work, he has made solid contributions to culture, and the proceedings against him are an indication of the low cultural level of the United States, of the predominance of those mob standards against which Pound has repeatedly affirmed 'the revolt of intelligence'. (It is possible that the more lasting values will reassert themselves sufficiently to prevent the taking of any serious steps against Pound.[4] But his formal condemnation, even as a gesture, is still a cultural condemnation of the American people.)

The same demand that the artist should conform to popular standards is seen in the prosecution of Max Harris for the publication of the 'Ern Malley' poems and other material in *Angry Penguins*. Here we see more especially the application of police standards to poetic work. In 'Night Piece', according to Detective Vogelsang (as reported in *Angry Penguins*, December 1944), there is a suggestion of indecency in that it seems to refer to people visiting a park at night — 'I have found that people who go into parks at night go there for immoral purposes'. The detective also finds a suggestion of indecency in the word 'incestuous' — though he admits that he doesn't know what the word means.

But police criticism is not the only noteworthy feature of this literary investigation. There are also literary pronouncements in the judgement of the magistrate (as reported in the same publication): e.g., 'Boldness in sexual reference is too often mistaken for brilliance. I think that the defendant should either endeavour to acquire that art of delicacy in the handling of sexual topics which is so necessary in literature, or avoid the topic altogether.' Thus the judge, presumably interpreting the law, lays down the law for literature. And it is a quite common belief that literature can and should be subject to such legal findings; indeed, 'legalism' — the setting up of legal standards to govern everything — is a quite commonly accepted position. But the more freedom-loving a people is, the less will legalism flourish, and the more will it be recognised, in regard to literature in particular, that, as A. R. Orage has it, 'the only check that ought to be placed on literature is criticism'.[5]

The charge of indecency is the one that the spokesmen of the populace always come back to. It has been made in many places against many forms of art, but especially of course against literature. Conventional criticism recognises that the great writers of the past had their 'lapses' ('in spite of which they were men of genius'); what it does not recognise is that men of genius naturally react against current taboos (of which the sexual taboo is by far the most powerful), that this is not something accidental but is inherent in their character. But, in dissenting from conventional criticism on this point, we should recognise that attempts at suppression are also not accidental, not something that we can turn off with a laugh — that 'wowserism' is rooted in popular thinking and needs continual criticism.

In fine, there is no country or people safe for literature; it must always, in Croce's phrase, lead 'a perilous and fighting life'.[6] Freedom in the treatment of sexual themes is one main ground of conflict, but there is a broader conflict, exemplified in the Pound affair, where nationalistic assumptions run counter to the independence of the poet. Equally, it is a gross misconception to think that literature can be given a safe place in education, that we can find poetry safe for pupils. The only proper mode of literary education is one which shows the weakness of the poetry of consolation and of the uncritical attitudes which it subserves. The greatest poetry is always heretical.

John Anderson

– 9 –
Art and Morality

The agitation against the recent prohibition of the importation of James Joyce's *Ulysses* into Australia did not last long; indeed, there was scarcely a protest when the Labor Minister for Customs confirmed the verdict of his predecessor. This, it may be said, is not surprising in circumstances of national emergency — people have more urgent matters to attend to, and there will be time enough, when peace is restored, to take up such special questions again. Now, while the question of culture in war-time is one which might profitably be argued much more fully than it has hitherto been, it is not my purpose here to go into that question. But there is, I think, an interesting parallel between literary and political censorship, between attacks on the 'obscene' and attacks on the 'seditious' or 'disloyal'.

While the main point of war-censorship is understood to be the prevention of the giving of information to the enemy, there is no doubt that very considerable limitations are placed, by censorship as well as by other means, on the expression of political opinions — in particular, those judged to be unfavourable to the national cause. And one implication of this is that the 'national cause' has already been defined beyond dispute. In the same way, in professing to speak 'in the name

First published in *Australasian Journal of Psychology and Philosophy*, XIX 3, December 1941.

of morality', the supporters of the ban on *Ulysses* assume that their conception of morality is one that all must accept. Their position would obviously be weakened if they admitted that they were speaking only in the name of *a* morality, if they had to uphold what we may call the morality of protection against the morality of freedom. To do so they would have to rest their arguments (in so far as they do argue and do not merely indulge in noisy denunciation) on some common ground — though this, to the same degree as it facilitated discussion, would make banning more difficult.

Indeed, the more we examine the position of the censors of the morally or politically unorthodox, the weaker do we find it to be. It is obvious that the orthodox view has immense initial advantages; and if those who support it do not want opposing views to be even stated, this would suggest that they doubt its ability to hold its own in free debate — from which it might further be inferred that the view they promulgate differs in important respects from what they really believe. Again (as has been regularly pointed out in discussions of this sort), they imply, in professing to be able to censor, that they themselves will take no harm from examining what they proceed to suppress; in other words, that there is a line of social demarcation between protectors and protected — a line which, since it is drawn by the protectors themselves, will always seem highly arbitrary to those who do not unquestioningly accept protection.

It is here, of course, that we are met with the plea of urgency — irreparable harm may be done while the question is being debated; even if in the end those who proclaimed themselves competent are shown really to be so, it may be too late; the 'enemy' may have gained a footing from which he cannot be ousted. Here we have the doctrine of the 'fatal attractiveness' of falsehood and evil. Though certain positions can be conclusively demonstrated, immature minds will rush to the contrary positions as soon as they are confronted by the problems. Accordingly, they should be subjected to authority; they should be kept away from these problems as problems, and be presented only with the solutions.

The glaring weakness of this position is that if moral or political 'minors' could be kept away from the problems, if these were something merely external to them, there would be no fatal attraction. It is because sexuality is part of the child's make-up, because the tendency to enterprise is inherent in the worker's social position, that 'indecency' and 'subversive' doctrines have so strong an appeal. And in keeping these things down, in seeking to abolish what arises in the nature of the case, the protectors are not merely falsifying the facts but are showing that they themselves have special interests, that their 'protection' embodies repression and exploitation. In a liberal regime 'subversive' tendencies are intellectually exposed and refuted (while, of course, considerable heterodoxy is tolerated); in an illiberal regime where, from lack of freedom, they are more deeply rooted, they are physically repressed.

One does not, of course, expect to find a purely liberal or democratic regime; but a regime, in so far as it is democratic, supports open discussion and, in so far as it censors, is anti-democratic. Censorship 'manufactures the evidence' of social solidarity. It produces *some* of the features of intellectual agreement, but a very different spirit is manifested in the two cases. Those who have come to terms with conflicting views and tendencies are far more vigorous and able upholders of a cause than those who simply follow authority; the latter are divided in mind and prone to panic, the former are adaptable and enterprising. At least, it should be clear that the question is not of the 'defence of morality' but of the existence of conflicting moralities, the morality of defence or protection being opposed by the morality of enterprise or initiative, according to which not having tackled problems directly, not having been subjected to 'temptation', is a moral defect, a disqualification for responsible living. From this point of view protectors and protected alike exhibit a *low* morality; there is no moral elevation without open discussion. And literary elevation is one particular case of moral elevation. Just as 'the only check that ought to be placed on literature is criticism' (A. R. Orage), so good literature is itself critical and revealing, and protective literature, the literature of comfort and consolation, is bad.[1]

But, whatever the detailed differences may be, the first point to be made is just that there are different moralities, opposing sets of rules of human behaviour. This is because there are different ways of life, different 'movements', each with its own rules of procedure for its members. Such rules, it may be noted, need not have been formulated; but the more important point is that, formulated or unformulated, they are not to be regarded as preceptual or mandatory. We speak of 'laws of nature', but by this is to be understood the ways of working which things themselves have and not anything imposed on them from without, anything which they 'obey'. In the same way, the moral question is of how people do behave and not of their 'obeying the moral law'; obedience, or the treating of something as an authority, is just one particular way of behaving, the moral characterisation of which has still to be given. The phrase 'how people do behave' may be misleading here. It is not a question of taking any type of activity in isolation; we do not have a morality until we have a way of life, a number of ways of behaving that hang together, that constitute a system — and it is in the conflict of such systems that rules come to be formulated. From this point of view it might be best to say that a morality *is* a way of life or a movement; and in that case the person who spoke in the name of 'morality' would be neglecting to specify the movement he represented.

That, at least, is one defensible usage. Alternatively, we might identify morality with the preceptual system, with living in obedience to authority — or, admitting that there are many authorities, we might speak of many moralities, while recognising that there is also a movement, a way of living, which rejects all authority but still has its own character (or again, we might recognise many 'free' movements). The multiplicity of authorities, however, is just what the authorities will not admit; each sets itself up as *the* authority, as laying down what is absolutely mandatory, what, in the nature of things and not relatively to any particular movement or director, is required of people. To speak on behalf of morality, in this sense, is to speak on behalf of the principle of authority — and so again (whatever the actual power may be that is thus metaphysically bolstered up) to support a low way of living. It is low, in particular, because it is anti-intellectual, because it is necessarily dogmatic. Some account can be given of the relation of a particular 'rule' or way of behaving to a certain way of life, but it can have no demonstrable relation to 'the nature of things'. To say that something is required by the nature of things is just to say that it is required — to say, without reason, that it 'is to be done'; and, as soon as any specification is attempted, the whole structure breaks down. If, for example, we are told to do something because God commands us to do so, we can immediately ask why we should do what God commands — and any intelligible answer brings us back to *human* relationships, to the struggle between opposing movements. In that region, to accept authority is simply to bow to superior force; but it eases the situation for both oppressors and oppressed to represent this as bowing to some Absolute, to the authoritative as such — in other words, to the unintelligible.

This does not mean that reasons can be found for everything we do; it can be shown that a particular line of action contributes to a more general form of activity, but such considerations of policy always lead back to activities for which no reason is sought, to activities in which we are actually engaged. In fact, ways of life are prior to policies, they *frame* policies, and, while different ways of life may have sufficient in common to permit of some compromise, some working arrangement, it constantly happens that what suits one does not suit another, that what from one point of view is a reason is from the other no reason at all. All they can do, then, is to fight it out — even the compromise depends on the exertion of a certain force by the various parties to it — and the struggle between different ways of life may be taken as the outstanding feature of social existence. But what the authoritarians, the 'moralists', maintain is that their reasons are 'essentially reasonable', that they are of a higher order than those of the non-authoritarians, and in this way they seek to disarm their opponents. The argument is of an ontological character; that which is binding-in-itself must have greater force than that which is not, just as that which exists-in-itself must be stronger than anything which exists under certain conditions — and ceases under certain conditions. And the freethinker is made to appear to be putting that which depends on something else above that which depends on nothing else, when he is really saying that there is no such thing as the latter, that the conception of the non-dependent is a confused one. Though this type of authoritarian argument (whether in its classic form, dealt with by Kant, or in more special forms) has been refuted again and again, it still imposes on the weak-minded; but even they would begin to see daylight under conditions of fair intellectual fight, and that is why authoritarians invariably add censorship, preventing arguments from being even heard, to intellectual crookedness.

The main point is the close connection between the upholding of a hierarchical doctrine of reality and the maintenance of a *social* hierarchy. And though, as already noted, we can distinguish various authoritarian movements (though there are different views of the proper order of the layers in the social pyramid), they all come together in this, that they recognise *some* order, that they deny the necessity or naturalness of conflict, i.e., that they take a solidarist view of society[2]; and thus it is that, in spite of superficial differences between them, they are regularly to be found working together in opposition to 'disorder'. The accusation that he is upholding privilege and servitude is, of course, one that the ordinary solidarist would indignantly repel, since he is maintaining that all are equally partners in the social concern; but it is by this very pretence at equality (as far as it is made plausible) that inequalities are covered over and the unprivileged are detached from the independent movements which are their escape from servitude. In fact, philanthropy implies inequality; it is 'relief' given by the privileged to the unprivileged, but it leaves privileges as they are. The best intentions in the world will not succeed by such methods in *bringing about* equality, in bringing the lower orders up to a higher level; it is by what they *are*, not by what they are given, that men will win release from servitude. If the philanthropist were really going to assist those he professes to be interested in, he would join their movements, he would *be* one of them. But he is not; and his philanthropy (his good intentions, his self-righteousness) is merely a means whereby their movements are weakened. It is curious that the philanthropic ideology is what nowadays passes as 'Socialist', but its purpose in its new setting is the same as that of ordinary bourgeois philanthropy, to pass off a hierarchical system as egalitarian, to sidetrack on the one hand, and on the other hand to justify the repression of, those independent movements which would alter the balance of social power.

Now all this is highly relevant to *Ulysses*. The position taken up by Joyce (as Stephen Dedalus) is above all a refusal to *serve*, a rejection of despotism, however benevolent its guise, a rejection of the master–servant relationship (with which is bound up the whole ideology of utility and social service), and hence a rejection of theology. More exactly, we are presented with Stephen's mental struggle against servitude, a servitude imposed upon him by the submission of his country to 'two masters ... the imperial British state and the holy

9 Art and Morality

Roman catholic and apostolic church' — and hence a struggle against Ireland itself, though this is something from which he can never be wholly free. To the bowelless critics of the book, steeped as they are in servility and easy social compromise, this struggle means nothing — and so they fasten on incidentals: the grotesqueries of style, the printing of the 'unprintable', the general 'unpleasantness' (i.e., the fact that the portrayal of any real struggle does not comfort and console). But, for the 'intellectual imagination' of Joyce, the makeshifts of the bourgeois world, and of the well-ordered universe which is its theological counterpart, are intolerable.

It is idle then, to call Joyce 'blasphemous'; that is only to say that the battle should not be fought — it is no answer at all to Joyce's intellectual attack, to his bringing out of the human, the servile, content of theology. His 'free thought' consists, in the first instance, not in rejecting theology, but in taking it quite seriously. If there *were* a master of the universe, then Joyce, to the extent of his power, would fight against him; he will not endure servitude, he cannot accept sacrifice and atonement, he rebels against the low conception of life, the base morality, which they imply. And this means that he is considering them in human terms (these being the only terms in which they are intelligible), that he recognises the arbitrariness of 'analogical reasoning', of the mystery-mongering which makes such things partly human and partly non-human. 'With me all or not at all.'

Ulysses, of course, is not a work of science. Dedalus works out no Feuerbachian reduction of the divine world to the human. Nevertheless, that is what is involved in his soul's crisis in the book. It is institutions, earthly authorities, that impose servitude in the name of heavenly authority. And it is the earthly content of theological conceptions that alone has psychic and social importance. 'My hell, and Ireland's, is in this life.' Hell, the self-alienation of the spirit, occurs here and now; it is something that has to be fought through, not something that we can avoid by propitiating human or 'cosmic' powers, not something that we can be protected from. He who remains in the circle of propitiation and protection remains in hell. He alone works through it who rejects the easy ways of escape — nodding at an image, repenting, letting one thing 'stand for' another — the whole system of anti-intellectual pretences. This is the central theme of *Ulysses*, and it is this that the Homeric material (the descent to and return from the shades, contentment with a swinish existence, mock-heroism and so forth) subserves. And it is because the theologians cannot meet this intellectual attack, while at the same time they wish to keep up the pretence at intellectuality which theology is, that they take refuge in accusations of blasphemy and immorality, of damage to immature minds — when in fact the issue raised is whether the life *they* uphold is not death to the spirit and when Joyce's free speculation is setting itself up as a *morality* (in the first sense suggested above), as a way of life opposed to precept and protection (which, as we have seen, is above all the protection of vested interests).

Actually, *Ulysses* would produce little or no effect on the immature; it is a book for the mature, but not for the servile, who are shocked by it because it confronts them with a freedom they have lost, because they can no longer face unpleasant facts and particularly their own defeats, because it attacks the ceremonial and fetishistic system by which they conceal these things from themselves. And because the immature have not yet been defeated and might come to see through the prevailing pretences, their guardians are anxious that they should not learn that anything but the ceremonial system exists. It is noteworthy that what they are not to hear about is above all *sexual* transgression; this is what 'immorality' has come to mean. Our censors do not say, 'This book portrays spite, that book portrays tyranny and greed, therefore children must not read them in case they should become spiteful, tyrannical and greedy.' There is a general misunderstanding that in a proper book evil conduct meets with some punishment; but, for the most part, such faults are not even noticed, and they are certainly not taken to be contagious in the way that *sexual* impropriety is supposed to be. Is the position, then, that sexual freedom has a particularly secularising tendency, that it cuts more sharply than other 'transgressions' across the hierarchical system? It is certain that, in moralistic theories, hierarchical conceptions are most strikingly applied to sexuality; thus it is demanded that sexual enjoyment be subordinated to reproduction, and the independent pursuit of it is regarded as a grievous sin. In fact, it is especially in regard to sexuality that the conception of sin finds application and that 'guilt' is felt; and it may be that, without exercising some command over the sexual life of the lower orders, authorities could never keep them docile.

9 Art and Morality

Feuerbach, in his *Essence of Christianity* (trans. Marian Evans; Trübner & Co., 1881), throws some light on this question. He connects Christianity's depreciation of sex with its individualistic character, its concern with personal salvation, and he says (p. 167):

> The true Christian not only feels no need of culture, because this is a worldly principle and opposed to feeling [i.e., to subjectivity]; he has also no need of (natural) love. God supplies to him the want of culture, and in like manner God supplies to him the want of love, of a wife, of a family. The Christian immediately identifies the species with the individual; hence he strips off the difference of sex as a burdensome, accidental adjunct. Man and woman together first constitute the true man; man and woman together are the existence of the race, for their union is the source of multiplicity, the source of other men. Hence the man who does not deny his manhood, is conscious that he is only a part of a being, which needs another part for the making up of the whole of true humanity. The Christian, on the contrary, in his excessive, transcendental subjectivity, conceives that he is, by himself, a perfect being. But the sexual instinct runs counter to this view; it is in contradiction with his ideal: the Christian must therefore deny this instinct.

Feuerbach, in fact, treats love (natural love) as the core of humanity, the central good; and it may be argued, along these lines, that freedom in love is the condition of other freedoms, that while in itself it does not constitute culture, there can be no culture without it, that it continually enriches and is enriched by the various forms of productive (enterprising) activity — Science, Art, Industry. Thus while, in general, a doctrine of individual salvation is calculated to weaken any *movement* of the enslaved and to nullify or divert their discontent with their place in the earthly system (their 'lot'),* the weakening of the fundamental

---

* Cf. Thamin, 'Saint Ambroise' (quoted by Sorel, 'Eglise, Evangile et Socialisme'; appendix to *La Ruine du Monde antique*, Riviere, 1925, p. 309): 'Faisant aimer aux pauvres leur pauvreté, aux humbles leur humilité, il [le christianisme] préparait pour ceux qui veulent avoir leur royaume ici-bas, des sujets dociles et des victimes volontaires.'

human tie is an important step in the process. It is also, I think, argued by Feuerbach, and it is in any case plausible, that what the religious person sacrifices is something that he values very highly, something that he glorifies by handing it over to divinity. Thus his sacrificed sexuality becomes an attribute of the divine, but, of course, in a distorted, 'idealised' form — and this idealisation further serves to keep his actual sexuality apart from the active life which it would fructify. It is, at any rate, not hard to see that the heavenly imaginings of the upholders of chastity are symbolic, that they have a hidden sexual content; there is, indeed much that is sexual in their manifest content, and one of the commonest forms of 'blasphemy', one of the earliest exercises in freethought, is to explode the mysteries by completing the earthly parallel. There is something of this in *Ulysses* but it is not prominent; the main point for Joyce is the falsity of it all. But that cannot be entirely separated from important social considerations — the central place of sexual repression in any repressive system, the way in which fear of sexuality carries over into fear of social disorder, the linking of chastity (which can never be other than *distorted* sexuality) with quietism.

That Joyce is interested in the question of sexual freedom is shown in his play, *Exiles*, where Richard Rowan 'wounds his soul' in his search for 'freedom from all bonds'. However, the main issue in *Ulysses* is still the intellectual one, and the sexual side of the book is only incidental to that. Even its printing of the 'unprintable' is to be taken mainly as an intellectual rejection of the customary — remembering always that there is a considerable element of sexuality in custom. The most bawdy conversations (e.g., in the lying-in hospital) fall far short of what is quite common in everyday life, and are governed by the intellectual and critical interest that characterises the work as a whole. Moreover, the characters are none of them pronouncedly sexual; Marion Bloom, who has been much referred to in this connection, says a good deal that is not usually recorded (again the attack on the customary), but it is to be remembered that Joyce is giving words to her half-formed nascent thoughts, and, that being understood, her attitude to sexual enjoyment is not at all abnormal. Her husband is more 'perverse', but even his peccadilloes are commonplace enough to those who have given any consideration to sex in society. There is no question, of course, of explaining away the sexual side of *Ulysses*. Sexual entanglements, cross-purposes, dissatisfactions, terrors, are an important feature of the hell of bourgeois existence. But the crux of the matter is servitude and the escape from servitude.

But now it may be asked why, if Joyce's rejection of authority is an intellectual one, he does not attack it scientifically instead of artistically, does not write a treatise instead of a novel. One answer is that the artistic attack is more effective. Intellectually, the exponents of hierarchy have not a leg to stand on, but they can *ignore* and promote ignorance. And here the work of science is more ponderous, it demands time and detachment, whereas the work of art is more pointed, it particularises, and so can bite through the defences of those whom mere argument would leave unaroused. But, again, the antithesis is not so sharp as might appear. The true scientist, who is not devoted to utility, to 'service', produces what may well be called a work of art. And the literary artist, in particular, has much of the scientist in him; he describes, he classifies, he correlates. So when Joyce speaks of 'the eternal affirmation of the spirit of man in literature', he is evoking a spirit which is scientific as well as artistic, and he is specifying what is his own escape from servitude.

It is interesting to observe here that Dedalus refers to what binds him as *history*. 'History is a nightmare from which I am trying to awake.' This awakening is art. Art is not concerned with dates, it is not concerned with the conditions and consequences of its subject-matter, though it may present a succession of phases *within* that subject-matter. Thus, while it may be said to particularise in that it presents something concrete and not a general formula, it may also be said to generalise, to present an 'eternal essence', as Joyce, through the medium of a day in Dublin in 1904, presents servitude and the escape from it as states of the human soul. What art, on this showing, is most sharply contrasted with is utility. Utility insists on conditions and consequences; its sharp distinction of means and ends is bound up with hierarchy, with the master-servant relationship. But for art all things are on an equality; they are all alike aesthetic material; in any one of them *character* can be discovered. Art, in other words, is concerned not with what things are 'for' or what they are 'by means of', but with what they are. And this is hard to find just because of utility, because in human life things become cluttered up with meanings and purposes. It is this which gives point to the description of the painter as restoring 'the innocence of the eye', breaking up conventional associations; and in the same way the literary artist can be described as restoring the innocence of our sense of humanity, as against adventitious commendations and condemnations. On this basis, too, we can see that the artist is supremely productive or creative — in fundamental opposition to the 'consumer's view'. That is to say, the good artist; for all arts can degenerate, and the bad artist is the supreme purveyor of consolation, the most efficient caterer to the consumptive or servile mentality.

Taking art, however, as good art, we find it diametrically opposed to preceptual morality; and what Joyce has shown us in *Ulysses* is the crisis in the struggle of a soul from bondage to freedom, from moral compromise to artistic integrity. It is thus a very special product; like all Joyce's larger works it is an essay in the theory of art as well as in art itself. It not merely does what art does but shows what art does; and, being thus a double attack on moralism, it is doubly attacked by the moralists. But, leaving this special case and taking art in general, we can say that it breaks rules, transgresses boundaries, that is, the rules and boundaries set up by human purposes; it follows the lines of the things themselves. In so doing it is dangerous as well as revealing; it stimulates new perceptions, but it runs foul of the safety system to which men cling. At the same time, such a system is never actually safe; safety or crowd motives (characteristic of bourgeois mentality) are, as already indicated, liable to panic. Thus the insights of art may often show the way out of a social impasse. When all is said, art occurs in society, in history; *it* has conditions and consequences, however little it may concern itself with such in its material. In brief, the struggle between art and moralism is the struggle between innovation and conservation in society; neither can conquer, but that is not to say that the artistic way of life can compromise (that way lies artistic death and social stagnation); it must still seek to *discover* and to push its discoveries as hard as it can against the inertia of custom and the 'protection' of privilege.

9 Art and Morality

Mr and Mrs Anderson on their honeymoon in Ayrshire, June 1922.

— 10 —
Ulysses

It is scarcely possible to discuss the work of James Joyce without referring to the censorship which prevents it from being so widely studied as it should be. Censorship, of course, is not a question with which aesthetics is directly concerned. It appears as a political expedient whereby a governing class secures the elimination from the circuses provided for the lower orders of anything which would make them reflect on their condition. But governments are assisted in the proscription of 'dangerous' topics by numerous philanthropic busybodies, who have a horror of anything of the nature of freedom, and who accordingly propagate the moralistic or censorious view of art.

The doctrine of the autonomy of art, of the free choice of themes, is thus of some moral and political importance. It involves not the irresponsible setting aside of moral considerations, but the rejection of the morality of prohibition. To say, for example, that *Ulysses* is 'obscene' is merely to say that it refers to matters the contemplation of which shocks certain minds. Thus if there is no shock, there is no obscenity. And, instead of resenting the absence of shock in other minds, the self-

---

An address to the Australian English Association, 25 September 1930. Offprint No. 3 of the Association as published was an edited censored version of the address; here, the censored passages have been restored and some of Anderson's marginal notes incorporated.

constituted guardians of morality would be well employed in curing their own obsessions.

To speak of the 'evil effects' of certain books is to neglect the fact that what is evil is some particular way of life which, if it does not find one means of expression, will find another. Thus the enormous interest in romantic fiction is symptomatic of an idle and hopeless way of living, but no one will pretend that the cure for this lies in the prohibition of the sale of cheap novels. The ability to deal decisively with facts of any order is the result of education and especially of aesthetic training. For aesthetic contemplation consists of the recognition of a thing as a balance of forces or sequence of phases, as against the confusion of it with its conditions or effects which is made by the panic-stricken moralist.

If, therefore, we are shocked by a book, we can stop reading it, and hope some day to be in a better frame of mind; while those who are not shocked may proceed to enjoy it — or, it may be, to condemn it as 'bad'. But this will merely mean that it fails in the presentation of its theme, or perhaps does not even have a theme. No other classification of books than that of the good and the bad, in this sense, can be upheld. To regard certain themes as 'improper' is to take up a position comparable to that exploded by Wordsworth — that there is a peculiar poetic language and certain specially poetic subjects. It is, in short, to make art, in Socratic language, 'an art of flattery'.

As an example of the inartistic treatment of 'certain subjects' we may take the way in which the Victorian novelists, e.g., Dickens, Thackeray and George Eliot, dealt with sexual matters. They worked by allusion and exhibited the 'awful consequences' instead of the thing itself — a procedure which had the incidental effect of promoting ignorance and superstition among their less mature readers. But this is merely an illustration of their general method, which is that of pointing a moral, i.e., working up a conclusion which falls outside the structure of the story, so that there is duality of theme or, more exactly, no consistently presented theme at all. Books of this kind, which inculcate a lesson, form one great class of bad books.

A similar incoherence is to be found in the work of Kipling. With him the great point is to be effective, to make a hit. This is seen in his straining after *mots justes* and in his conception of art as magic, and is connected with the extraordinary prominence given in his work to vindictiveness or 'scoring'. And this again is just a feature of that public school code from which he derives those fixed ideas — of the white man's mission, of chivalry, playing the game and so forth — which serve as the 'morals' of his tales.

This confusion reaches its height in the romantic theory that there is only one artistic theme, Life, and that art has to bring out its value or significance. Thus from the idols of Kipling and the 'poetic justice' of the Victorians we pass to the great fetish to which, in the 'philosophical' works of Shaw, art is finally and deliberately sacrificed. The artist is set to producing sermons, he is required to be helpful and uplifting, even if he has to falsify his material to do it.

How widespread such delusions are is shown by Bennett's description of Joyce as having a 'colossal down on humanity' [*Things That Have Interested Me*, second series], because *Ulysses* is largely concerned with human degradation. Such a theme, according to the romantic, should be developed so as to show the 'silver lining'. The classical doctrine on the other hand is that of the independent theme working itself out in its own way. Joyce's works, largely influenced by the classics, are to be appreciated as classics, i.e., as works of art.

In the works of Homer, though they are described as epics, the material is the same as that of the novel, viz., human beings, and thus the same sort of theme is possible. The theme of the *Iliad* is *wrath*, specifically the wrath of Achilles, and this is presented against a background of general wrath-war. The *Odyssey* has as its theme the exile, or, perhaps better, the home-seeking, of Odysseus, and again the background, against which the hero appears, is one of general homelessness or desolation. That this theme is an important one for Joyce is seen not only in *Ulysses* (the many parallels between which and the Odyssey have been pointed out in Gorman's *James Joyce: His First Forty Years*), but also in his play, *Exiles*. The classical character of his works is shown by the definiteness with which he announces his themes and the thoroughness with which he works them out through their successive phases.

In *A Portrait of the Artist as a Young Man*, which deals with the early years of Stephen Dedalus (who, as he appears here and in *Ulysses*, is clearly Joyce himself), the theme is given out in a striking passage.

The spirit of youth is presented as the *profane joy* which the young artist feels, when an encounter with a girl stirs his interest in the life which is to be his material.

> Her image had passed into his soul for ever and no word had broken the holy silence of his ecstasy. Her eyes had called him and his soul had leaped at the call. To live, to err, to fall, to triumph, to recreate life out of life! A wild angel had appeared to him, the angel of mortal youth and beauty, an envoy from the fair courts of life, to throw open before him in an instant of ecstasy the gates of all the ways of error and glory. On and on and on and on!

The element of romanticism here is a characteristic of youth. But this in itself shows the position to be an unstable one; the last phase of this development is the opening of a new struggle. The crisis of youth is the birth of the soul, and the soul is born to estrangement, with the breaking of former ties.

> It has a slow and dark birth, more mysterious than the birth of the body. When the soul of a man is born in this country there are nets flung at it to hold it back from flight. You talk to me of nationality, language, religion. I shall try to fly by those nets.

It is with the escape from exile, with 'flying by those nets', that *Ulysses* is concerned. The theme is given out in the scene in the Dublin National Library, where Stephen discusses *Hamlet* with certain Irish *literati*:
'Where there is a reconciliation, Stephen said, there must have been first a sundering.'
And again (in a quotation from Maeterlinck): 'If Socrates leave his house today he will find the sage seated on his doorstep. If Judas go forth tonight it is to Judas his steps will tend.'
The theme is thus expressed as exile or sundering from self, and the search for reconciliation with self. This reconciliation is to be found, as we learn later when Stephen's steps have led him to the other exile in Dublin, Leopold Bloom, in 'the eternal affirmation of the spirit of man in literature'. As in the *Odyssey*, then, the hero is seeking escape from exile, and here also there is a background of exile — Ireland,

divorced from free development. But here the effect is heightened by the concentration on exile as a state of mind or 'soul', and by the juxtaposition with Dedalus of Bloom, whose wanderings from and return to his home and to his far from pining Penelope are on a different plane of exile, but who, as a Jew, suffers from the historical exile of his people. Stephen also feels in his own person the sufferings of Ireland from British and Roman rule, with the consequent material and spiritual impoverishment. 'I am the servant of two masters, an English and an Italian ... and a third there is who wants me for odd jobs.'

'History', Stephen says again, 'is a nightmare from which I am trying to awake.' The subjection of man to history is the state of sundering from self; as the affirmation of the human spirit, the recognition, as Nietzsche has it, of the world as an aesthetic phenomenon, is the release from servitude. Odysseus descends to and returns from the shades — an episode which has its closest parallel in the 'orgiastic' scene, as Bennett calls it, in Dublin's night-town, but which is paralleled in a more general way by the whole book. For the state of sundering from self is the state of being damned; the theme, in one of its formulations, is Hell and the escape therefrom.

What is notable about Joyce's work is that, as an artist in human material, he concentrates on the exhibition of hell as a state of mind, and not, like Dante, on externals, on the apparatus of torture, however vividly portrayed. True, there is the background of damnation, in Dublin as in any great city, and especially in oppressed Ireland. But it is in the souls of the leading characters that the real issue is fought out; and, in comparison, the *Odyssey* too seems episodic. The desolation of the heart of Odysseus stands out against the desolation of the scenes he passes through, but it is not developed as a theme; it is only there. Dostoevsky's *Crime and Punishment* is likewise great as a work with human material, because he presents crime and punishment as developing conditions of the mind of his hero, Raskolnikov. He is well aware that these are social phenomena; the appropriate social background is present. But the theme is a mental one and is developed in its own terms.

In *Ulysses* the theme as hell and the escape from it is indicated in a number of passages, as when 'the mocker', Mulligan, says of Dedalus —

'They drove his wits astray ... by visions of hell. He will never capture the Attic note. The note of Swinburne, of all poets, the white death and the ruddy birth. That is his tragedy. He can never be a poet. The joy of creation ...'
'Eternal punishment,' Haines said, nodding curtly. 'I see.'

And again in the night-town scene, where his dead mother appears to him —

> *The Mother*
> *(With smouldering eyes)* Repent! O, the fire of hell!
> Stephen
> *(Panting)* The Corpsechewer! Raw head and bloody bones!

And below this, from Stephen — '*Ah non, par example*! The intellectual imagination! With me all or not at all. *Non serviam!*' This recalls *A Portrait* —

> I will not serve that in which I no longer believe, whether it call itself my home, my fatherland, or my church: and I will try to express myself in some mode of life or art as freely as I can and as wholly as I can, using for my defence the only arms I allow myself to use — silence, exile and cunning.

But before he can enter upon the work of affirmation, he has to escape from his self-alienation, his exile from self.

In *Ulysses*, then, Dedalus and Bloom stand out from the surrounding crowd in the 'hell on earth' which is Dublin, because for them there is a solution. Bloom, by accident, Stephen, by design, stand apart from nationalism and can escape the other nets — the latter because he is an artist, the former because he is a Jew and also, as one of the characters remarks, 'a bit of an artist', a man in whom curiosity has not been killed. The rest are sundered from self without hope of reconciliation; and all their drinkings and blusterings, songs and lovemakings, are but the antics of the damned, pretending that freedom does not matter, that illusions are best. They are Circe's swine, and would fain bring others to their own level. It is they whom Stephen challenges when, in Circe's palace (in its more particular re-creation as a disorderly house in Dublin's night-town), he shouts, 'Break my spirit all of you, if you can!'

The return from Hell is marked by the meeting and mutual recognition of Bloom and Stephen (Ulysses and Telemachus), Bloom finding in Stephen one who can fulfil his aspirations, and Stephen finding in Bloom material for his greatest creative work. And the story ends with the long monologue of Mrs Bloom (Penelope), who, after all her wanderings in the mazes of desire, finds such reconciliation as she can aspire to in the memory of the moment when she accepted her husband.

A number of important aesthetic reflections are suggested by *Ulysses*. The whole book is a demonstration of the artistic possibilities of the theme, and the folly of the objectors to 'wallowing in human degradation'. The conception of literature as showing us the 'bright side' of things is purely commercial. The sole question is that of the presentation of a coherent structure, whatever the material may be. Again, the dramatic form of the *Walpurgisnacht*, or 'orgiastic' scene, illustrates the point that, since both deal with human material, there is no real difference between the novel and the play; and so, the Homeric comparison reminds us, with the epic. It is also worth noting that only an unaesthetic emphasis on the upshot, as contrasted with the working out of the theme, occasions the popular distinction between tragedy and comedy.[1]

Objection has been taken to the mixture of styles in *Ulysses*. Now this is not, as has been suggested, mere experimentation or fanciful innovation, but the objective treatment of style — the rejection of the distinction between matter and manner. The way in which words are arranged is just as much a part of the content of the work as the words themselves or the incidents presented. Everything, even Stephen Dedalus, is presented objectively and impersonally; Joyce is nowhere 'addressing the reader'. The style is part of the incident, as when the Gerty MacDowell (Nausicaa) episode is narrated in the language of the novelettes which form Gerty's notion of 'life'. So the succession of styles (amounting, almost, to a history of English literature) in the scene in the lying-in hospital indicates at once the transition from *the calm of the twilight* to the frenzy of the night-scene, and the strange variety of characters who had collected as guests of the young assistant doctor. Naturally, as in *A Portrait*, this is only a beginning. First a breaking away from ties; then the discovery of a solid foundation; after this the work of affirmation will follow. Hence, when her crisis is past, there is a toning down of style to the reconciliation (as far as she was capable of it) of 'Penelope', Mrs Bloom in a return to an affirmation of her acceptance of her husband as her 'poetical moment' whatever may happen to her afterwards.

> he said I was a flower of the mountain yes so we are flowers all a womans body yes that was one true thing he said in his life and the sun shines for you today yes ... O that awful deep-down torrent O and the sea the sea crimson sometimes like fire and the glorious sunsets and the figtrees ... I was a flower of the mountains yes ... yes and how he kissed me under the Moorish wall and I thought well as well him as another and then I asked him with my eyes to ask again yes and then he asked me would I yes to say yes my mountain flower and first I put my arms around him yes and drew him down to me so he could feel my breasts all perfume yes and his heart was going like mad and yes I said yes I will Yes.

Such thorough classicism makes it hard to grasp the book as a whole, even when (as by Bennett) special passages are admired. But, in terms of Joyce's aesthetic creed (stated in *A Portrait*), this is not sound appreciation. Appreciation consists in recognition of the wholeness, harmony and radiance of a thing; when it is apprehended as *one* thing, as a *thing*, and as the thing that it is. *Ulysses*, then, is to be thought of as portraying one peculiar thing — the escape of the soul from hell, from its own dissociation. But no theme can be dealt with purely or universally; there are always peculiarities of the circumstances and the actors. It is such variations, along with the abiding traits of human nature, that make possible the classical tradition of European literature, which Joyce follows. The discussion of Hamlet is only one of many suggestions of parallels with and influences from other writers — Homer, Dante, Shakespeare, Goethe, Dostoevsky and Shaw.[2]

Perhaps the greatest influence on Joyce is that of Ibsen. This influence is seen in *Exiles*, and the dramatic part of *Ulysses* not only illustrates the general Ibsenite thesis (which is indeed the basis of drama) that thoughts are things, but is directly connected with *Peer Gynt*, and with Peer Gynt's answer to the question what it is to be oneself.

> The Gyntish Self — it is the host
> Of wishes, appetites, desires, —
> The Gyntish Self, it is the sea
> Of fancies, exigencies, claims,
> All that, in short makes my breast heave,
> And whereby I, as I, exist.

It is these wishes, appetites, desires, taking personal form as in dreams, that make up the dance of the shades (just as in dreams we have the 'deformation and reformation of words', as Colum puts it, which is characteristic of Joyce's latest publication, a fragment of a work dealing with 'the night-side of our lives', *Anna Livia Plurabelle*). The conquered souls of *Ulysses*, then, are so many Peer Gynts, making false selves out of their fancies, instead of affirming the spirit of man.

But all these parallels and influences do not affect the originality of Joyce's work. They simply show that he is in the tradition of great literature.

– 11 –
The Banning of *Ulysses*

In Anatole France's *The Revolt of the Angels*, the uncle of Maurice d'Esparvieu, on being introduced to Maurice's guardian angel, expresses doubt as to his genuineness. 'My faith in Jehovah,' he remarks, 'is not sufficiently strong to enable me to believe in his angels.'

> 'Monsieur,' answers the angel, 'he whom you call Jehovah is really a coarse and ignorant demiurge, and his name is Ialdabaoth.'
> 'In that case, Monsieur, I am perfectly ready to believe in him. He is a narrow-minded ignoramus, is he? Then belief in his existence offers me no further difficulty. How is he getting on?'

It is, in fact, not at all difficult to believe that narrow-mindedness creates a God in its own image and for its own protection. It creates a whole system of protection, of which censorship is an integral part. And it is not surprising that Joyce, that 'relentless foe of social and business success,' should be subjected to censorship, for his work in general, and *Ulysses* in particular, is a direct attack on the system by which men protect their illusions.[1]

From *Honi Soit* (published by the University of Sydney Students' Representative Council), 25 September 1941.

The fatuities of Federal Ministers are neither here nor there. The fact remains that, if anything should be censored, *Ulysses* should be, that, if obscene, blasphemous and seditious mean anything, Joyce is all three — literature is all three.

'The eternal affirmation of the spirit of man in literature' is the dragging into the light of day of the things that men conceal from themselves and one another. 'When the soul of a man is born in this country there are nets flung at it to hold it back from flight. You talk to me of nationality, language, religion. I shall try to fly by those nets.'

How far Joyce succeeded in flying by those nets is a question on which critics will differ. It seems to me that *Finnegans Wake* is a failure — that it tries to 'beat time' in a merely temporal sense, and loses grip of what is permanent in culture. But the Icarian flight in *Ulysses* is a magnificent success. The artist fights his way through the 'hell' of estrangement to the acceptance of all things as artistic themes and the rejection of taboos.

And it is not a merely personal success. In the struggle between literature and censorship, between free-thinking and phantasy, the protective system has its share of defeats; and Joyce's work has given a distinct turn to contemporary writing — it has emboldened the critically-minded and given a set-back to the purveyors of consolation. It is to be expected, of course, that objectors will direct their fire on the crude forms of 'obscenity' and 'blasphemy' which Joyce exhibits as incidental to his own larger denials; but it is these that really rankle — or, perhaps better, it is the majestic indifference with which Joyce sweeps over the ordinary avoidances.

Much has been made of the 'all life in a day' formula for *Ulysses*. The 'day' does not matter; but Joyce is certainly concerned with all life — all activities, all characters, all styles. *Ulysses* has the encyclopaedic character which is a mark of great works. And this is possible because Joyce has brains, because he is not merely an artist but a thinker — just as the piffling little 'audacities' of a Galsworthy derive from intellectual feebleness (and the denunciation of 'subversive activities' from incapacity for dealing with them intellectually).

In fine, as against those who would save themselves or their juniors from hell, Joyce demonstrates that the protected, bourgeois life itself is hell ('My hell and Ireland's is in this life'), and that salvation in any non-phantastic sense, the emancipation of the human spirit from bourgeois values, lies in uncensored art.

– 12 –
James Joyce

Estimation of the literary achievement of James Joyce is complicated by the variety of his work — poetry, short stories, drama, novels — and also by the peculiarity of that part of it which is still 'in progress'. One must, of course, leave out of account police criticism, though the conception of improper themes still makes its appearance in what are presumed to be literary circles. Taking a general view of Joyce's production, we can scarcely doubt that *Ulysses* is his outstanding contribution to letters; indeed, it so overshadows the work of his contemporaries that a discriminating and forthright public would call for the disappearance of most of them from the literary scene.

There are certainly many non-aesthetic reasons for the treatment of *Ulysses* as a phenomenon. There is the absence of 'reticence' — though this may be taken to indicate, on the aesthetic side, a more thorough working out of the theme than is customary in the market-place. There is the limitation of the action to less than twenty-four hours; there is the mere length of the book; there are the variations in style; there are other matters of 'technique' — all of which may be considered aesthetically in relation to the subject, but which, taken by themselves, may be made matters of sensational or journalistic comment. However trivial some of these considerations may be, critical appreciation of the book will

---

First published in *Hermes*, XXXIX, Michaelmas Term, 1933.

at least have to dispose of the charge of heterogeneity, of slapdash workmanship, and of general unintelligibility.

Ulysses is undoubtedly a difficult work to follow in detail, as compared, for example, with Joyce's earlier work, though there is nothing in it to compare with the difficulties encountered in 'Work in Progress' [published as parts of *Finnegans Wake* in 1939]. In the latter case many points may be made clear when we have the whole work before us, but under the most favourable conditions there will, I think, remain much that will defy the most acute interpreter. But in *Ulysses* the difficulties are all of a minor character, and the book can be objected to on this score only by those who think that a work of art should reveal its whole content on a first inspection — a demand the untenability of which is widely recognised in regard to music, and which is equally untenable in the case of any other art.

It is clear that anyone who does not know Dublin will miss many of the allusions; a knowledge of the relative positions of different parts of the town, streets, buildings, etc., will bring out a number of connections that would otherwise be passed over. But the same may be said of any book dealing with an actual place or, similarly, with an actual period; and, while knowledge of such facts may illuminate some details, ignorance of them leaves the main connections unaffected. It is perhaps more necessary that something should be known of the actual persons introduced and how they are alluded to; thus 'A.E.I.O.U.', in the library scene, will appear a pointless jingle, unless it is realised that the narrator means that he owes money to Mr George Russell (A.E.). But to miss this point scarcely affects the appreciation of the incident in which it occurs — Stephen's exposition of *Hamlet*.

The form of presentation of the thoughts of Stephen and Bloom occasions more serious difficulty to many readers. But this is due more to the way in which they are intermingled with narration than to any difficulty in the thoughts themselves. In such a passage as the following —

> He had come nearer the edge of the sea and wet sand slapped his boots. The new air greeted him, harping in wild nerves, wind of wild air of seeds of brightness. Here, I am not walking out to the Kish lightship, am I? He stood suddenly, his feet beginning to sink slowly in the quaking soil. Turn back.

— it is easy enough to distinguish narration from Stephen's thoughts, though even the narration is affected by Stephen's interest in verbal imagery. But in many cases the distinction is not so easy, especially when thoughts are coming in rapid succession, one cannoning into another. Still, there is no passage which a little attention will not clarify, and, as has been observed by Gorman, the well-marked difference between Stephen's way of thinking and Bloom's is of the first importance in the construction of the story. It may be noted that we need not imagine that the words 'Here, I am not walking out to the Kish lightship, am I?' actually passed before Stephen's mind. Here, and still more in the rapid succession of thoughts, it is a question of indicating how the person would express himself if his nascent thoughts received full formulation, and not of a detailed verbal meditation that actually takes place. At the same time verbal fragmentariness is used quite successfully to indicate a greater rapidity or disconnectedness of thought.

The case is similar with the variations in style throughout the book; they are essential to the development of the subject-matter. The insertion of mock-heroic material in the Barney Kiernan chapter brings out the mock-heroic character of the Citizen and of the Irish national movement in general (this being one of the main forces with which both Bloom and Stephen collide). The narration of the Gerty MacDowell episode in the style of cheap romance brings out the character of Gerty herself and also a particular strain in Bloom's mentality. The succession of styles in the scene in the lying-in hospital is another matter. A comparison is apparently intended between the development of English literature and embryological development, but it is not clearly worked out and seems to be a merely accidental analogy. The case is otherwise in the night-town scene, for there fancy (hallucination, nightmare) is the very substance of the episode, and identification, or, to use the Freudian term, 'condensation', is a ruling principle. Drunkenness, as in the hospital scene (which, of course, leads up to the nightmare scene), may have similar effects of condensation and displacement; nevertheless, the comparison of the stages of the embryo, the stages of English literature and the stages of drunkenness, is far-fetched and seems alien to the development of the general theme. This, I should contend, is the one weakness of *Ulysses*; but it is not serious, considering that through this chapter itself the main subject goes on, and that we can separately admire the exercises in style which it embodies.

The method of condensation or identification of related things is carried still further in the 'Work in Progress' which, according to Padraic Colum in his preface to *Anna Livia Plurabelle*, deals in its entirety 'with what is nocturnal, with the night-side of our lives, and with no other side'. This will account for what Colum calls 'the deformations and re-formations of words in James Joyce's later works', for such word-play, as Freud has shown, is characteristic of dreams. Nevertheless, whatever the dream-work may be, the dream takes its material from the 'other side', the waking side, of our lives; and even if something of the nature of a dream is taken as the theme, it has to be worked out in logical order. Allowing then that by identification the Liffey can be 'enlarged until it includes hundreds of the world's rivers', we have still to find what is conveyed by the naming of these rivers in the text. 'How many rivers,' Colum asks,

> have their names woven into the tale of *Anna Livia Plurabelle*? More than five hundred, I believe. 'She thought she's sankh neathe the ground with nymphant shame when he gave her the tigris eye.' In that sentence four of the world's rivers are mentioned and the associations we have with 'nymph' and 'underground' give us two more river-references.

But, when all these associations are allowed for, the appreciation of the text itself still remains to be undertaken.

A similar identification of cities takes place in *Haveth Childers Everywhere*; Edinburgh, for example, being introduced as a city of seven hills. But this is not enough to explain the meaning of 'Braid Blackfordrock, the Calton, the Liberton, Craig and Lockhart's, A. Costofino, R. Thursitt', i.e., why Craiglockhart, Corstorphine Hill and Arthur's Seat should appear under these curious disguises, and what either the disguises or the places themselves have to do with the subject. Again in *The Ondt and the Gracehoper (Tales of Shem and Shaun)* we find similarly worked into the text the names of various insects and the names of various philosophers (e.g., 'schoppinhour' = shopping hour +

Schopenhauer). This may suggest some identity between philosophers and Aesop (as alike manufacturers of fables). But what has the word 'schoppinhour' or a phrase 'a schelling in kopfers' to do with all this or with the theme of providence and wastefulness? Such questions may merely indicate failure in appreciation; it is quite certain that condensation of the kind in question *can* very forcibly convey a point; but it would also appear in the general consideration of word-play that it can be so far-fetched as to miss its mark.

It is scarcely possible to adopt the view of Stuart Gilbert, in his commentary on *Ulysses*, that Joyce actually accepts the mysticism, theosophy and identity-mongering which appear in that work also. Such an interpretation seems incompatible with passages like the mock-communication with the lately deceased Paddy Dignam.

> Interrogated as to whether life there resembled our experience in the flesh he stated that he had heard from more favoured beings now in the spirit that their abodes were equipped with every modern home comfort such as táláfáná, álávátár, hátákáldá, wátáklását and that the highest adepts were steeped in waves of voluptcy of the very purest nature. Having requested a quart of buttermilk this was brought and evidently afforded relief. Asked if he had any message for the living he exhorted all who were still at the wrong side of Máyá to acknowledge the true path for it was reported in devanic circles that Mars and Jupiter were out for mischief on the eastern angle where the ram has power. It was then queried whether there were any special desires on the part of the defunct and the reply was: *We greet you, friends of earth, who are still in the body. Mind C.K. doesn't pile it on.* It was ascertained that the reference was to Mr Cornelius Kelleher, manager of Messrs. H. J. O'Neill's popular funeral establishment, a personal friend of the defunct, who had been responsible for the carrying out of the interment arrangements.

An abundance of similar material would appear to show that identification is a method with Joyce, and not a belief — if it were, he could be taken as identifying himself with Homer. And, whatever admiration for Homer Joyce may have, the 'Homeric' passages in the Barney Kiernan chapter and elsewhere are clearly satirical. For example:

The figure seated on a large boulder at the foot of a round tower was that of a broadshouldered deepchested stronglimbed frankeyed redhaired freely freckled shaggybearded widemouthed largenosed longheaded deepvoiced barekneed, brawnyhanded, hairylegged ruddyfaced sinewyarmed hero. From shoulder to shoulder he measured several ells and his rocklike mountainous knees were covered, as was likewise the rest of his body wherever visible, with a strong growth of tawny prickly hair in hue and toughness similar to the mountain gorse (*Ulex Europeus*). The widewinged nostrils, from which bristles of the same tawny hue projected, were of such capaciousness that within their cavernous obscurity the fieldlark might easily have lodged her nest. The eyes in which a tear and a smile strove ever for the mastery were of the dimensions of a goodsized cauliflower. A powerful current of warm breath issued at regular intervals from the profound cavity of his mouth while in rhythmic resonance the loud strong hale reverberations of his formidable heart thundered rumblingly causing the ground, the summit of the lofty tower and the still loftier walls of the cave to vibrate and tremble.

Nevertheless, the method (of identification) is pursued so far in the later work that it may be doubted whether anyone but Joyce himself can follow it. It is not merely, as Colum says, that Joyce is 'as local as a hedge-poet' and 'writes as if it might be taken for granted that his readers know, not only the city he writes about, but its little shops and its little shows, the nick-names that have been given to its near-great, the cant-phrases that have been used on its side-streets.' He assumes a knowledge of everything he knows himself, of the results of his studies as well as of his immediate observations. Similar remarks have, of course, been made about the allusiveness of other writers, for example, Browning; but Joyce goes to unprecedented lengths in this matter. Still, when we recall what has been said about *Ulysses*, we may consider it possible that 'Work in Progress', when we have it as whole, will be just as illuminating and will fully repay continued study.

This question may be linked with that preoccupation with himself which Joyce's presentation of Stephen Dedalus seems to imply, and in connection with which it has been said that, apart from Bloom, he has failed to create any character but himself. This, however, is not the case; characters like Lenehan, Gerty MacDowell, Mr Garrett Deasy and Malachi Mulligan are certainly 'created', even if they are not treated in such detail as the two chief figures. And Mrs Bloom's monologue thoroughly establishes her as a definite character. The references which enable us to identify Stephen with Joyce are numerous, but the convincingness of the presentation of Stephen has nothing to do with this identification. The presenting of thoughts, for example, is just as successfully used in the delineation of Bloom and also of Mrs Bloom, and the implication in both *Ulysses* and the *Portrait* that Stephen is the author of *Dubliners* in no way detracts from the objectivity of the material. It is indeed often a sign of artistic crudity and amateurishness that an author makes his leading character an author, but it is by no means bound to be the case that a man's interest in himself conflicts with his artistic interest; and Joyce's novels precisely prove this point — just as Freud's *Interpretation of Dreams* is an outstanding example of the interest a man has in himself not conflicting with but reinforcing his scientific interest. In Joyce's case, the introduction of questions of art and aesthetics enables us usefully to combine criticism of aesthetic theory and of the artistic character with aesthetic estimation of the works themselves (and, similarly, study of Freud helps us to an estimate of the scientific character).

It is especially in *A Portrait of the Artist as a Young Man* that aesthetic views are presented (though in *Ulysses* the important *Hamlet* chapter introduces considerations of the artistic character as exhibited by Shakespeare), and for the estimation of Joyce's further work the account given of pity and terror is of considerable importance.

> Aristotle has not defined pity and terror. I have. ... Pity is the feeling which arrests the mind in the presence of whatsoever is grave and constant in human sufferings and unites it with the human sufferer. Terror is the feeling which arrests the mind in the presence of whatsoever is grave and constant in human sufferings and unites it with the secret cause. ... The tragic emotion, in fact, is a face looking two ways, towards terror and towards pity, both of which are phases of it. You see, I use the word *arrest*. I mean that the tragic emotion is static. Or rather the dramatic emotion is. The feelings excited by improper art are kinetic, desire or loathing. Desire urges us to possess,

to go to something; loathing urges us to abandon, to go from something. The arts which excite them, pornographical or didactic, are therefore improper arts. The esthetic emotion (I used the general term) is therefore static. The mind is arrested and raised above desire and loathing.

There is some confusion in this exposition between the question of the aesthetic character of a thing and that of its effect on us, but this does not affect the main implication of the theory of *stasis*, viz., that the aesthetic object is being considered not for the sake of anything else or in terms of any purpose but as it is in itself. As regards pity and terror, the subject of *exile* is especially present to Joyce's mind as something grave and constant in human sufferings, and this comes out in the play *Exiles* as well as in *Ulysses* — the wanderings of a modern Odysseus. But whereas *Exiles* (and to a large extent also the later poems — *Pomes Penyeach*) treats of the grave and constant factor of loss of love and exposes the 'secret cause', *Ulysses* is more concerned with the escape from exile, the return from the shades, the waking up from the nightmare of history, through artistic affirmation.

Richard Rowan, the hero of *Exiles*, exhibits the tragic character when he tells his friend, Robert Hand, that

> in the very core of my ignoble heart I longed to be betrayed by you and by her — in the dark, in the night — secretly, meanly, craftily. By you, my best friend, and by her. I longed for that passionately and ignobly, to be dishonoured for ever in love and in lust. ... To be for ever a shameful creature and to build up my soul again out of the ruins of its shame.

But this ignoble longing is not yet the deepest cause of loss of love. Richard says that he has acted 'from pride and from ignoble longing. And from a motive deeper still.' What this deeper motive may be is made clearer at the end of the play when Richard says to Bertha,

> I have wounded my soul for you — a deep wound of doubt which can never be healed. I can never know, never in this world. I do not wish to know or to believe. I do not care. It is not in the darkness of belief

that I desire you. But in restless living wounding doubt. To hold you by no bonds, even of love, to be united with you in body and soul in utter nakedness — for this I longed. And now I am tired for a while, Bertha. My wound tires me.

Bertha, for her part, longs for Richard as he came to her first — 'O, my strange wild lover, come back to me again!' For Richard, freedom from all bonds carries with it loss of love, loss of 'the luminous certitude that yours is the brain in contact with which she must think and understand and that yours is the body in contact with which her body must feel'. For Bertha, it is loss of love that brings the imposition of bonds. In both the source of exile is the division between 'understanding' and 'feeling', between aesthetic and possessive emotion.

This is only a rough description of the conflict. But it may be remarked in passing that, in terms of the theory suggested, the work of the critic purges him of pity and terror — of terror because he has *exposed* its secret cause, and of pity because he is no longer at one with the victim to whom it remains a secret. It is on some such basis as this that criticism appears to be cold-blooded, while sympathetic 'enjoyment' of a work may be quite unaesthetic. But there is no ground for saying that the critic or aesthetic theorist *loses* enjoyment; it is simply that he replaces sympathy by *aesthetic* enjoyment, which will find satisfaction, of course, as much in non-human material as in human material. The fact is that the operation of sympathy is a considerable obstacle to the aesthetic consideration of human material in novels and plays, as we note in statements about 'liking' and 'disliking' various characters, and it unfortunately extends itself into expressionistic or humanistic 'appreciations' of non-human material (e.g., music). The cure, if there is one, is the emphasis on stasis.

This element comes out very markedly in *Ulysses*. 'History,' says Stephen, 'is a nightmare from which I am trying to awake.' And the escape from exile, from the hell of mental dissociation, is secured not simply by standing apart from the movements of the day, as is suggested in the *Portrait* — that rather is one of the complicating factors — but by finding a form of activity in the creation of the static or aesthetic, in 'the eternal affirmation of the spirit of man in literature'. Solution is found in the presentation of things themselves, not in uplifting or romantic or progressive treatment of them; not in the propagandism or up-to-dateness of a Lawrence or a Huxley, but in classicism. It is this classicism alike in the development of the theme and as part of its substance that makes *Ulysses* the outstanding work that it is. The question to be considered when the 'Work in Progress' is completely before us will be whether it marks a departure from the static to the kinetic. Meanwhile, the recognition of the monumental character of *Ulysses* does not imply that its subject-matter excludes struggle, but only that it is devoted to no cause, to no upshot, beyond the working out of the theme itself.

– 13 –
James Joyce: *Finnegans Wake*

The character of James Joyce's writing is not wholly that of *Finnegans Wake*. Indeed, one might almost say that Joyce stands or falls as an artist by his main production, *Ulysses*, for in any judgement of his work, the importance of *Finnegans Wake* lies rather in the fact that it sheds light on the opinions and character of its author, than that it is of very high aesthetic merit itself. It is to be admitted that even in evaluating the earlier works, one's judgement is to some extent a judgement of the opinions of Joyce himself — in the poetry, the presentation of romanticism and classicism as different attitudes of the one person; in the prose, the literary arguments in *A Portrait of the Artist as a Young Man*, and those in the library scene in *Ulysses*, the latter of which gives an interesting though not particularly important view. But these opinions are neither so extensive nor so pervasive as they are in *Finnegans Wake*, and so they are less of a weakness aesthetically.

Despite the fact that *Ulysses* has more kinship with the earlier works, some of its features foreshadowed the later *Finnegans Wake*. For example, there is the section in which a number of different happenings in Dublin are presented simultaneously; and even more apt is that concerned with the lying-in hospital, especially its culmination which uses the distortion and condensation of language that is the very stuff

---

Address to the Literary Society, 23 April 1940.

of *Finnegans Wake*. Yet *Finnegans Wake* itself cannot be said to be literature in any exact aesthetic sense. It is supposed to deal with the night-side of our lives, the whole work being an enormous extended dream, containing condensation of language and various kinds of dream-work. And it is to be noted that the description necessary for an understanding of it comes from the author *outside* the work and not from the work itself or from him as a character in the story; and this is a definite aesthetic weakness such as we find also in writers like Meredith and Kipling, Shaw and Wells.

Part of its dream-like material is composed of the desire, often given expression to in dreams, to have all times at once, to have, as it were, the knowledge of age with the activity of youth, and so to be able to undo the error and defects of earlier years — the desire, in other words, for 'another chance'. In *Finnegans Wake* Joyce treats of this not only in the case of an individual, but in the case of all history itself. The influence of Vico is seen in the distinction he seeks to present between the temporal and the eternal (the very name of the hero — Earwicker — may be associated with the German for 'eternal') and while Joyce may or may not have accepted Vico's doctrine, a presentation of the opposition of the eternal to the temporal as itself a theme is impossible in a work of art. There is really no such theme, and such a conception is merely illusory. In fact, the presentation of *any* theme is the eternalising of it. It is the seeing of the universal and the eternal in the particular and the temporal. While *Finnegans Wake* presents some kinds of clashes between people with aesthetic interests and people with historical interests, these occur merely as strains in a great slab of material, and Joyce does not really succeed in bringing out the universal character of the opposition between the artist and the utilitarian.

But he is, indeed, much concerned with the problem of time, just as Meredith, for example, is in his poems. This concern has already appeared in the hospital scene in *Ulysses*, and in *Finnegans Wake* we find it openly stated in the question 'By holy St Martin, why can't you beat time?' It is this very question of beating time, of being eternal, of not passing away that is connected with his attitude to the Irish National Movement, cf. *A Portrait*. His want of sympathy with it is the particular example of his general opposition to history and of his setting up the eternal against the temporal; and it is by means of *Ulysses*,

13 James Joyce: *Finnegans Wake*

by establishing himself as an artist, that Joyce flies by the 'nets' of history.

It might also be mentioned in this connection that Joyce at all times insists that it is necessary for the artist to escape from what is current — to escape, for example, from the notions of patriotism and religion, both accepted by the herd. Those who do not escape remain servile beings degraded like the companions of Ulysses who became Circe's swine. Yet it is curious that with this idea, there goes an interest, in the later work, in Folk — not, to be sure, the herd, the modern crowd: and here we are made aware of the distinction between *myth*, the living sign of what is to come, and *convention*, the sign of that which is already dead.

The theme of *Ulysses* has important relations to aesthetic questions. It might be called either one of estrangement, or the recovery from estrangement, the reconciliation with self, for the novel makes it clear that there can be no such reconciliation without a previous sundering from self. This is a way of presenting the whole literary position, especially noticeable in drama, where there is first a complication (sundering) and then the resolution (reconciliation). Joyce is taking Drama itself as a drama, and this theory of drama is a large element in his work. Just as the wrath of Achilles is presented against a background of general wrath or war, and the homelessness of Ulysses against a background of desolation, so is the dissociation in Stephen's mind — which Joyce calls hell — presented against the hell which is Ireland, 'My hell and Ireland's are in this life', and the minor characters who impede him and help to drive him distracted are a 'chorus of the damned'. The presentation of Hell in *Ulysses* is linked with the Sermon in *A Portrait*. Stephen's wits are driven astray by visions of Hell and his development as an artist obstructed. But it was just through such alienation that the serious artist developed. Those who fail to develop remain alienated from self and retain the character of servile beings, degraded like the companions of Ulysses when turned into swine.

Ulysses, of course, has links with Homer, but ignorance of Homer would hardly affect our appreciation of Joyce. The concept of hell, or exile, as a state of mind is more characteristic of modern developments in literature than of the presentation of them that we find either in Homer or in Dante, both of whom treat hell in a more external fashion than Joyce does. But the European tradition gives us certain problems. Was Joyce linked with Virgil as well as with Dante? Did Shakespeare also suffer from the sundering from self, as it is suggested in the library scene that he did? The highlight of *Ulysses*, the orgiastic scene, is connected with Goethe's *Walpurgisnacht* and with Ibsen's *Peer Gynt*; and we know that Joyce was considerably influenced by Ibsen and by the Ibsenite thesis that 'thoughts are things'. In the notion of Ireland as Hell — though this is also linked with the sermon in *A Portrait* — there is a conscious reference to Shaw[1] with whose works James Joyce was familiar. But in taking Hell as a state of mind, he is much more akin to that other great European writer, Dostoevsky, who presented both murder and punishment as states of mind. Is there any question of the one being influenced by the other, or is it simply that they are both great European literary figures?

Joyce, by being what he is, raises the problem of the artist as critic, aesthetician and intellectual. As a thinker, he was distinguished from the great mass of his contemporaries, and it is interesting to see how much the artist with 'brains' gives evidence of them in his work. Joyce is all the time concerned, not only with the production of artistic work, but also with artistic material. This cannot be the case in other (non-literary) arts. Again there is an important connection between words and human behaviour and the fact that human speech is the medium for literary work dealing with human beings, gives to the work a wholeness and completeness not found in physical science. Nor does Joyce separate matter and form or style. He uses styles appropriate to the persons most important in the scene, cf. the 'novelette' style for Gertie MacDowell, and the mock-heroic manner for Barney Kiernan, where he brings out the character of the Irish National Movement and the Citizen representing it ('the tear and the smile') by satirising Homer. He is not entirely successful in the lying-in scene, where progressive incoherence is meant to represent the stages of drunkenness as well as a comparison of the development of the embryo with English Literature. And the question and answer section is not particularly good.

There is an important connection between words and human behaviour, and the fact that human behaviour is the author's material and words his medium, makes him more inclined to theorise than artists in other fields. Joyce poses the question to what extent it is an aesthetic advantage that a writer in his work should raise problems of interest to intellectual readers. One need not settle the question here, but the fact that Joyce could not write without thinking about literature constitutes one of his greatest attractions for me.

Yet his work is very far from being an intellectual exercise, as might be feared from the above remarks. He wrote about the common people, and so got more quickly to serious and 'eternal' issues. 'Society' and its members lend themselves more readily to satiric treatment, but concern with illusions of a broader and more human character makes the working out of 'large' themes more possible. And with certain weaknesses, some of them already mentioned, *Ulysses* is worked out. There is, at the end, the indication that Stephen found in Bloom the artistic material he was seeking, and that the 'eternal affirmation of the spirit of man' stood for more than a 'shout in the street'.

― 14 ―

Exiles

Exiles comes between *A Portrait of the Artist as a Young Man* and *Ulysses* and has a certain kinship with both. Its theme, as the title indicates, is one form of the theme of *Ulysses* which deals with the wanderings and home-seeking of people — a type of question in which Joyce was especially interested. In this work, however, we cannot identify Richard Rowan directly with Stephen and so with Joyce, even though there is a good deal of Stephen Dedalus in Rowan. Richard's attitude to his mother, for instance, shows a difference between his position and that of Stephen, though she still fights against him in his head. But there is some resemblance, and it might be that the good and the bad sides of the same mother are presented in the two works. On the other hand, there *is* a direct resemblance between the fathers of the two men. Rowan, again, is not intended to be a writer of *fiction* as Stephen promises to be, but rather of *criticism* and the position that he is being considered for is that of Professor of Romance Literature. Thus, while there are certain resemblances, there is not here the same identification with Joyce as there is in *Ulysses* and the *Portrait*.

Before considering *Exiles* let us look back to what Dedalus says of pity and terror in the *Portrait:*

Reconstructed from notes for an address to the Freethought Society, Newport, 1942.

Aristotle has not defined pity and terror. I have. ... Pity is the feeling which arrests the mind in the presence of whatsoever is grave and constant in human sufferings and unites it with the human sufferer. Terror is the feeling which arrests the mind in the presence of whatsoever is grave and constant in human sufferings and unites it with the secret cause. ... The tragic emotion, in fact, is a face looking two ways, towards terror and towards pity, both of which are phases of it. You see I use the word *arrest*. I mean that the tragic emotion is static. Or rather the dramatic emotion is. The feelings excited by improper art are kinetic, desire or loathing. Desire urges us to possess, to go to something; loathing urges us to abandon, to go from something. The arts which excite them, pornographical or didactic, are therefore improper arts. The esthetic emotion (I used the general term) is therefore static. The mind is arrested and raised above desire and loathing.

This is connected in two ways with the subject-matter of *Exiles*. The notion of possession, of making things yours (especially in the amatory sense), is an important thing in the play. Also the general notion of the material of tragedy is important; exile is something which is 'grave and constant in human sufferings'. Estrangement is what Joyce is concerned with both in *Ulysses* and in *Exiles*. In the former it is estrangement from one's self; in the latter, it is estrangement from one's fellows, especially those who are near and dear. The two things are not altogether separable but there is some distinction. Heraclitus says: 'They are estranged from that with which they have most constant intercourse,' and Joyce is suggesting that familiarity breeds estrangement, that habit and even institutions lead to loss of love — and this is another thing with which Joyce is much concerned, for loss of love is the theme in his early work, *Pomes Penyeach*.

Love is the subject, or a considerable part of the subject, of much modern literature and yet it is not treated with any sort of thoroughness. This is so in life also; there is no kind of analysis of love. Yet if love is a field of goodness, comparable to the fields of goodness of science, art and industry, we should expect to have 'works of love', developed perceptions and built-up structures which could be appreciated. Novels in general are not very illuminating; their personages and their authors fail to grasp the matter in any but the simplest way. *Exiles* does attempt some kind of analysis. While concerned with loss of love, it is, at the same time, an examination of the character of love, which in most novels is taken for granted. People are afraid to discuss it and feel that there is the possibility that a scientific discussion of love would destroy it. But I think it would rather be destroyed by habit, by the not having any refined perceptions about it. In Cabell, we see the repetition view of love as a mere again, again and again thing. *Jurgen* is always coming back to the same thing without any refinement of perception or any development at all, mere repetition without variation.

In *Exiles* Richard Rowan rejects the longing for possession. There is a confrontation of Robert Hand and Richard, Robert speaking of the urge to possess, Richard rather taking love as 'to wish her well'. He asks Robert whether he feels that his is 'the brain in contact with which she must think and understand' and his 'the body in contact with which her body must feel'. The formula here may be criticisable in some ways; it suggests a certain inferiority on the part of the woman. Richard does not also ask whether he feels that hers is the brain which will rouse him, or hers the body which will make him feel. And it comes out again and again in the play that Richard is the leading spirit, although Bertha has some refined perceptions not found in Richard. Bertha is, in fact, presented as a creation of Richard. But can a doctrine of complete mutuality in love be supported? We may have to recognise different types of love, or the question may be one of having as much equality as possible, though one is the leader and it is generally the man.

On any showing there is an attempt made here to get behind the façade; love is not taken for granted. This is important in another way, because there is a suggestion that an acute consciousness like Richard's is itself a state of exile or estrangement. Is there, then, a drama of consciousness? How far does consciousness enhance and how far hinder some types of human activity? There can be no simple answer to this, but there is a suggestion in Joyce of moments or phases; of a passage through the phases of consciousness and unconsciousness (or being merely natural), and of the existence of love (and perhaps of any high cultural activity) being dependent on these phases. Familiarity is not the best of conditions for artistic work, and in Joyce there is the notion that a 'life-partner' is a deadening influence. But it is not, in the main, cultural conflicts that arise in marriage, and the working out of these marital conflicts may actually mean loss of strength for the cultural ones.

Gorman expresses himself as being thoroughly puzzled by the play and unable to place it in the line of Joyce's work, while he finds the four principal characters and their interactions not to be very explicable. There is something in this. It *is* a puzzling play but there is much that is puzzling also in Joyce's other novels. This may be due to the fact that he is, in some measure, putting out material which is unfamiliar to us. Also, in *Finnegans Wake* and *Exiles* and partly in *Ulysses*, he rejects the whole notion of a story; it is as if he were satirising those who want to know 'what happened', those who want to be told all — when really nothing happened or just the same thing as always happens. So in *Exiles* there is an indecisive ending. The characters have all been in exile and still are. All of Tchekov's plays are such studies in hopelessness, in dead ends; that is how he presents life in Russia. But in *Exiles*, there is the suggestion that this phase will pass and there is hope of a renewal in productiveness — the suggestion that Richard does not despair entirely though he is tired for the time being of his 'wound of doubt'. It might be said, also, that the play is a sort of spectre-dance of the four figures in it. In their uncertainty of each other, and in the pervasive intellectuality of the group, they have all lost life to a considerable extent and move around in a ghostly sort of way. Beatrice is a really ghostly figure for she has given up the struggle; but they are all puzzled by their surroundings; they are trying to understand things which are generally taken for granted and such an attempt might well lead to a loss of vitality. The life of exile is, in many ways, a spectral life.

Looking at the position of love in culture, one would be inclined to say that it is one field of culture. But there is the other position — that of romanticism — which makes it the content of all culture, especially of art. It makes the heart the clue to every art and thus runs all the arts together. This leads to expressionism, the making of every art the expression of human feeling. Denying this position, we recognise the heterogeneity of the arts. The notion, also, that every human activity subserves love does away with the objectivity of art — and of science. Now Robert Hand is not a specially romantic figure in the ordinary sense, but for him love is the end for which culture is the means. He is a man of some culture, but he treats gratification or possession as that to which all culture leads. There is, however, a third view — that love is not a field of culture at all, that it is not artistic (so that there are no 'works of love'), but rather that love is something that leads the way, or opens the gates, to culture, that it releases the spirit for cultural activities. This is not to say that it is a mere 'that-whereby' — that it is a means of passing from humdrum existence to something livelier. Possibly there would be no release for free spiritual activities unless we wanted love for itself and not as a means; but being, or having been, in a loving phase would release us for artistic activities; then we could go back to loving and so on. Thus, from the point of view of the cultural activities, love would be a means. This position would have a certain kinship with Richard's position as romanticism has with Robert's.[1]

In this third position, there are similarities with Ibsen's treatment of the 'inner' and the 'outer', and just as the solution there did not lie completely in either the one or the other, so it is not a denial of either the spontaneous or the 'mechanical' that leads to culture. The notion in *Exiles* is of a sort of alternation, even a struggle, between the point of view of emotion leading to productive work, and that of habit; and it is out of this that culture comes; for the 'secret cause' of loss of love lies in the seeming irreconcilability of the one with the other — of following the one to the exclusion of the other. This is connected with Richard's attitude to love with its 'luminous certainty' and its 'wounding doubt'. He does not realise that if there were doubt all the time, love would not have been established; and that if there were 'luminous certainty' all the time, love would be in danger of being taken for granted — of becoming a habit. Doubt and certitude are moments, or phases, of love. In his yearning for perfect freedom from all bonds, he is illustrating the romantic notion of 'keeping by losing', which Bernard Shaw presents in *Candida*. And there are other enigmas and riddles here like those which are to be found in *Emperor and Galilean*. In the spectre-dance of the characters of the play there is the suggestion that the life of the intellect is the death of the body; while an even closer analogy with Ibsen is the notion of the mutual implication of Jesus and Judas, though it is not worked out so fully. This is significant for the play. Robert speaks of the faith of a disciple in his master as a strange thing, while Richard presents as stranger yet the faith of a master in the disciple that will betray him (cf. Ibsen's world-spirit working through contradictions even by means of treachery; and the notions, in Nietzsche, of Apollonian and Dionysian, or subjective and objective — the conditions of a work of art as contrasted with those of the life of the artist).

There is also in *Exiles*, a suggestion that there is a necessary 'agony of the thinker' (or of the artist), that struggle is necessary to his being an innovator. A heightened consciousness is what he gets through his struggle, but it is also a condition of his deepest agonies. Here again, Joyce is attacking artistic problems directly; he is concerned with the artist and his position in human society. If we agree that this theory of an alternation is correct, we can see that for an artist in human material the struggle will be all the more acute. He is constantly forced up against contradictions which he is not able to solve in passing. The plastic artist and the musical artist will have more of a real chance by plunging into love, and so will more easily gain replenishment. They have less of this agony of the literary artist — an agony which is the 'secret cause' of the grave and constant fact of exile as it is presented in this play.

While Richard is conscious to the last iota, Bertha grasps things naturally. She does not understand why he should torment himself, and the suggestion is that self-torment is characteristic of the thinker. And there is a desire in Richard to torment as well as to be tormented. To Bertha Richard comes along with his machine-laid plans of freedom, of breaking all bonds. She just does not have these desires; she rather wants freedom from his plans. His trying to escape all bonds only leads him into convention, and Bertha hits the nail on the head when, at the end of the play, she cries for her 'strange, wild lover' to come back to her again — he *was* freer then. All this brings out the artificiality of the notion of breaking all bonds. Richard wants to intellectualise all reality and so he does not, and cannot, get replenishment. This consciousness, without any change, leads to a terrible tension for him and for those around him. Part of his solution would seem to be — another of the 'contradictions' — that other people have to have a sort of enslavement to him for him to be free of all bonds.

Exiles seems to cast some doubt on the whole notion of friendship. There is the betrayal of Richard by Robert; but Richard has never been very much attached to him, and has never had that spiritual certitude about him which would be needed for friendship and which, perhaps, is impossible without bodily relationship. First we find Richard saying that Robert, as his friend, should have wooed Bertha openly; later he speaks of an ignoble longing that he should be betrayed by him and by her. But this is not yet his deepest motive. He speaks of wishing for doubt, for restless doubt, and of desiring her nakedly. It is another aspect of his desire for freedom from all bonds, from all that is customary and commonplace, by which love is lost. But the point of the play is that this attempt makes him lose that feeling of 'luminous certainty' which also is love. The suggestion is that however one takes the matter, whether one gives in to the customary or refuses to be influenced by it, one cannot avoid an estrangement in the end. Bertha, being far less conscious, takes the matter uncritically. She simply records the loss of love, and does not try to solve the problem; she had taken it as natural that Richard and she should remain lovers. So estrangement is bound to come from following a single line, whether it be the customary one or one of one's own. There is need for alternation by which we get to new works, a need to return to Dionysianism, to forget consciousness now and then. Needless to say, the problem here would be much more difficult if there were two intellectual lovers. Beatrice and Richard could have had only a tortured relationship. There is more chance of renewal and replenishment for Richard with a less intellectual woman.*

Joyce does not quite bring out the solution I have been suggesting — that alternation is required for lastingness, that we need at times to reject conscious values, that love is something which releases production, something to which we must return if these productive activities are to go on; but I think that it is along these lines that an understanding of the play is to be found.

---

* The tragedy of exile is more acute for those who are not content with the customary, as, for example, the ordinary people in *Ulysses* who are, as it were, Circe's swine. They are quite content to do as others do, not to try to think out things for themselves, no matter what pretences they may make.

– 15 –
The Applecart

This play indicates more than anything else the snobbery of Shaw. As usual, in his latest manner, he produces something on the lines of a variety sketch, with just that spice of 'intellectual daring' that appeals to his petty-bourgeois public, who want to believe that they are thinking while they are being entertained. In case the pretence should wear thin in the reading of the play (and Shaw's public is mainly a reading public), he adds a further little intellectual exercise in his preface: and naturally, his broadcast speech has to be preserved for posterity.

We have, then, the very daring idea (in these days of democratic shibboleths) of a king who is a 'man' and not a 'rubber-stamp'. This is a conception that goes straight to the heart and lifts us above all cheap theatricality — like that of poor Bill Boanerges who, however, blossoms out under the refining influence of kingly manners. Manners (i.e., assurance) is the mark of the superior persons, the people with capacity, who alone can get us out of our troubles, can give us *orderliness* in place of 'breakages'. The struggle of *both* royalty and democracy against plutocracy is a most original idea — if Shaw hadn't prigged it from Belloc — and gives us a new opportunity of finding capacity in the people with place (superiority in superior station).

Mrs Anderson observes that this is an informal piece which was probably written in 1932.

One can see now what Shaw finds to admire in the Bolsheviks. They have *arrived:* they have organisation: they have a great administrative head (Stalin): everything goes by clockwork. And yet they are 'men', too, not 'rubber-stamps'; they have *grades,* and the right man can get to the right place (compare a remark in the Introduction about the ideal extension of governmental order — 'we could then have a graded series of panels of capable persons for all employments'). So long as there is something that can be called State organisation, Shaw's Fabianism is satisfied and he does not discriminate between Stalin, Mussolini and King Magnus. All this is 'Socialism': and just as 'we' had to have a measure of Socialism to keep us going through the war, so we have to have more now when we see 'big capitalist enterprises running to the Government for help as a lamb runs to its mother'.

Now the name of this kind of Socialism (without the working-class) in these times is *rationalisation:* it is the scheme of the Second International for keeping capitalism going. We eliminate as much 'wastage' as possible (i.e., as much of the working class) and we keep the rest going to *capacity:* they are in their proper grade because they are unable to solve 'our economic and social problems': they are only swayed by mob orators and the press, whereas clever people like Shaw can think for themselves. So while, as he has said, ' Marx made a man of him', he shows himself totally ignorant of Marxism and of the working-class movement, of social capacity and social forces.

His play is very like *press-cuttings:* in fact, he seems to get most of his ideas from the press — or rather he is the same sort of Sophist as pressmen are. For instance, the reference to 'the abandonment of politics by the old governing class' is the silly sort of notion that we get in the papers: as if politics were anything but the activities of the governing class, with, of course, the opposing activities of the governed. And again 'we cling to the little scrap of individuality you have left us' — as if economic realities were affected by mere declarations of independence, which undoubtedly are a part of the window-dressing which Shaw calls 'politics', but are no criterion of real (economic) independence. Certainly there is the later statement that government will stay only at a *real* centre of gravity, but with all the guff about kings and parliamentarians, this becomes only another phrase from a leading article.

15 *The Applecart*

If Shaw had wanted to make a farce out of some of these political figure-heads taking themselves seriously, it wouldn't have been so bad. But the fact remains that they don't, that they know which side their bread is buttered on and what they are there for. Shaw is playing his own sycophantic part, too, in pretending that there might be 'real capacity', some socially valuable force, in these quarters: just like A. J. Cook when he staged his come-back to respectable Trade Union leadership by congratulating the Prince of Wales on his philanthropic efforts.[1]

The play, then, is an exercise in non-existent manners — the Court Guide versus the world. We are reminded of the first Labour Government, with Sidney Webb, Ramsay MacDonald and others in court dress. Fabianism joins up with royalty, and the union of all the superior people has the task of keeping the mob (i.e., 'the industrial class' which, as A. E. Taylor shrewdly points out, includes capitalists as well as workers) from breaking up *Society*.[2]

The theme of 'ability', being a mere catchword of social humbugs, cannot be presented in its native character in this play. There is a very little satire on *admiration* for ability or for place, but as Shaw shares this himself, he can hardly carry it right through the play or see how far it goes. There could, of course, be a good play about social snobbery and humbug (the 'intelligence' of the governing classes) but this isn't it.

There are a few neat phrases: 'I never resist temptation.' 'All men are fools and moral cowards when you come to know them.' This second could be neater, but it is all in the line of Shaw's preaching, of his tickling the ears of the 'emancipated', following in Ibsen's footsteps. But nothing like the way Joyce follows Ibsen in *Exiles*, for instance, getting into the human heart. There is no terror and pity in Shaw — only trickery.

It occurs to me that the phrase 'I never resist temptation', though neat in its way, is really rather silly. In the first place, it suggests a merely conventional distinction between tendencies or impulses which are to be called 'tempting', and other impulses whose function is resistance to temptation. Actually, each would resist the other and each would tempt us to resist the other. Conventionally, certain impulses are called 'temptations', but this is a matter of how people regard them and not of what they are themselves. The phrase, then, would be reducible to the form, 'I never resist impulse'. Now, if any man says he has never experienced *resistance*, a clash of impulses such that he can't go on with both of them, he is simply a liar or a poseur. The phrase, then, is humbug, though it might still be interesting (were it not for the general sketchiness of the play) in bringing out exactly what kind of humbug Magnus was.

15 *The Applecart*

Faculty at the University of Edinburgh, probably 1925. Anderson is sitting third from right. Beside him, in the centre of the photograph, are Professor A. E. Taylor and Professor Kemp-Smith; Rush Rhees is standing in the back row, far right. Anderson lectured at Edinburgh from 1920 to 1926.

– 16 –
George Bernard Shaw

One of the main points that have been made in criticism of Shaw, is that he is a preacher rather than a dramatist, and Shaw himself would not be at all displeased with such a judgement. When, in *The Doctor's Dilemma*, Sir Paddy Cullen exclaims, 'Bernard Shaw? I never heard of him. He's a Methodist preacher, I suppose,' this is not a mere Shavian quip, but a remark behind which there is a serious meaning; for Shaw really thinks of himself in particular, and the artist in general, as having a mission to teach people how to live better than they do.

Now it may be argued that artistic appreciation does enable us to live better, apart from the question whether appreciation is not itself a way of living well — or a good activity. But it is quite a different matter to say that a work of art *tells* us how to live better; that it actually points to our faults and demands their correction; that it gives us a sense of sin. If works of art are to do this, then we shall have to have one interpretation of art for a work in human materials, such as the novel or the play, and another for one which deals with non-human materials, like music, painting, sculpture or architecture. Upholders of the didactic view of art tend to give a *human* interpretation to all the other arts — as Shaw himself does to music in *The Perfect Wagnerite*.

An address delivered to the Literary Society, 10 April 1933, and reported in the *Union Recorder*, 20 April 1933.

But even he cannot carry this interpretation right through, and has to distinguish between music-drama on the one hand, and pure music (sound patterns) on the other. In *The Sanity of Art* he admits that Brahms can, and does, produce such musical patterns, but even there he moralises as much as possible and criticises Brahms for putting across a paltry moral in his music, describing him as 'that greatly gifted absolute musician and hopelessly commonplace and tedious homilist, Johannes Brahms'. Consequently we are not surprised to find that Shaw, in reply to Max Nordau's *Degeneration*, maintains that the sanity of art lies in the fact that it teaches moral lessons.

The solution here lies in the opposite direction. In all art, if the same criterion is to be applied to all, including art using human material, the question is one of the working out of a formal pattern, of the treatment of a theme; it is a question of the work itself. And this question, and the question of what effect a work of art has on us, are quite separate. This is clearly shown by the different effects the same work has on different people, and by the fact that all sorts of things, inartistic as well as artistic, can uplift us, can show us our prevailing sins, or turn us onto 'the straight and narrow path'. It could be said, that when a work points beyond itself, has a moral, or requires further working out on the part of the spectator or the artist, we have artistic failure; for it is the artist's business to present a whole, i.e., a work where the point of importance does not lie outside it. In general, the precept or the awful warning is a different matter from the material to which it is attached, the moral being arbitrary, and depending on what we happen to be reminded of or what we are incidentally told to look out for — like Wagner's symbolism as explained to us by Shaw. Even in the case of his own plays, Shaw frequently finds it necessary, in order to make sure that we grasp the lessons they are meant to inculcate, to become their interpreter himself, as he does in *First Aid to Critics* attached to *Major Barbara* — thus showing that he has a sense of his own dramatic inadequacy. Or the point may be driven home more or less crudely within the play itself. Instead of trusting to De Stogumber's words and actions in the course of the play to convey to us the information that he is a bigoted nationalist, Shaw makes him say outright in *Saint Joan*, 'No Englishman is ever fairly beaten' — an opinion which he would never have expressed in the circumstances, though it is worth noting that the words would have been quite suitable for a farce, however inapt they are in a serious drama.

In his general criticisms, much of which has an effect upon his art, Shaw is attempting to popularise in England the works of Ibsen, Nietzsche and Marx. He has the notion, derived from Ibsen, that society is maintained by following certain ways of living; whence comes his own formula that when ways of living harden into convention and prejudice, they must be given up in the interests of progress. This is all the easier for him, since he sees law as at best a convenience (like the rule of the road), or, at worst, a fetter. It is not for Shaw a question of what kind of organisation laws and regulations are linked up with. Believing in an evolution of manners, i.e., in a moral society, and therefore not, incidentally, in a class society, he poses the question in a solidarist fashion. In accordance with these theories, he examines social practices in general, and property relations and the institution of marriage in particular, asserting that we think our property and marriage arrangements are the only possible ones, and that, in order to keep them going and to persuade ourselves that we are getting satisfaction out of them, we have built up a web of illusions about them — especially those of marriage. Therefore, he is concerned with exposing such illusions for, he argues, such ways of living may not be fundamental to society at all; and, if that is the case, progress will depend on departing from them.

Ibsen suggested something like this in *The Doll's House*, where Nora left her husband because their life together was not a real marriage, she being only his 'little skylark', 'his doll', and not a responsible human adult. This play was generally taken as an attack on the home and was greeted with outbursts of indignation. But in Ibsen's *Ghosts*, on Shaw's interpretation, we see the horrible results of a woman adhering to current social morality and not leaving her husband when she should have done so. Shaw himself makes a further and characteristic contribution to the question of sex and morality in *Mrs Warren's Profession*. Here he deals with the matter of prostitution, showing how people who condemn it continue to live in, and approve of, the very system that keeps the profession going. Vivie Warren does cast off her mother rather than be kept as a lady on the proceeds of brothels, but it is worth noting that though Shaw is anxious to drive home the *social* responsibility of everyone, there is no suggestion of any obligation on Vivie's part to pay back to her mother the money that was spent on her education; she simply cuts herself off to make her own living by doing the work that now lies open to her. It is in his treatment of questions such as these that Shaw presents himself to us as an 'immoral dramatist', one who questions current morality by showing people what they are *really* doing and reveals to them the implications of what on the surface does not seem harmful at all, because it is the customary way of living.

Now drama may accomplish a showing-up of illusions, tragedy when the illusions are recalcitrant, comedy when the characters see through their pretensions. It may criticise manners and thus help the spectators to criticise manners as painting may help them to criticise landscape. But to say that a drama criticises morals is not to say that it criticises the spectators, even if it enables them to criticise themselves as painting cannot do — though as pictorial critics they might learn to know when they were blots on the landscape! The important thing is to have drama, the interaction of characters with characters and characters with situations, in order to bring out certain ways of living or certain attitudes; and learning something from that, or living differently because of it, is a further question. Presumably nothing we study fails to influence to some extent our future actions; but we must not confuse, as Shaw does, the criticism of the play with the soul-searching criticism in which the spectators may indulge and which is not expected in the case of works of music, painting or sculpture, though on any positive theory of aesthetics it would need to be equally present. Criticism on the basis of effects is, therefore, bad criticism. It is the work itself — the thing in itself — that must be criticised.

This attitude to art, this estimation of it by its effects, is a romantic and idealistic one, and Shaw with his preaching, his moralising and his teaching of lessons, shows himself both a romanticist and an idealist. Further, in *The Sanity of Art* he says:

> ... as a dramatist I have no clue to any historical or other personage save that part of him which is also myself, and which may be nine tenths or ninety nine hundredths, as the case may be ... but which, anyhow, is all that can ever come within my knowledge of his soul.

Such subjectivism on Shaw's part, is a denial of literature, with its objectivism, its endeavour to present things as they really are; but it fits in well with his journalistic characteristics which enable him to take any kind of material and make what he wants of it. He has an extraordinary power of assimilating things and he cashes in on European giants like Nietzsche, Wagner and Marx, putting them over watered-down to the British public, without entirely understanding them or dealing fully with the questions they raise, but acquiring a ready way of treating every difficulty. This sophistic cleverness is to be found in his plays. It is not without merit, but like the sophists and journalists, he will deny at one time what he asserts at another, and be plausible all the way if we do not watch him closely. It is, however, responsible for the shallowness which shows itself often in his dramas and for the fact that we do not always have from him a properly worked-out theme. Along with this sophistic attitude goes his self-styled character of progressive, looking for the most up-to-date morality, and praising it because it is the latest, though the new morality may be no better than the old. Posing, too, as an evolutionist, he claims to belong to a movement for social betterment, and he clouds the issue that social progress lies in the *clash* between social forces by presenting goodwill as a social solvent and money as a means of salvation (cf. *Major Barbara*).

These, then, are some of the defects of his position, defects which influence his literary work. Nevertheless, in spite of his own romanticism, he has made good attacks on romanticism itself (cf. Preface to *Plays Pleasant and Unpleasant*, vol. 2, as quoted in 'Some Questions in Aesthetics'). Amidst all his moralising and sophism, he is trying to get at a 'genuine natural history' which will present men and women in their true characters, not taking their word for what they are or what they are doing, but letting them act and show what they really are by their own speech and actions. An endeavour to penetrate appearances is a definite and sound position aesthetically. Any artist has to bring out the actual character of things, but Shaw, in addition to the defects mentioned above, is sometimes hampered in his attempt to do so by the romantic illusions he holds about art itself.

Generally, he thinks of the artist as a preacher and teacher, but at times he presents him as if he were some sort of magician and in *The Dark Lady of the Sonnets* he talks, among other things, of 'the black magic of words'. This romantic conception of art is responsible for his failure to make of Dubedat (*The Doctor's Dilemma*) a convincing figure. We have to take the word of his wife and of the doctors for his genius as a painter and we get no insight into the combination of his scoundrelly and his artistic activities. Of the former, and of his immense nerve, there is abundant evidence, but of the latter there is no dramatic evidence at all. In *Candida*, the poet is a much more coherent character with less of a division between his artistic abilities and his general ways of behaving, though Shaw cannot refrain from talking of 'the secret in the poet's heart' and we have the romantic notion of keeping love by losing it. Nevertheless, in spite of this somewhat mystical approach, there is in *Candida* a real analysis of Morell, who for once is confronted by someone who can outpreach him and show up his hypocrisy; but there is no culmination in the play — no thorough working out — it simply stops.

In the presentation of his plays, Shaw follows in the footsteps of Ibsen, a writer of dramas of everyday life and domestic complications, whose methods he found more suited to his purposes than works about nobility would have been where the characters seem so far removed from the problems of the ordinary man. Even in this favourable 'natural' setting, it is surprising how much of his romanticising, his Puritanism and his incurable theorising manages to break through. We have already seen how, in *Mrs Warren's Profession*, he has been concerned to show that, as money made from prostitution is the same as any other money made in a single economic system of society, the whole audience, being bound up with the money system, has a certain social responsibility in the matter. In *Widowers' Houses* and in *Major Barbara* we are again presented with the popular view that only *some* money is tainted, but in the latter play, while we are shown how we are all involved, it is also argued that nothing can be done without money; and we find present the notion of salvation by money — the notion of a safe life. This is another example of his romanticism, for there is no safe life — there is always risk; and though there may be a certain amount of sarcasm in Shaw's thesis that poverty is a crime and money the means of salvation, it fits in too well with the rest of his theories for it not to be his real belief. As a progressive, we must remember, that he wants to get things done so that human society may move out of chaos to a well-ordered and well-administered community — the ideal of all true Fabians. For that, as Wells points out in *Mr Blettsworthy on Rampole Island*, as Mr Crotchet suggests in *Crotchet Castle* and as Shaw himself knows very well, much money will be needed. Given the money, however, salvation *can* be acquired — of that Shaw has no doubt; for 'you imagine what you desire: you will what you imagine: and at last you create what you will' (*Back to Methuselah*). And when the will of man can finally operate unhampered by lack of means (cf. Ibsen on the 'will' in *Emperor and Galilean*) then, Shaw avers, there will be a soaring of the spirit, and everyone will be free not only from the bondage of poverty but from other bonds as well.

Some of these bonds are dealt with in *Back to Methuselah*, where Shaw, departing from his theories of a 'natural' history, creates a dream world instead of presenting a real one. In this play human beings are depicted as living to a great age, and there is the notion that age of itself makes for excellence. It is to be remembered that Shaw himself was now growing old, and though old age is satirised in *The Philanderer*, when personal history is identified with social history, there is naturally a desire for immortality — 'of life only, there is no end'. This long-lived human race has not yet attained to 'life eternal' when there will be no people, only thought, a vortex of pure thought; but in accordance with Shaw's notion of the perfect human society, it *has* evolved towards an extreme purity, to the stage of the egg-born human being. There is none of the coarseness that Miss Miniver refers to in *Ann Veronica* and risks are reduced to a minimum. There is even learning without study and experience, and art has been quite outgrown — for is it not a mere imitation of life, of real things, comparable to the toys that children play with, to be thrown away when the human race has reached the heights? This is the logical outcome of Shaw's aesthetic position — his interpretation of music, in particular, as the imitation of human emotions, and of art, in general, as moral lessons.

In *Man and Superman*, following his usual style of presentation, Shaw also theorises about the universe — this time showing the way to progress for the human race. How it is to arrive at the goal depicted in *Back to Methuselah* he does not make clear but he introduced the Life Force, which is, of necessity, aspiring to 'higher organisation, wider, deeper and intenser self-consciousness and clearer understanding'. It is

Jack Tanner who exemplifies the theory as the play develops, telling us at intervals that he is in the grip of the Life Force, when all we can see is a man who, in spite of his insight into the character of the woman who is determined to marry him, finds it impossible to escape from her. None of the other males in the play seem to be similarly afflicted and Tanner's exclamations strike one as simply farcical. The same may be said about the position of Ann. Shaw has the theory that women are particularly concerned with the preservation and improvement of the race, and the implication is that Ann's determination to marry Tanner is an example of the Life Force at work, driving her to seek a father for the superman; for when Ana (her incarnation in the Hell Interlude) vanishes at the end of it, she is 'crying to the universe: "a father — a father for the Superman!"' Again, none of the other women in the play seem to be urged on to such a search, although it is described as a cosmic force. This notion of a superman, this theory of the Life Force, this transcending of ordinary morality and reaching to cosmic proportions is like Shaw's interpretation of *The Ring* as cosmic drama — the drama of man. The Life Force cannot be brought on to the stage, though the Hell Interlude is an attempt to do so — by discussion. Shaw's insistence on discussion — as if dramas could ever be developed and presented except in terms of what people say and do — simply amounts to the fact that he is more concerned with pointing the moral — driving the lesson home — than with letting the play speak for itself. His aim is always to arouse people to a sense of their political, social and religious responsibilities, and *Man and Superman* he describes as 'A Comedy and a Philosophy'. 'It might,' he goes on to say,

> have been called a religion as well; for the vision of hell in the third act ... is expressly intended to be a revelation of the modern religion of evolution ... however fantastic its legendary framework may appear, is a careful attempt to write a new book of Genesis for the Bible of the Evolutionists. (Foreword to the popular edition of *Man and Superman*, published in 1911)

For all this high-sounding talk, the play is simply farce and sermon juxtaposed, and without the Hell Interlude, the farce is clever and amusing.

I have not touched on Shaw's novels at all, and his plays are too numerous to be dealt with here in any sort of detail. Those who read and study them will find how his economic, political and religious ideas have prevented him from showing 'us ourselves as we really are' (*Man and Superman*), or the world as it really is. In spite of all his teaching and preaching, he has had little effect anywhere — not even in his drive for clearer thinking — while Dickens, who exposes not a whole society like Shaw, but merely parts of it (cf. Dotheboys Hall) did have some influence, according to Chesterton.[1] Shaw raises many interesting questions, though he cannot convincingly deal with them, and in the prefaces to his plays, even though the arguments may be sometimes weak, there is much good material; those dealing with the Bible and with parents and children are outstanding. As an artist he can build good dramatic structures such as those we find in *Plays Pleasant* and in *Androcles and the Lion*, while *Arms and the Man*, though of minor importance, is a bright comedy with its exposure of military illusions. *The Philanderer*, a criticism of the Ibsenites, is his best comedy, curiously devoid of uplift; and General Burgoyne, in *The Devil's Disciple*, is excellently and dramatically treated. Both of these plays, incidentally, contradict the accusation often brought against Shaw — that he can create no character other than himself; that Caesar, for example, is only Shaw. Shaw himself gives colour to such an accusation by some words of his own (vide supra), and there are certainly times when we think he has created a character to give utterance to the beliefs of George Bernard Shaw. But he often wrought better than he knew, and Burgoyne, at least, is an example of it. As a rule, his earlier works are his best, for in those written after the war we do not see an artist of any eminence. There is some good work in *Heartbreak House*, but *The Applecart* is simply feeble, and most of the others are imitative of earlier works or too ridiculous to be considered in any serious way. But he is not a mere charlatan or cheapjack, though his later works, like those of Kipling, leave him exposed in that character. Usually he has a fine dramatic core, and if the players forget the moral (though this is not always possible) the play may go well. Shaw has submerged the artist in him to the preacher and journalist and he attacks art the more because he is himself definitely an artist.

— 17 —
The Perfect Wagnerite

An examination of Fabianism and its by-products may appear to many to be a post-mortem or a piece of antiquarian research. Actually, of course, this social tendency is not a thing of the past; it has achieved the 'permeation' at which it aimed and now speaks as the official voice of labour. And Shaw himself has not changed with the years. It is just because he is still devoted to 'getting things done' in an 'orderly' manner that he can lavish admiration impartially on Mussolini, Stalin and Hitler. And he has always been a useful adherent of the cult of administration because he could give it a 'cultural' touch — because, while Webb sought support in Blue Books, Shaw found it in music and literature, in Wagner and Ibsen.

It is idle to speculate on the critical work he might have done if he could have avoided Fabianism. Certainly, being 'a very clever fellow', he finds real connections and distinctions among things; again, having some acquaintance with Socialism, he can cleverly play the iconoclast and drum academic timidity out of town. But always there is the bureaucratic moral. He gives Fabianism a 'philosophic' sanction by showing that its petty regimentations are in line with the one increasing

---

This paper first appeared in *Manuscripts*, 13, May 1935.
The Perfect Wagnerite: A Commentary on the Niblung's Ring, by G. B. Shaw, was first published 1898. References here to the Third Edition, 1913.

purpose which is gradually ordering the universe, making it a moral whole. Art, too — especially when it embodies 'thought' — can serve this purpose, and lead us onward and upward along the track of the Life Force. It is the 'philosophic' character of *The Ring* that gives it its greatness; it is Wagner's 'vision of the world' that makes him a Master.

Shaw has a like vision in *Back to Methuselah* of the Life Force leading beyond all the confusions of art, politics and other forms of child's play, to beings who can spend aeons in contemplation (contemplating sweet vacancy). Being, like Wotan, 'unable to force on the word the pure law of thought' (p. 11), he makes it gradually purify itself until it becomes a pure thought-vortex. Here freewill and necessity unite, as in Wagner's conception of his hero, Siegfried, as the 'Freewiller of Necessity' — a conception exasperating to 'Englishmen with a congenital incapacity for metaphysics' (p. 68). Such a final solution is what Shaw thinks is the object of philosophy, but it is only the moralist's Paradise, where all is pure and rational — 'when from sin and sorrow we are free'.

Shaw, then, is a romantic, a dealer in uplift; and as such he has a contempt not only for art but for science and philosophy as they really are. Pursuing the 'ultimate' he cannot accept the actual. Hence his girdings at love, which is too fleshly and solid for his taste — which is, indeed, for the puritan, the chief source of evil. For it can release us from our inhibitions, our puritanical 'sense of sin', and make us think that there is nothing the matter with the secular life. On this very account it serves to advance actual goods; it removes hindrances to artistic and intellectual activity. Undoubtedly there is a tendency to make love the actual *substance* of artistic work, and it can be linked with all sorts of romanticising. But acceptance of it, flesh and all, is certainly a great seculariser. Shaw, however, wants release not from religion (inhibition) but from the flesh. Thought, he admits, cannot reach as far as the pure vortex, but creative evolution can bring about the time — first brought to consciousness in the prophetic thought of G. B. Shaw — when we shall pop out of synthetically produced eggs and there will be none of 'the horrible coarseness' (to use Miss Miniver's phrase in Wells' *Ann Veronica*) which so shocked Eve when the serpent put her up to it.

17 *The Perfect Wagnerite*

But, of course, this is not romanticism; it is philosophic thought, *a vision of the world* comparable to the main part of *The Ring* — for at the end even Wagner becomes romantic. We find (pp. 71–2) that

> at the point where *The Ring* changes from music drama into opera, it also ceases to be philosophic and becomes didactic. The philosophic part is a dramatic symbol of the world as Wagner observed it. In the didactic part the philosophy degenerates into the prescription of a romantic nostrum for all human ills. Wagner, only mortal after all, succumbed to the panacea mania when his philosophy was exhausted, like any of the rest of us [presumably after we had endured the philosophy].

Overlooking Wagner's backsliding, then, we can avoid romanticism by following *not love, but life* (p. 76).

> The only faith which any reasonable disciple can gain from *The Ring* is not in love, but in life itself as a tireless power which is continually driving onward and upward — not, please observe, being beckoned or drawn by *Das Ewig Weibliche* or any other external sentimentality, but growing from within, by its own inexplicable energy, into ever higher and higher forms of organisation,* the strengths and the needs of which are continually superseding the institutions which were made to fit our former requirements.

Meanwhile, the elevation of life above love can be helped on by Fabian schemes of eugenics, grandiloquently urged. The dilemma of 'the few who are capable of government', either to hold down the many or to be destroyed by them

> will persist until Wotan's inspiration comes to our governors, and they see that their business is not the devising of laws and institutions to prop up the weaknesses of mobs and secure the survival of the unfittest, but the breeding of men whose wills and intelligences may

---

* Just like the British Commonwealth of Nations ('Wider still and wider', etc.).

be depended on to produce spontaneously the social wellbeing our clumsy laws now aim at and miss. [p. 67]

A father, a father for the superman! And though we do not yet have 'a race of men in whom the life-giving impulses predominate', the eugenic process is certainly helped along when the comparatively capable shoot down the incapable, as in the Paris Commune, for 'one efficient sinner is worth ten futile saints and martyrs' (p. 107).

Wagner's declension to opera and the nostrum of love, then, was due to the demonstration, between 1848 and 1871, of the fact (as Shaw puts it in the preface to the Third Edition), 'that the passing away of the present capitalistic order was going to be a much more complicated business' than it had at first appeared. Marx was too simple-minded to see this, but Wagner (p. 105) was comparatively 'a practical man' — he had enough Fabianism in him, it seems, to recognise the historical necessity of efficiency.

> ... The one fact that could not be denied was that when it came to actual shooting, it was Gallifet who got Delescluze shot and not Delescluze who got Gallifet shot, and that when it came to administering the affairs of France, Thiers could in one way or another get it done, whilst Pyat could neither do it nor stop talking and allow somebody else to do it. True, the penalty of following Thiers was to be exploited by the landlord and capitalist; but then the penalty of following Pyat was to be shot like a mad dog, or at best sent to New Caledonia, quite unnecessarily and uselessly. [pp. 100–1]

It is obvious, since the Communards were beaten, that they had not a true 'vision of the world' and were not well-bred representatives of the Life Force. They had not learned to do

> the political and industrial work which is now being done *tant bien que mal* by our Romanoffs, our Hohenzollerns, our Krupps, Cadburys, Levers, and their political retinues. And in the meantime these magnates must defend their power and property with all their might against the revolutionary forces until these forces become positive, executive, administrative forces. [pp. 104–5]

— after which, of course, the magnates will bow to the Life Force and gracefully withdraw. And it is not in the least by struggles like that of the Commune that revolutionary forces *acquire* capacity. After all, parliament is bit by bit bringing about the changes Bakunin wanted (p. 76), and private capitalism 'is, by the mere necessities of the case, giving way to ordered Socialism' (p. 78). Wagner's Bakuninist hero, then, was not yet administrative enough to run the world; hence the declension to the peddling of nostrums. The Communards could not take his place, for, being shot or sent to New Caledonia, they showed that they were not necessities of the case but accidental impurities like love — surds in the cosmic system.

But, even though Wagner modified his world-view or failed to work it out, it is out of such 'political philosophy' that the drama of ideas is made. Art may originate as a surd but it can become a number; it can be purified and raised to a higher power as the vehicle of *thought*. For Shaw, as for Hegel, there are degrees of spiritual significance, degrees of articulation of the meaning of things. What is inarticulate in art may become articulate in philosophy, high art may express what lower art cannot, and what is sensuously adumbrated in emotion may be integrated and transcended in an ideal content. Thus *Wagner's view of the world in 1848* has a certain degree of adequacy to the world itself, and a 'dramatic symbol' of that view has a certain adequacy to it; and so we are carried by a progressive series of representations nearer and nearer to the heart of things.

Now, all this, as well as being romanticism of the first water, is charlatanism. It may indeed be said that notions of human destiny and cosmic evolution are vague substitutes for certain quite earthly objects which analysis could discover. But it is also important, taking these professions just as they stand, to observe that the distinction between 'ideas' and things is an illogical one. If by 'ideas' were meant only the sort of things that could be thought about (the 'content' of thought), then the material of any work of art would be just as much *ideas* as that of any other work of art or of anything else. Since, however, ideas are regarded as something special, something we have to rise to, they must be considered as 'principles', the driving forces behind things, the bureaucratic organisers of the Fabian cosmos. But when we come to look for them, they are not there; we have only 'their representatives', existing forces, the *status quo*, which nevertheless is reinforced by having this cosmic sanction. Thus the *force majeure* of Thiers should be accepted as the immediate representative of cosmic force, as a stage in the onward and upward movement of life; and while it is true that *in the sphere of thought* 'Anarchism is an inevitable condition of progressive evolution' (p. 78), in the sphere of practice the Commune has shown itself not to be. The political opportunism thus expressed by Shaw is matched by the critical opportunism, the sheer aesthetic bankruptcy of the whole exposition.

The charge of imposture applies, indeed, to all expressionist or representationist treatments of art. The statement of the *spiritual equivalent* of any theme or part of a theme, whether it be the individual or the universal spirit that is in question, is simply bluff; it is a camouflage 'that reminds me', escaping by means of its obscurity the ridicule that commonly falls on the mere banality of this method. When, in particular, we are told that *the world* is the underlying theme, we may admit that this theme cannot be directly presented — but neither can it be represented; as in the case of the 'ideas' there is nothing to represent. It is, of course, impressive to be told that what is presented has cosmic significance, that the cosmos can be expressed to us through 'its highest achievement, man', that a certain agent represents a cosmic force, either directly or mediately as representing a social force. A skilled journalist like Shaw can put up quite a plausible case for such interpretations, such fancied approximations to the ultimate, guarded as they inevitably are by philosophical vagueness at critical points.

Nevertheless, this sort of interpretation can never demonstrate the *working out* of the complication. It was not accidentally that Wagner had to patch up the piece, if he proposed to give a cosmic account of human history in the form of 'man's destiny'; for he did not know it. It would be dramatic to show men mastering mythological and romantic illusions, or again being taken in by them. But to hold that the struggle with illusions is man's 'fate' is to be oneself under illusions, and any construction on that basis can only be a patched-up affair. Love will serve as well as any other human material to do the patching; it is itself a subject of human illusions which can be tacked on to the illusory cosmos. But Shaw is dissatisfied because he would like a romantic solution on the plane of *cosmic* illusion — like his own 'aeons of contemplation' — and love is too actual, too unrepresentational, for him.

Turning now to the musical side of the question, we find the same expressionist bluff in Shaw's dramatic interpretation of the music as in his cosmic interpretation of the drama — and the same criticism applies to any attempt to state what feelings or 'thoughts' a piece of music expresses or denotes. 'A Beethoven symphony', we are told (except the articulate part of the ninth), 'expresses noble feeling but not thought; it has moods but no ideas. Wagner added thought and produced the music drama' (p. 138). What are we to understand by 'expressing' noble feeling? Presumably not that the composer felt 'noble' (superior?) when he wrote the music. Is it then that on hearing it *we* feel noble or find ourselves thinking about nobility, whereas in other cases we think about 'thought'? If the structure of the music does remind us of the structure of 'noble feeling', this may be due to any sort of accidental association; and Shaw says nothing to show in what way the music could actually 'have moods' (as, of course, it could not), or what sort of mixture of music and feeling he supposes *the symphony as appreciated* to be.

As before, Shaw's distinction between thought and things has to be rejected; thought-content is nothing but things, and things are not, by being thought, raised to a higher power. Both feelings and sounds are, as they stand, thinkable objects, and they neither require nor admit of any 'interpretation' whereby they may become charged with 'ideas'. Again, if a part of the ninth symphony is articulate, what does it say? And what is the difference between just *saying* that and writing 'articulate music'? Does Shaw merely mean that, where there are words *along with* the music, the music means these words? This would be making criticism, as the discovery of 'spiritual equivalents', a shade too easy; and it would imply that either words or music could be dispensed with. Actually, nothing but the music is 'articulated' in the music; and as to its making Shaw or us *think of* something else, there is no music of which this might not be said. Anything, indeed, may become associated with anything else — and that is a decisive objection to all symbolist and representationist theories.

Shaw's criticisms, then, merely show his own limitations, and he fails to make good his distinction between music with moods and music with ideas. In the same way (pp. 128–9) he does not succeed in distinguishing between merely musical structure (in which, e.g., 'the second stave is usually a perfectly obvious consequence of the first') and what we might call supra-musical structure.

> The other and harder way of composing is to take a strain of free melody, and ring every variety of change of mood upon it as if it were a thought that sometimes brought hope, sometimes melancholy, sometimes exultation, sometimes raging despair, and so on. To take several themes of this kind, and weave them together into a rich musical fabric passing panoramically before the ear with a continually varying flow of sentiment, is the highest feat of the musician.

After such bathetic verbiage we are not surprised to learn (pp. 134–5) that the symphonies of Beethoven made it certain 'that the poetry that lies too deep for words does not lie too deep for music, and that the vicissitudes of the soul, from the roughest fun to the loftiest aspiration (!), can make symphonies without the aid of dance tunes.'

All this striving after the soulful equivalent of music does not advance us one step in musical appreciation. We may have a certain flow of soul in the presence of an object, and, in the case of a manufactured object, this may be substantially the same as the flow of its creator's soul while he was making it; but all that leaves the character of the object itself still unspecified. And, if what we are to appreciate is really the creator's flow or our own, we have still to consider *its* structure and criticise it objectively. Expressionists may, of course, contend that we appreciate it by going through it. The fact remains that there are objects and soul-states that we do not enjoy, and this raises the objective problem which no amount of soulfulness will solve. That being recognised, we see that soul is no more entitled to be considered *the* aesthetic object (or material) than anything else. In fact, as has been said, this whole line of criticism is bluff; we are *told* that Shaw or someone else has a remarkable 'flow of sentiment', but we do not have it presented to us. All that we get is a glorified version of 'pleasure' as the aesthetic criterion — exemplified, on the side of 'appreciation of Nature', in the well-known lines, 'And then my heart with pleasure fills, and dances with the daffodils.' To show that his heart is thoroughly filled the expressionist lays claim to every variety of feeling and 'aspiration'. The wider the range, the more he is 'in tune with the infinite' — and the more he is absolved from bothering about *structure*.

Similar criticisms apply to Shaw's exposition of the musical character of *The Ring*. With reference to its 'themes', he says (p. 119) that

> when it comes to forming the necessary mental association with the theme, it may happen that the spectator may find his ear conquering the tune more easily than his mind conquers the thought. But for the most part the themes do not denote thoughts at all, but either emotions of a quite simple universal kind, or the sights, sounds and fancies common enough to be familiar to children.

Here once more we have the bad distinction between 'thoughts' and other things, e.g., emotions. We have also the admission that certain arbitrary associations have to be formed. That being so, a particular musical arrangement may suggest a particular arrangement of the associated things. And it may be true that Wagner, in aiming at an effect of this kind, 'was the literary musician par excellence' (p. 137), i.e., that he used musical material for literary purposes. But to go on to say that 'he could not, like Mozart or Beethoven, produce decorative tone structures independently of any dramatic or poetic subject matter, because, that craft being no longer necessary for his purpose, he did not cultivate it', is to beg the critical aesthetic question whether Wagner has any subject-matter — whether he has either a literary or a musical theme, or, again, if that be possible, a jointly literary and musical theme. At any rate, the distinction between 'decorative' and 'dramatic' is one to be rejected. We can say of drama, and of 'music drama' if such a thing exists, that the presentation of its material will be just as 'decorative' as any other aesthetic presentation.

As regards the possibility of 'music drama', then, it would appear that its material *includes* that of drama. Of course, according to Shaw, even the dramatic material of *The Ring* is to be taken representationally, as having not only a cosmic but a social reference. The Preface to the Second Edition informs us that Wagner's 'picture of Niblunghome under the reign of Alberic is a poetic vision of unregulated industrial capitalism as it was made known in Germany in the middle of the nineteenth century by Engel's *Condition of the Labouring Classes in*

England.' A 'poetic vision' is apparently one which presents the thing without its coarser qualities, as the helmet, e.g., is a refined version of the top-hat. But, of course, this is mere convention; the one is no more 'poetic' than the other. And, to take the most important point, if *The Ring* differs from capitalism, in not being squalid or 'prosaic', then, however much it may *remind us* of capitalism, we have no ground for saying that the conflicts of capitalism are the theme, or part of the theme, of *The Ring*. If Wagner said to himself, 'That is the capitalist, that is the top-hat, these are Law and the Church', this is of interest to the critic of Wagner but not to the critic of *The Ring*. What we choose to *associate* with *The Ring*, be it the history of 'the world' or the condition of society, is of no aesthetic importance. We certainly could not get actual history out of *The Ring*, and if Wagner thought he was expressing 'the ideas of 1848', that merely indicates his romantic misconception of 1848, and how in consequence he could afterwards make his peace with the powers that be. Prestige is certainly gained by making out that a work means something big, but as critics we are concerned not with what it 'means' but with what it is.

As representation, then, the work is bound to fail. In extenuation of that failure Shaw tells us (p. 30) that 'there is only one way of dramatising an idea; and that is by putting on the stage a human being possessed by that idea, yet none the less a human being with all the human impulses which make him akin and therefore interesting to us.' But, if there is such a thing as an idea, it should be presented in its own structure; and if that is not dramatic structure, then any drama which is alleged to deal with the idea does not do so. This is apart from the fact that the 'idea', as conceived by Shaw, is a driving-force behind things, something which by definition cannot be presented, and which therefore cannot be represented either, since there is no structure which the given structure could make us think of. It is, of course, possible to be reminded of *presentable* material; and it might be that, just as in looking at a flat picture we are to think of a three-dimensional structure, so in *The Ring* we are to think of a certain conflict or complication which is not physically present. The interest which Shaw admits we may have in what *is* present ('human impulses', etc.) might then be irrelevant to the real work of art or object to be appreciated — though what is present might conceivably also be a work of art. But actually the supposed underlying conflict is *not* represented by *The Ring*. If we had a separate belief in it, we might, as Shaw does, see connections; but we cannot attend to *The Ring* and see that conflict as we can look at a picture and see the solid. And if the actual history of society is not to be found in *The Ring*, the non-existent 'destiny of man' cannot even be connected with it.

We are brought back, then, to the actual proceedings of the characters, Siegfried, Wotan and the rest, and we find them to be dramatically trivial. On the dramatic side, *The Ring* can be regarded only as a show, a *pantomime* with real giants, a dragon and tons of real water — as Shaw, indeed, admits it is (p. 1), if it is divested of its cosmic and social significance. And if the drama cannot have these meanings, then obviously the music cannot — though if it had, it should be allowed to speak for itself and should not require to be helped out by spectacular displays. But, for Shaw, the music simply means the action that goes with it and the action means some phase of the world-struggle; and these arbitrary interpretations are all that we get by way of elucidation of the term 'music drama'. It is quite apparent that Shaw has not even begun the musical interpretation of *The Ring*; and his aesthetic bankruptcy and the imposture of his 'Wagnerism' are completely exposed. It appears also that any attempted 'musico-dramatic' consideration of such work will give us at most a *dramatic* theme.

Certain possible relations of music and drama remain to be considered. It may be argued that music can assist dramatic presentation. For example, singing might be, like a blank verse, a convenient way of putting a dramatic point across; or our interest in the drama might be enhanced by incidental music — though, if our attention had to be stimulated by such external means, this would raise a suspicion either of weakness in the drama itself or of critical weakness on our part. On the other hand, the human voice might be a useful addition to the orchestra for a particular musical purpose; and various stage-effects might get us and keep us in the right frame of mind for appreciating certain orchestral music. Nevertheless these effects would be outside the aesthetic picture; and it might well be argued that they would tend to make us *less* critical rather than more so, that they would hamper our appreciation of the music as accompanying music may hamper our appreciation of the drama. Shaw himself admits (p. 95) that in Die Götterdämmerung 'the extraordinary storm of emotion and excitement which the music keeps up' helps to conceal from the public the extreme conventionality of the dramatic side of the work.

This is what commonly happens with opera. Having the multiple titillation of drama, spectacle, and music, we can be highly entertained by stuff that is dramatically null, like *The Ring*, or musically null, or both. We may be 'stirred' at once by the music and by our 'interest in the fate' of the hero. But what has stirring to do with art, or great stirring to do with great art? Wagner is, doubtless, very stirring. But we have found that all the devices whereby our attention is directed to what the music 'means', make it possible for Shaw to dodge the critical problem and profess to be discussing the music when he is actually discussing something else. It may be that these tricks, in fact, the whole operatic apparatus, enable Wagner *to dodge the musical problem*, to cover up his musical weaknesses by distracting our attention or making us too excited to be critical — carrying us off our feet, after the manner of 'not a dry eye in the house'.

It may be contended, then, that whatever may be said of opera as a form of entertainment, music and drama are separate aesthetic forms, and there is no structure which is jointly musical and emotional. On the basis of expressionism, any material may be combined with any other material, since what is appreciated is the 'spiritual significance' of each. But we have found such interpretations to be of an arbitrary and falsifying character. Thus, unless we can find a theme which is definitely both musical and emotional in nature, we must regard opera and the like as mere juxtaposition of materials, and not as having any concatenated structure. We can, as was noted, have emotional structure with incidental music or musical structure with incidental emotion, though these incidentals may be more of a hindrance than a help to critical appreciation. Indeed, the prevalence of emotional interpretations of music and other arts is enough to indicate the readily confusing effect of 'incidental emotion', and to make us doubt whether it is ever even of educative value; nay, more, this fact by itself would lead us to cast doubt on any alleged structural combination of emotional and other material. At any rate, we can say definitely that *The Ring* is not such a combination, and that, though it is not a musical whole, whatever value it has lies in the music. The rest is spoof — exploitation of 'eerieness' and other forms of *Das Heilige*.

17 *The Perfect Wagnerite*

Photograph of Anderson submitted with his application for the Challis Chair of Philosophy at the University of Sydney, 1926.

– 18 –

Emperor and Galilean

Emperor and Galilean deals with the struggle (351–363 AD) between Julian the Apostate and the Christian Church. It consists of two plays — *Caesar's Apostasy*, ending with Julian's rebellion against Constantius, and *The Emperor Julian*, concerned with his tenure of the throne until his death. This duality suggests that there is here no working out of a single theme. If it was worked out in the first play, there would be no need for a second; and if the second is required for the working out, we should expect just one, and not two plays. There is, however, some force in the notion that the working out of one subject naturally leads to another. *A Portrait of the Artist as a Young Man* deals with the youthful artist as *Ulysses* does with his maturity, and in these two novels there is at least *some* passing from one phase of Stephen to another — though Bloom is important only in *Ulysses*; but in the first is completed the phase of youthfulness, with all the romanticism which is the characteristic of youth. Again, in his two sets of poems, youthful love is the theme of *Chamber Music*, and in a sense this is worked out, but it leads naturally to *Pomes Penyeach* where the theme is loss

---

This article is a composite of: (1) an address to a Socialist meeting in Stonehouse, Lanarkshire, circa 1920; (2) an address to the Sydney University Literary Society, 28 April 1932, reported in the *Union Recorder*, 5 May 1932; and (3) an address to a Congress of the Sydney University Freethought Society, Newport, 1942.

of love, the poem 'I Hear an Army' being the natural link between the two. A phase of a sequence, then, can be treated as a theme and yet lead naturally on to another theme. But we cannot say that this is the case in *Emperor and Galilean*. Though in point of time and in the continued development of Julian's character *The Emperor Julian* follows naturally on *Caesar's Apostasy*, no theme can be said to be worked out fully in either of the plays, and there is a good deal of overloading in the presentation of the work.

This dramatic weakness is connected with the historical material with which Ibsen is dealing. The struggle between Christianity and Paganism in which Julian is involved lasts for twelve years, the first play in five acts and with no formal scenes stretching over ten of these years, and ranging from Constantinople to Athens, Ephesus, Vienna and two places in Gaul. The second play covers two years, with scenes located in Constantinople, Antioch and the plains beyond the Tigris. While strict observance of the unities of time and place is not an aesthetic necessity, perhaps in consequence of the utter disregard of them which we find here, the plays seem episodic, a series of collisions and crises rather than the working out of a single theme. Without going further into details of their aesthetic merit, the first play may be judged less episodic, more forceful and more coherent than the second which is padded a good deal and in which the situations are less dramatic; at best, perhaps, it could be said that the second serves to underline some parts of the first play.

The historical character of Ibsen's material is a matter of importance, for special questions arise in connection with historical works of art. They require, for instance, a double criterion — that of artistic coherence and that of historical accuracy. These two are independent; there can be works of art based on history which are artistically coherent but not historically accurate, and works which are historically accurate but not aesthetically satisfying. In the writing of *good* history itself, some artistic canons must be observed, even if the work of the historian is largely determined by his fidelity to facts. Some historians have little theory, little notion of what their story is, and tend simply to relate one event after the other. Croce has a more artistic approach; for him history is the story of liberty, and on this view all the events related will assume what significance they have in the light of that conception and be built up around it. For the *literary* artist in historical material, there is always the problem of cutting off one situation or one section from the general flow of history — since in spite of the tendency to regard history as the drama of the human race, the history of the race is not a single theme at all and cannot be dramatised. It may be argued that this selection, this cutting off of material for the building up of a work of art, is a problem for every artist, but it is perhaps a more difficult one for the writer of historical novels and plays because of the necessity to be as faithful to the facts as possible. In any case, the artistic criterion will always be the extent to which the events connected with the situation have been seized upon by the author and presented in logical order. And though literary presentation can increase the forcefulness of the social or historical point, history is not to be confused with literature, and it is to be noted that merely literary criticism of a work which has a historical point is not enough, and may even be unimportant.

In the case of Ibsen, his literary ability (his ability to present states of mind through the deeds and words of his characters) illuminates the historical crisis with which he is dealing. Even if *Emperor and Galilean* is not an aesthetic whole, even if Ibsen were wrong in certain historical details, if it does have the essential political and historical content, it can still be illuminating. Ibsen himself thought it was his best play, and though we may not agree with him, it cannot be denied that he has dealt very convincingly with his human material, has presented a certain psychological conflict and has treated dramatically, in its historical context, a clash between the ideals of men and the realities of things. We cannot help noticing the difference between the force of Ibsen in *Emperor and Galilean* and the weakness and sentimentality of Merejkowsky in *The Death of the Gods*, a book which deals with the same historical period as *Emperor and Galilean*. It, too, is episodic, and the sentimentality arises from the failure in handling human relationships and from the idealisation of the characters involved.

We discover, in tackling the plays, that Ibsen has certain views about history and about the way things come to pass in the social struggles of a people; and we must admit, even if we disagree with him, that he puts the points across in a forceful way. Whether there is a continuous theme throughout history is a question raised especially in the first play, where he puts forward the notion of a world spirit acting through men, taking them from one phase of history to another; and he tries to show the working of this world spirit in the events of the historical period he has chosen, and in the lives of his characters, especially that of Julian, the Emperor. This conception of a continuous theme in history is held also by Vico with his idea of a guiding thread which he calls Providence, running through the maze of events. Vico's Providence might be considered simply as the personification of the laws of society, the laws of history, and Ibsen also is personifying what he believes to be the laws of history, for in neither case is this spirit something external, something forced upon events; it is just something that is supposed to be observable in the working out of events. Ibsen's world spirit does not guide, however, but works through opposition, and though there are marked differences between his conception and that of Vico, they have one thing in common — namely, the idea that the people concerned do not know what they are really doing. On Ibsen's theory, the very having of a certain intention can be the instrument for the opposite coming about, as Julian's opposition to the Christian religion could be said to be the instrument by which that religion was definitely established. The notion of this opposition permeates the whole of the first play, with the suggestion that Julian is in line with Cain and Judas — Cain who by opposing a sacrificial creed thereby advanced it, and Judas who, by betraying the Galilean, actually played an essential part in establishing Galileanism.*

Closely bound up with this notion of a world spirit that works through opposition is the recurrence in the plays of enigmas and riddles, and there is a considerable amount of quoting of texts because many of these riddles are embodied in the Christian religion itself. In the second act of the first play, in Julian's mock trial before the Christian Gregory, he ridicules the latter by means of the text 'Render unto Caesar the things that are Caesar's — and unto God the things that are God's' and there are continual references to this enigmatical command

---

* We might here instance the Bolsheviks who intended to do certain things but achieved something very different from, and even opposed to, what they intended. Lenin, in particular, aimed at liberation but ended by establishing a peculiar tyranny which would not otherwise have come about.

throughout the play. Victory and defeat, too, have an enigmatical relationship, for 'he who saveth his life shall lose it' and 'what shall it profit a man if he gain the whole world and lose his own soul?' At the end of the play, before and during Julian's last battle on the plains beyond the Tigris, all the enigmatical strands in the work seem to be interwoven. While Julian's army, with the help of a body of soldiers who believe in the Galilean whom he hates and persecutes wins a miraculous battle over the Persians, Julian himself is mortally wounded by a spear hurled by a Christian soldier ('the Roman's spear from Golgotha'). In the moment of his great success we find him dying with the conflict in his soul unresolved. 'No lamentations!' he says, 'Do we not all love wisdom? And does not wisdom teach us that the highest bliss lies in the life of the soul, not of the body? So far the Galilean is right, although —; but we will not speak of that.' His very last words were 'Beautiful earth, — beautiful life — Oh, Helios, Helios — why didst thou betray me?' This opposition between an 'inner' life and an 'outer' one, between spirit and body, between God's kingdom and Caesar's empire is an important one in the play, and it can at least be said that Ibsen is truly interpreting the Christian doctrine, or one particular variant of it — the necessity for the sacrificing of the 'outer' for the 'inner' — in his presentation of the events and characters concerned in the play.

But there is the further notion of the giving up of the earthly for the heavenly, where heaven is not something inward and spiritual but something future and outer — mansions in the sky after death — a material reward for those who make the required sacrifices during life. It is interesting to note that an insistence on an inner, extreme spiritualism results in materialism, including a concern with signs and portents. Ibsen is being straight out Hegelian here with the notion that the more we emphasise one extreme, the more we run into the other. Elias Jones, in *The Road to Endor*,[1] brings out the fact that so-called spiritualism is actually extremely materialistic (in the bad sense), that it is concerned with rewards and, in general, with fleshly things, not spiritual things at all. With him we might compare Feuerbach, who argues that the heavenly is always a way of presenting *human* things, with some of the features voluntarily removed — faith removing logic, so to speak. Julian, a man of extreme inwardness, 'alone in earnestness', is presented to us as continually looking for signs and portents and as suggesting, by his behaviour, that there is a non-natural character of things.

This work of Ibsen is really a drama of power. Already in the title the opposing forces are indicated and it is against a background of the struggle for power between the Empire and Christianity that the struggle in Julian's soul takes place; for he, too, had been a Christian and he has to fight the Galilean in himself. We are presented with the problem of whether there is an 'inner' power (cf. 'The kingdom of Heaven is within you') or whether power depends on externals. On the one side there is the notion that if all is well with the soul, if the Kingdom of Heaven is within, no external power can harm one, for defeat will be victory and death will mean eternal life; or, alternatively, that one will have power over events (cf. faith removing mountains). On the other hand, there is the external power, the power of empire with all the apparatus of government and the working with external things.

Julian can find peace neither within nor without. In his extreme inwardness, in his extreme concentration on himself, in his desire to discover *his* peculiar destiny, he pays no attention to how things work and he can never go forward confidently on any course of action. He can adhere to no cause and his position can be bolstered up only by dragging in signs and portents. From the very beginning of the first play we find him seeing significance in all kinds of happenings. He takes the dream of his friend, Agathon, for example, as a sign that he, Julian, is to go to Athens to contend with the philosophers and to uphold Galileanism. Indeed, when he wants anything, if signs and portents are not at hand, he tries by all kinds of trickery to get others to suggest what he wants — conduct which is very much in keeping with that of the world spirit and its indirect ways of working. Apart from these means he has nothing but his will to carry him along; in fact, it is his will all the time for in the arbitrariness of his extreme individualism he insists on giving his own interpretations to the visions that the mystic, Maximus, conjures up so that he makes it seem that it is *they* who are pointing out to him the way *he* wants to go. And if no interpretation can be found in accordance with his desires (as happens often in the second play), he simply goes his own way — or what he thinks is his own way. In one of his sessions with Maximus, Julian asks: 'What is my mission?'

The Voice:	'To establish the empire.'[2]
Julian:	'What empire?'
The Voice:	'The empire.'
Julian:	'And by what way?'
The Voice:	'By the way of freedom.'
Julian:	'Speak clearly! What is the way of freedom?'
The Voice:	'The way of necessity.'
Julian:	'And by what power?'
The Voice:	'By willing.'
Julian:	'*What* shall I will?'
The Voice:	'What thou must.'

And when later in the scene, Maximus conjures up before his eyes Cain and Judas, he refuses to be the 'third great freedman under necessity'. He denies necessity, saying 'I will not serve it! I am free, free, free!' As in *Brand* Ibsen is here concerned with the problem of *will*; and the suggestion is that the man who *merely* wills, who claims to be a person of strong will, is really in no better position than he who 'follows the gleam'. Since Julian's grasping of power is not a positive, creative thing, he is bound, like Macbeth whom he somewhat resembles, to fail after he achieves it. In opposing Christianity he has only his own egoism and the abstract power of empire to fall back upon. He thinks of power as a *possession*, as something he *has*, and so we find him complaining to Maximus: 'Is not that very thing divided among many which the ruler of the world should possess in fuller measure than all besides, nay, which he alone should possess?' (Cf. the notion of the unity of power as found among the Christians — 'For thine is the kingdom, the power and the glory'.) 'Everything,' he concludes, 'even renunciation and seclusion, becomes a power to oppose my power. But the crucified Jew is still the worst of all.' This point about power is connected with notions of pure individuality, pure inwardness and lack of content, and it is in keeping with the working of the world spirit that extreme urge to power leads to utter lack of it.

The question of causes is one of the most important that the play brings up. It is an example of the working of the world spirit that a cause regularly shows nobility in adversity and loses its spirit in success, though it may regain it in renewed adversity.* In *Emperor and Galilean*, we are confronted at the very outset with the wrangling Christians whose religion has become, under Constantius, the established religion of the Empire. Constantius does not support Christianity because he believes in it but because he is seeking to find peace for his soul tormented by the many murders that he has committed. And it is a further refinement of the juggling of the world spirit that the religion of peace thus set up brings anything but peace to a Church that was supposed to stand for it. In this successful Christianity we see a variety of quarrelling sects with their worldly and egotistic attitudes, and in Constantius himself only suspicion, superstition and fear.† When he dies, however, the Christians once more in subjection, this time to the Emperor Julian, close their ranks and unity is again achieved in the Christian Church. No longer in a state of receptivity, of getting benefits, of being safe from persecution, many of those who fell away or were corrupted in the period of prosperity return to the fold, some even embracing martyrdom, and the general body of Christians recovers in its adversity its erstwhile nobility of purpose.

Is there a simplification of the main issues presented in *Emperor and Galilean*? We can indeed see something in the idea that it is only in wrestling with obstacles, in opposition, that causes *can* work. Liberalism, for example, as a cause, must always be in opposition —

---

* In modern times the cause, describable as Socialism, illustrates the thesis underlying Ibsen's play. In opposition it was generous, self-sacrificing, disinterested, but as a form of rule, with its insistence on power, it could not but be bad, and lose much or all of its original socialist character. Like Julian, the Emperor, the Stalinists degenerated; they thought they had a criterion that they were automatically right, that they had *arrived*. They, too, were absorbed in signs and portents, in shows and spectacles, in rhetoric and in superstition.
† There are many analogies with Bolshevism in Ibsen's characterisation of arbitrariness and tyranny, and the Stalin regime, where the murder of rivals is possible, is comparable to the reign of Constantius, who had Julian's brother, Gallus, murdered (in circumstances recalling the murder of Tukachevsky) and who attempted to murder Julian after having nominated him his successor.

'agin the government' as its position used to be described; it must not become an established power on pain of ceasing to be liberal. But is it simply a question of the 'inner' and the 'outer'? Ibsen himself seems to recognise that opposition between them cannot be maintained completely, for he refers in the play to a Third Kingdom where the two will be reconciled, where flesh and spirit will work harmoniously together, and the old beauty of Paganism go hand in hand with the new truth of Christianity.

There is something of this notion of a reconciliation between the two — not as a kingdom or power, but as the interconnecting, the working together of the 'outer' and the 'inner'. If a person concentrates on inwardness as Julian did, he degenerates as Ibsen shows. If he is bound up with a movement, with a cause, he has more chance of achieving a harmony of the two, for then, even in oppression, he can keep a certain measure of freedom. In connection with the opposition of the spirit and the flesh, Feuerbach makes the point that it is not spirituality divorced from fleshliness nor fleshliness divorced from spirituality that has any value. It is the growing intercourse between the two that we can call progress or freedom; neither alone can generate anything but a very low kind of life. As against Marx, who in the *Theses on Feuerbach* rejects the difference between the 'inner' and the 'outer', it is more true to the facts to insist on co-operation between the two. There *is* a certain distinction between them even without arguing that the mind is not bodily. It might even be better to state the solution as a balance between two bodily (or two mental) tendencies.

Ibsen himself satirises the notion of spiritual purity in Helena, the sister of Constantius — treatment which contrasts with the presentation of Solveig in *Peer Gynt*. Julian takes up an attitude of adoration and worship of her purity; but she turns out to have been 'impure', to have indulged in secret gratifications of the flesh. The suggestion is that she had been the lover of Gallus, Julian's brother, before his death and before she married Julian; then, having no relations with Julian, she had turned in secret to others. This is all put into a special form to satirise the asceticism of Christianity; she is even said to have had relations with a priest who is supposed to be Jesus in the guise of his servant. Finally she is poisoned by Constantius, and the body of this 'pure' woman is reputed to be able to work miracles and cure of their diseases those who touch her bier. Thus bad conditions are brought about by the cleavage between flesh and spirit, by the insistence on the spiritual, whether or not Julian is meant to be the one most responsible for what happened. This particular question is only a minor one in the play, but it illustrates not only the evil that follows from complete separation of the two, but the way in which the world spirit provides Julian with the opposite of what he longed for and what he thought he was receiving when Constantius gave him Helena to wife.

We have, then, in *Emperor and Galilean* what might be called a drama of ideas, an exposition of Ibsen's views on history and human nature by means of the dramatic interaction of historical characters and historical events. Artistically we must reject the notion that the work presents Julian's fulfilment of his destiny to establish Christianity by opposing it. If we do not, we go beyond drama, for the notion of a world spirit involves the operation of forces that cannot be brought upon the stage. But if we consider drama as the exploding of illusions then, whatever weaknesses there may be, we can say that this is done here. We see the outcome of Julian's egoism, his inability to co-operate, his obsessions, his delusions of power. As in the case of Lear, who had the illusion that he could divest himself of his royal powers and still be treated as a king; and in that of Macbeth who, like Julian, desired power as something he could simply possess and by which he thought he could bring about what *he* wanted, the power to which Julian lays claim, the power to control destiny, is exposed as being unequal to events; and because like Lear and Macbeth he cannot see through his pretensions, like them he is destroyed.

All this again is connected with the Ibsenite idea, most clearly expressed in *Peer Gynt*, that thoughts are things; that delusions and metaphysical notions are realities in the minds of the persons who hold them, and that they have an actual working out. In psycho-analysis, these things are worked out in the consulting-room, in the mind of the patient; in drama they are worked out by means of the speech and actions of the characters in the play. In the case of *Emperor and Galilean*, these delusions are presented not only in the 'inward' (mental) dramatic way through the speeches and actions of the characters but also in an 'outward' way by the dramatisation of the delusions themselves, and we have, for instance, Julian actually seeing Cain and

Judas in the 'table-rapping' scene. This kind of thing *can* have dramatic value, even when it is presented on the stage, on the understanding that it is the kind of thing in which all or some of the characters believe — just as we can have some stage device for Macbeth's dagger in which Macbeth alone believes. But if the dramatic development *depends* on these things being there, apart from being supposed or believed in by the characters concerned, this would be dramatic weakness. If there is any force in the drama as an exposure of delusions, it should be possible to have the theme worked out without asking the spectator in any way to share in the delusions.

The play, then, may not be historically accurate but it does embody important general historical notions. The main basis for our *aesthetic* judgement of it is the fact that Julian is presented as a coherent character, striving to bring about certain things in the troubled times in which he lived. He is a tragic character, because he is defeated without ever finding out what were the illusions which led to his downfall, though they are sufficiently exposed to the readers or the spectators of the play. Ibsen very forcefully and convincingly presents Julian's clash with his epoch, his struggle for power and his inevitable failure, and in these respects *Emperor and Galilean* is good drama.

– 19 –
Kenneth Grahame

Kenneth Grahame's writing belongs to what might be called the literature of the countryside. Not only does it deal with the significance of common things, of growth, of open-air delights; it draws attention to the way in which the countryside is significant in history. These qualities are to be found also in Chesterton and Belloc, the latter of whom has enshrined them in the poem at the end of *The Four Men*:

> He does not die that can bequeath
> Some influence to the land he knows,
> Or dares, persistent, interwreath
> Love permanent with the wild hedgerows;
>   He does not die, but still remains
>   Substantiate with his darling plains.

George Bourne, in his *Memoirs of a Surrey Labourer*, makes it quite clear that such historical significance resides in persons. There is nothing 'literary' about his attitude; he describes country life as it is lived and his description is direct and free from literary allusions. With Chesterton, Belloc and Kenneth Grahame there is at least a hint of the pathetic fallacy, and little description of country life as it is actually lived

---

A very early paper, probably written in 1920.

by those whose lot it is to till the fields and tend the crops and animals thereon.

Perhaps Kenneth Grahame comes nearer than either of them to the 'John Barleycorn' attitude, even though the very titles of the first two *Pagan Papers* — 'Romance of the Road' and 'Romance of the Rail' — indicate the romanticism which is expressed in Kenneth Grahame's case by his somewhat learned and literary views, and there is a strong suggestion that the countryside is being described from the point of view not merely of the 'educated' but of the comfortable class. In this respect Chesterton, and to a greater extent, Belloc, achieve a more objective attitude, though their Romanist views do not permit of a quite non-sentimental outlook (cf. Chesterton's interpretation of history in the matter of the Crusades).[1] In none of them, of course, do we get simple nature-worship; all recognise the importance (or the necessity) of work and toil, yet sometimes, in *Pagan Papers*, there is a suggestion of literature and life (especially that of the countryside) as amusement, as reflection for the jaded — not as something that is actually lived. Connected therewith, there is a certain 'insincerity' — a search for the *mot juste*, for *neat* ways of saying things, for the sake of neatness and not for the things. This characteristic also appears in the literary style of the 'I' of *The Golden Age* and illustrates how 'fancy' can lead to *inconsequence*, to having things praised for their associations and not for themselves. At other times, again, there is a suggestion that men seek, and have sought, the idyllic: that there is a real and possible life of this kind, with its own economies and its own enjoyments: that, at least, it is a kind of life into which one can sink for awhile, and in which, if one could stay, it would be well. Then, again, there is the notion that all we have are glimpses of something that is now unattainable.

For Kenneth Grahame, the golden age was in the past, both as regards the race and as regards individuals. In *The Lost Centaur*, he asks if the lamentable cleavage between men and animals that has taken place somewhere along the line of development might not have been avoided, thus leaving the world with beings of a 'dual nature', comprising 'the nobilities of both and the baseness of neither'. And of ourselves, he says: 'As we grow from our animal infancy and the threads snap one by one at each gallant wing-stroke of a soul poised for flight into Empyrean, we are yet conscious of a loss for every gain, we have some forlorn sense of a vanished heritage.' What most endears these pagan worlds to him is the absence of didacticism, and though the rhythm of his prose gives an effect of rhetoric, there is thus often the saving grace of a certain ironical criticism of business and of systems of ends (i.e., of definite objects or goals), ranging from that of the strenuous holidaymakers in 'Loafing', 'their voices clamant of feats to be accomplished', to the more whimsical paper, called 'Deus Terminus', with its final request for a 'fat and succulent stationmaster' to be offered up on 'the altar of expiation'. There is, too, evidence of a certain *satyric* mentality (cf. his fondness for the musical god, Pan) which has none of the sadness of Belloc or the buffoonery of Chesterton; but there is, unfortunately, not enough of either quality to save the work from being judged both 'literary' and cathartic — something to amuse, to distract and 'interest'.

It is in *The Golden Age* itself that we find this ironical criticism of convention as the world is seen through the eyes of a child. *He*, for example, is not allowed to do as he likes, but *they* (the Olympians) are, only they have forgotten how to like (cf. the wish that fails because it never acts).

> These elders, our betters by a trick of chance, commanded no respect, but only a certain blend of envy (for their good luck) and pity (for their inability to make good use of it). ... Having absolute licence to indulge in the pleasures of life, they could get no good of it. They might dabble in the pond all day ... they were free to fire cannons and explode mines in the lawn; yet they never did any of these things. No irresistible Energy haled them to church o' Sundays: yet they went there regularly of their own accord, though they betrayed no greater delight in the experience than ourselves.

Even in *The Golden Age*, 'fancy' intrudes to some extent. Instead of the recognition of play as useless work for its own sake, we have the children's activities glamourised. The impracticability of the 'practical' is not to be shown by means of 'fancy' or romance, but by means of things themselves as contrasted with ends or purposes. The earth and the children's kinship with it are not presented directly, but are treated with an insistence on the joys of retrospection, which comes perilously near the 'Cult of Immaturity'; but if it is a cult of anything, it is the cult of romance, which is not a childish thing at all. There is a certain amount of romance in Cook's 'Littlemen' in *The Play Way*, but through it all, these 'Littlemen' are eminently practical. One might rather say that Grahame puts a romantic flavour over things that would later in life seem romantic, but were not so at the time. It is true that tales of knights and chivalry were far less interesting than paddling and other childhood activities, but Grahame sheds on these the light of romance that comes with memories in after years.

This is a good book, a better book than *Pagan Papers* and superior, too, to *Dream Days*. It is nearer to things themselves and has fewer allusions, though it is still burdened by romance. Its excellence lies in the fact that it shows the working of simple motives, the going direct to some object, the cultivation of things in themselves — things not tied up with other people's expectations. In a word, it deals with the age of innocence, a theme which is strongly grasped; and for that reason alone, it is not a children's book, but quite simply a work of art, with certain incongruities like the foisting of literary enthusiasms on 'I', etc., but good in spite of that.

In *Dream Days* we find a greater tendency to epigram, much longer stories (suggesting a spinning out, or the intrusion of alien material) and more 'grown-up' stories. The title, too, is bad, standing as it does for the development of one of the defects in the previous book. There is also some affectation, a certain striving after 'fine writing' and, as a result, the poses are no longer boys' poses — they are too thoughtful. This preciosity leads to making fun by mixing up childishness and grown-upness — by a notion of the incongruity of a child's imaginings. But this position is not really sound for the child does not mix toys with his 'grown-up' adventures.

Perhaps the suggestion in the title is that we have here a halfway stage between the Age of Innocence and the Age of Convention — a conventionalised innocence, as it were — a compromise. But (except for the absence of 'Edward'), the background seems much the same, and the ages of the children very little different; the age is not yet the age of puberty. At any rate, the stories are told from a more external point of view — that of making fun of the child instead of entering into his diversions. They are *pictorial* rather than dramatic, and the atmosphere partakes too much of the 'jolly-good-fellow' spirit, of Bohemianism as well as of reflectiveness. The last story in the book is much the best; it captures some of the spirit of *The Golden Age* and avoids the smartness that has crept into much of *Dream Days*.

In *Books and Persons*, Arnold Bennett describes *The Wind in the Willows* as 'an urbane exercise in irony'. What we have in Kenneth Grahame generally, and *The Wind in the Willows* in particular, is a criticism of *habits* as contrasted with spontaneous activity; *or* of straight lines as contrasted with cycles — a criticism, in a word, of rigidity (i.e., of 'morals'). This is presumably the function of all comedy, whether in the form of irony or not, and just as it stands for criticism against 'morals', so it stands, in general, for art and literature, for things themselves against pretences (for the removal of hypotheses), for variety against uniformity — in a word, for beauty.

At the same time, there are in the book (cf. the chapter headed 'Wildwood'), objections to 'adventure without responsibility', such as those indulged in by Toad, as much as to 'responsibility without adventure'. These attitudes on the part of the author are both inartistic, for art is not *random* (as moralists assume); it is not a mere outbreak; it has rules. The important point is to follow the rules of things themselves, not to set up rules over and above them, i.e., not to set up standards from without. Things *have* measures. In addition to this defect, there is, as in the other books, a certain amount of 'fine writing' and some incongruity as in Otter's description of the snow.

But in the wonderful Pan episode ('The Piper at the Gates') we have the sense of great moments; of the lifting of veils; of inspirations that cannot be recaptured, but that somehow lead us on thereafter. There is also a sense of security, of a watcher and helper, of 'nature' that carries us though in *spite* of our efforts; not end, nor yet origin, but being (cf. 'the god who made things as they are'). We have, too, a notion of harmony behind strife; of value behind valuation. This is all romanticism (yet of a realistic sort), and may be compared with *Jurgen*, which is much more romantic and gives far less sense of actuality.

Kenneth Grahame achieves this sense of actuality in many ways. For instance, among his animals we find the notion of servants, of foreigners, of tradesmen and all sorts of specialists just as we find them in real life. Yet over the whole work he casts a poetic spell, perhaps because he gives such lively expression to our own longings for 'adventure'. It is interesting to see how he treats adventure itself in the four main characters of the book. Mole embarks upon it from ignorance and interest; Rat from poetry (romance) and because he enjoys it; Toad from vanity and Badger from necessity — he is quite willing to undertake adventures when they have to be undertaken, but he is fundamentally fond of peace and security. As Arnold Bennett says, 'they are human beings, and they are meant to be nothing but human beings. ... The superficial scheme of the story is so childishly naive, or so daringly naive, that only a genius could have preserved it from the ridiculous'; and it is 'no more to be comprehended by youth than *The Golden Age* was to be comprehended by youth'. It is, in fact, an unusual and wonderful work, and both in it and in *The Golden Age*, Kenneth Grahame, although his output is so small, shows himself an artist of very great ability.[2]

Elizabeth Anderson, John Anderson's mother, in the garden.

— 20 —

Kipling

It is perhaps peculiar to begin a series of discussions which is to embrace European literature, with the study of a writer who is as insular as Kipling. He does, of course, include in his 'insula' certain preserves or back blocks which go by the name of India, the Sudan, South Africa and so on; and there is, besides, always value in contrast, though this connecting of literature with civilisation, European or any other, must not be taken to imply a social criterion of literature. Aesthetics remains independent even if we allow that there is a connection between aesthetic and social views and between these and artistic work.

Although this address concerns itself solely with the prose work of Kipling, the whole body of his works indicates a certain outlook — an attitude which could be called servility, one aspect of which is pragmatism, the doctrine that *truth is what works*. There are, it might be said, two types of false thinking — the servile and the sentimental, as contrasted with the realist; and this difference might be otherwise expressed as comparativism and superlativism against positivism, or in Comte's terminology as theology (including mythology) and metaphysics in contrast with the scientific outlook. Kipling's position is largely theological and mythological. He presents agencies and forces

---

Address to the Literary Society, 2 July 1931, reported in the *Union Recorder*, 9 July 1931.

which can control, dominate and divert natural affairs *at will* as compared with the orderly working out of things, the logic of events. For him, there are no true universal propositions, no 'laws of nature'. Whether a thing of a certain class will turn out to have a certain character or not, will depend on what spirit is guiding it, or what force or spell is laid upon it, and some new factor is liable to turn up at the psychological moment, introducing the quality of magic into the work. With this may be connected his treatment of psychic compulsions, obsessions, psycho-pathology and dreams. His theological outlook manifests itself particularly in the social sphere, with the servility of his treatment of characters in a hierarchical system such as feudalism and imperialism, which is a kind of feudal capitalism. All this does not prevent him from treating 'nature' itself as a factor, a force; indeed the expression 'nature' and the kind of references we ourselves often make to its 'laws' are themselves examples of mythology.

These ideas are connected with the *content* of his work, but as I hope to show, there is no real distinction between form and content. In any piece of literary work, we are bound to find the expression (both conscious and unconscious) of the views of the writer, who is always limited by his intelligence, his knowledge and his beliefs, in presenting a tale, however faithfully he may think he is doing it; and Kipling's material leads straight to his aesthetic. There is a lack of balance in his themes from the start. He insists on race or breed, so that there are bound to be inconsistencies in his created world. He uses his stories (and this is one way in which his 'propagandism', his elevation of certain agents above circumstances, acts) to uphold the tradition of his country and class (in his case, country as seen by class). He is feudalistic and imperialistic, and his 'pragmatic' method comes out in all sorts of trickery and lying. He is ever the Magician, as Hardy is the mean Fate that governs *his* creatures and as Conrad is the more gaudy Doom of his.

Let us begin, then, on the social side, remembering that while he treats the world as a field for the exercising of personal prowess, 'gifts' and magic, he treats society, in particular, from the point of view of breed or class. He has the usual views of the English Tory about Ireland, and what does he do with them in his art? He creates (in *Life's Handicap*) a Himalayan half-caste, Namgay Doola, son of Tim Doolan (a deserter, presumably from the British army in India) and a hill-woman, and makes him, true to type, refuse to pay taxes, and (sweetest touch of all) cut off a cow's tail at night! (This is a reference to the Irish cattle-maiming outrages.) Namgay's 'breed' is then described by 'I who went forth and spoke to the King,' saying

> Thou canst either hang him from a tree, he and his brood, till there remains no hair that is red within the land ... Or thou canst, discarding the impiety of the cow-maiming, raise him to honour in thy Army. He comes of a race that will not pay revenue ... *This is the nature that God has given him.*

Here, then, we have Kipling's comment on Irish history. Social struggles in Ireland are not due to historical factors, least of all to English oppression, but to a peculiar brand of Irish life-force! And so Namgay Doola, rechristened Patsy Doolan, becomes the head of the hill King's army.

This kind of treatment of social affairs runs right through Kipling's stories, each nation, each race, each class, each person having his God-given place in the hierarchy. There is, for instance, the matter of 'the white man's burden', where again lying enters, this time in relation to the Boer War in *Traffics and Discoveries*. Laughton O. Zigler, an American inventor, having fought in the war and been captured by the British, declares that he is not a naturalised burgher because he is 'white'. 'Would *you* be a naturalised Boer?' he asks his captor. 'You can hold any blame opinion you choose, but I'm a white man, and my present intention is to die in that colour.' The point is further emphasised in the remarks of the Kentuckian later in the same yarn: 'A little thing like a King's neither here nor there, but what *you've* done is to go back on the White Man in six places at once.' One simply cannot credit the fact that Americans, including one that fought *for* the Boers (as did a number of Irishmen), would regard Boers as other than white. After all, a considerable number of Dutchmen went to the making of America, and although Americans, who are not exactly European, may suffer from a transmuted English insularity, it is not on behalf of the English themselves — the Anglo-Saxon race, whom they would never regard as the only 'pure' whites. Again in 'A Sahib's War' and

'The Comprehensions of Private Copper' (*Traffics and Discoveries*) we read about Boer atrocities and broken treaties in a country that British troops were making safe for Rand millionaires. These tales are all very sentimental, some of them servilely so, as we should expect to find in art where events are being related not logically and realistically, but in order to bolster up a particular point of view, and where we have the glorification of an author's likes and dislikes, instead of the objective treatment of a theme.

Kipling's feudalistic or hierarchical conception of the working class is indicated in a story in *The Day's Work*, in which he makes one of a group of horses attempt (in the accepted agitator's manner) to corrupt the others into an attack on their master, Man, and who gets thoroughly kicked for his pains. The relation between master and worker is made one of possession — of slavery, and one, too, of absolute biological distinction. Workers are inferior, lower animals who, if domesticated, will keep their proper place and do their day's work for a 'fair wage'; and the agitator, trying to revise this order of things, is put down by his servile mates. The same attitude is expressed in 'The Mother Hive' — the same belief in a hierarchy, in the fixity of the nature of things, with the addition that the agitator in this case is an alien — the wax moth. This theological version of social affairs, this belief in race and station, clearly implies incommunicable differences, rooted in superstitition and involving disbelief in education.

Coming next to what is more obviously 'magic', with special reference to psycho-pathology (which seems particularly to dominate Kipling's recent work), we find all the paraphernalia of the magician — mind-reading, dreams with their interpretation, second sight and telepathy. There are curses and there is the lifting of curses; there is devil-doctoring and there is voodoo. It may be argued that Kipling is seeing what can be done with the themes — that they are, as it were, suppositions. But we have seen the superstition of what he really believes socially, and it will be interesting to examine how much that is in keeping with his psychological and aesthetic beliefs, and how it all affects his artistic product.

In *Life's Handicap* we have 'The Mark of the Beast', a presentation of lycanthropy. An evil spirit is laid on a man for an offence against a temple and taken off again. For a time, then, he was obviously 'possessed' by that evil spirit. In *Actions and Reactions*, there is the story of 'The House Surgeon', where gloom is laid on a house by the gloom of someone thinking of it at a distance — caused by the spirit of a dead person trying to 'explain'. In *A Diversity of Creatures* a man in the horrors, sees a dog ('The Dog Hervey') belonging to a woman who is willing him back to her, and in *Traffics and Discoveries* is found 'They', the story of a blind woman in whose house the spirits of dead children live and play. This tale is an example of what can only be called a deep and foul tenderness in Kipling's work.

More characteristic still are the stories of dreams and nightmares. *A Diversity of Creatures* furnishes us with 'In the Same Boat', where two persons have regular nightmares of a fixed kind, these being representations of terrifying events that happened to their respective mothers shortly before they, the children, were born. Here we have the straight handing on of impressions — the effect is like the cause — and these impressions can afterwards be removed! This is, like the stories we have mentioned in *The Day's Work*, a denial of the process of learning — in this case, a denial of the fact that the basis of obsessions and compulsions is in a person's own history and struggles, and that methods of healing are related thereto. These tales are the sort of lies that an obsessive might tell to himself to avoid recognising the real source of conflict, 'getting away with it' by accusing fate, magic or witchcraft. Worst of them all, perhaps, is 'The Brushwood Boy' (*The Day's Work*) in which a man and a woman who had seen one another only once, as children, discover that they have been living the same dream adventures ever since; and decide that it means wedding-bells in the present, whatever it may mean in the 'hereafter'.

Kipling carries his theory of 'possession' over into literature. The artist is the man 'inspired', the wonder-worker, the magician. If Kipling had had a serious conception of the artist and his productions, of the worker and his work, he could not have indulged in all this fancifulness. In 'Wireless' (*Traffics and Discoveries*), we have the production of literature on a parallel with magnetic induction. A man (1) working in a chemist's shop (2) suffering from consumption (3) in love with a girl called Fanny Brand — instead of Brawne — (4) having just walked out with her in a cold night round by a church called St Agnes, goes off into a semi-drugged trance, and begins composing 'St Agnes' Eve' — or something very like it. The man never read or even heard of Keats, but these similarities in his life and activities bring him, so to speak, within the magnetic field of Keats, or the field which also charged Keats; so that, after struggling with 'St Agnes' Eve' for a while, he finally begins shaping the last lines of 'Ode to a Nightingale'. 'Power snatched him. But this time the agony was ten times keener' than before. In spite of it all, the nearest he could get to the actual lines before he woke from his trance, was:

> Our magic windows, fronting on the sea,
> The dangerous foam of desolate seas —
>   For aye.

We have a similar effort in the period of Kipling's decline, dealing with an induced Chaucer — a Chaucer induced by a set of pictures. 'There was a castle in the series; a knight or so in armour' etc. — Kipling's mind flying to the feudal age he admired so much. In the case of Keats, Kipling works on the actual poems and produces a story that might be interesting if it could be true. But it is really a fanciful lie, a pretence at a 'wonder' which is quite imaginary. In this later tale he produces an unknown Chaucerian fragment, the outstanding lines of which are:

> Ah Jesu-Moder, pitie my oe peyne,
> Daiespringe mishandeelt cometh nat agayne.

Hence the title of the story — 'Dayspring Mishandled'. It should perhaps be 'Chaucer Mishandled', when a few pictures are supposed to inspire a man to be a Chaucer, and to produce the above and other lines, e.g.,

> For what his woman willeth to be don
> Her manne must or wauken Hell anon.

'Dayspring Mishandled' is an outstanding example of how Kipling gets his morals all wrong. They are really the morals of an English public-school boy — of the sort that conforms to the common manners but has angels and devils of his own within his breast (i.e., English conformity and suppression). Costerley, the story goes, had loved a woman 'in his own way', and after her death, because she had refused him, he had denigrated her — though the reader is never told what was said. This unchivalrous conduct gave a purpose to the life of Manallace, who had also loved the woman and helped her until she died — a purpose which was fulfilled by using the Chaucerian fragment he had composed, with such accompanying fakery of ink, paper, etc., that Costerley, who had by this time become a great Chaucerian authority, was completely deceived by it. The plan was that he should be allowed — encouraged rather — to publish a book on it, after which Manallace would expose him, and make of him a laughing stock. However, Costerley died before the work was published, and the book went out and remained unexposed. The important point is that Kipling here presents a man who devotes his whole life to such a pitiful revenge, as being upright and praiseworthy through it all. It is almost as bad as *The Picture of Dorian Gray*! But Kipling's stories, even the earlier and better ones, are dominated by such juvenile conventional morals, by righteous indignation and, above all, by the spirit of revenge; or, on a lower level, by taking-down, this being the punishment a gentleman inflicts on a cad, i.e., on one who doesn't know his social place, and steps into the ranks of gentlemen where he doesn't 'belong'.

This school-boyish outlook, with its fundamental falsehood or distortion of things as they are; this elevation of exclusiveness and all it implies (revenge on the interloper, chivalry to dames, playing the game, 'scoring') into the supreme human quality or virtue, is naturally very marked in *Stalky and Co.* Here also we see the lying character of Kipling's work. He presents his own school, introducing a character (Beetle) who is clearly himself, and who proceeds with two companions (Stalky and McTurk) to score off masters and others in a way which one of the trio, Stalky — D. in real life, says never happened.[1] It is boasting and by that the less can it be literature; for the boasting is not dealt with as a theme, but treated from the point of view of the 'scorer'. Yet Kipling professes an objection to bullying! We have surely a trace of psycho-pathic division here!

This leads us straight to Kipling's aesthetic theory. We have already seen his notion of art as magic and how he treats it also as 'scoring', as hitting things off. This latter quality is, for him, part of the web and woof of things, for Nature, the great artist, 'defeats us every time' — scores off us, produces greater wonders, better surprises, more striking tableaux than we ever could imagine. In *A Diversity of Creatures*, when Bat Masquerier ('The Village that Voted the Earth was Flat') saw the genuine society of Flatearthers after he had played a prank on the Village by having one of his theatrical groups descend on it in that character, he was sick with envy. 'Curse Nature,' he muttered, 'She gets ahead of you every time. To think I forgot hymns and a harmonium!' The story is, by the way, another drama of revenge, with its schoolboyish sense of humour and its inflexible desire to 'score off'.

To a certain extent, Kipling sees through the game; he has his critical moments, but he remains faithful to his class — the public school class, the military class — of both of which he is a privileged slave and flatterer, a court jester. In that he is always aiming at effects, he is a romanticist, part teacher, part propagandist, part moralist. In his artistic game of scoring off, he is concerned with upshots, conclusions, repartees, and not with themes and their development. It is his insistence on effort and success (success being the goal and effort the means), instead of process (the sequence of phases and balance of forces which are the mark of the work of art) that mars Kipling's work, making it definitely unbalanced and discordant. And while we do not describe his aesthetic achievement by his aesthetic intention, we can see that his intention has actually affected his achievement. He solves problems, complications and entanglements by external, and often magical means, just as he often bridges gaps by supernatural agencies. The intrusion of the 'I' in so many of his stories breaks the continuity of the development, for 'I' is not treated as a character, but intervenes to put forward Kipling's own views (cf. 'Namgay Doola'). There is a certain artlessness in his tales, but it is not a true artlessness; it is a feigned, sophisticated artlessness. And there is always deception; *Kim* is a drama of deception. Kipling, like Manallace, is a faker, and so we might describe his work substantially as fabrication instead of construction. In spite of what might be termed his 'artfulness', his search for the *mot juste* and his terse prose, etc., although these help to make him readable, he is still unaesthetic — not a first rate artist but a quite good artist of the second rate.

My main purpose, however, has not been to pass a detailed aesthetic judgement on Kipling. I have been concerned to show his predominant characteristics, all pointing to one — servility. There is much to indicate that his failings are the fault of his environment, of his class. We see many signs that he himself feels the oppression of the servile system, and there are fragments of better work, uncompelled, unmagical, unobsessive. It is the possible works of art that his better works suggest to us, that lead us to appreciate Kipling.

– 21 –
George Meredith

I do not propose to consider George Meredith's work in great detail, but I shall try to touch on every side of it — novels, poems, the *Essay on Comedy* and the fantasy, *The Shaving of Shagpat*. In particular, I should like to deal with what might be called the 'Meredithian position', for Meredith had definite views concerning the art which he practised, as well as the place of that art in society, and he tended to introduce these views in his artistic works.

According to Arnold Bennett who wrote of him mainly as a novelist, Meredith was not so much the last of the Victorians, as the first of the modern school of writers. 'Between Fielding and Meredith,' he says, 'no entirely honest novel was written by anybody in England. The fear of the public, the lust of popularity, feminine prudery, sentimentalism, Victorian niceness — one or other of these things prevented honesty' (*Books and Persons*). Yet since his works were a product of the Victorian age, Meredith did not succeed entirely in breaking away from the Victorian tradition, and he was a good deal more Victorian than might at first sight appear. A definite moralistic strain, for example, runs through his writing, indicating a wish, so characteristic of the Victorians, to improve the world, to treat it, in Shaw's phrase, 'as a

---

Address to the Literary Society, 14 April 1932, reported in the *Union Recorder*, 21 April 1932.

moral gymnasium'. Thus it is not surprising to find that his first novel, published in 1859, has an ordeal for its theme; though for the matter of that his fantasy, *The Shaving of Shagpat*, which appeared earlier in 1856, was also concerned with an ordeal — the thwackings undergone by Shibli Bagarag in his struggle to 'master the Event'. In *The Ordeal of Richard Feverel*, Meredith gives us a straightforward novel, without allegory, in which he presents Richard's reaction to the training of his strong-minded father — an upbringing which had results far other than those which were intended. On the whole, Arnold Bennett's criticism of this book is a just one.

> What a renaissance! ... It was the announcer of a sort of dawn. But there are fearful faults in *Richard Feverel*. ... The separation of Lucy and Richard is never explained, and cannot be explained. The whole business of Sir Julius is grotesque. And the conclusion is quite arbitrary. It is a weak book, full of episodic power and overloaded with wit.

Here it may be said in passing, that Meredith's novels suffer from a weakness in plot. Coincidence is overstrained, and excessive use is made of accidental occurrences, especially in the dénouements. His critics never forgave Meredith for the death of Lucy in *The Ordeal of Richard Feverel*, and, indeed, it might be said that his characters die on insufficient provocation. In spite of the judgement of one critic [R. H. C. Crees, *Meredith: A Study of his Works and Personality*] in his comments on *Rhoda Fleming* — 'We feel that Dahlia must die' — all this dying is irrelevant to the theme. It may be necessary for the *story*, when the characters must be disposed of somehow, but the result is both sentimental and mechanical, with the author playing fate instead of allowing the theme to work itself out in its own terms.

Almost as great a defect as this weakness of plot is the emphasis laid by Meredith on wit and brilliant conversation. The world which he depicts is a wealthy one, the world of the country house, and his characters are the ladies and gentlemen of that society. There is an abundance of conversation, where wit flashes fire and epigrams are tossed about so fast and so freely that the reader has a great deal of sympathy with Lady Culmer who, in praising the lively conversation at Sir Willoughby Patterne's lunch table, remarks:

'Though what it all meant and what was the drift of it, I couldn't tell, to save my life. Is it every day the same with you here?'
'Very much.'
'How you must enjoy a spell of dullness!'

This emphasis on witty conversation is important, however, because it is bound up with Meredith's view of art, of society and of the position of women. Generally speaking, he thinks that it is only when women live on an equality with men that there can be a cultivated society, and 'the Comic Muse', he said in *An Essay on Comedy* (1877), 'is one of their best friends. They are blind to their interests in swelling the ranks of the sentimentalists. Let them look with their clearest vision abroad and at home. They will see that where they have no social freedom, Comedy is absent.'

It is in *Diana of the Crossways* (1884) that Meredith's views on art definitely emerge. Art and the world are both in need of improvement, but neither can be improved 'before our systems shall have been fortified by philosophy'. Philosophy, it appears, will operate first on the art of the novelist and on that of the historian, and 'we can then be veraciously historical, honestly transcriptive. Rose-pink and dirty drab will alike have passed away' for 'philosophy is the foe to both' and 'bids us see that we are not so pretty as rose-pink, nor so repulsive as dirty drab: and that ... the sight of ourselves is wholesome, bearable, fructifying, finally a delight.' Now, if the study of philosophy does anything to us, it enables us to see things as they are, to see the facts of the case, and it is sentimentalism on George Meredith's part to assume that after a course of philosophy the sight of ourselves must be 'wholesome, bearable, fructifying, finally a delight'. 'Rose-pink' and 'dirty drab' are really ways of looking at things; they are attitudes or, perhaps, the same attitude which despises some things and elevates others, and these attitudes come to be read into things, or people as the case may be. For the artist, they are something to be presented in a work of art through the medium of characters who look at the world in either of those ways, reacting with situations and other characters in a novel or a play. Nevertheless, in spite of his confusion in the matter, we can discern that Meredith is groping after reality in art, a real world where the 'inner' as well as the 'outer' of things and people is presented: 'and to love comedy you must know the real world, and know men and women well enough not to expect too much of them though you may still hope for good' (*An Essay on Comedy*).

While it is possible that philosophy or the Comic Muse may improve us, that does not imply that an author must be actively engaged in aesthetics or philosophy, or be interminably witty, in the works that he produces — that he has to be deliberately setting about the improvement of manners. Meredith does do all this, holding up the story with long dissertations in order to drive home the lessons he would like to have us learn. This didacticism is one of his great weaknesses, and is found in all his works, with the possible exception of *Shagpat*.

His pious hope for improvement also is as weak and sentimental as the 'abstract optimism' of men like Victor Radnor which he satirises in *One of Our Conquerors* (1891). Shallow optimism was apparent in all of Radnor's social undertakings, and naturally it coloured his politics as well. At the election meeting which he was to address (but collapsed and died before he could do so) his daughter Nesta, while waiting for the speech,

> set herself to study a popular assembly. It could be serious to the call of better leadership, she believed. Her father had been telling her of late of a faith he had in the English, that they (or so her intelligence translated his remarks) had power to rise to spiritual ascendancy, and be once more the Islanders leading the world to a new epoch abjuring materialism: — some such idea: very quickening to her.

Meredith, too, has a notion of a leadership necessary to improve the world and guide the men and women in it to higher things. Partly it is a political leadership — a leadership of the lower orders by the cultivated classes feeding them 'brainstuff', for 'matter that is not nourishing to brains can help to constitute nothing but the bodies which are pitched on rubbish heaps' (*Diana of the Crossways*). But 'brainstuff' is also necessary for women oppressed and at the mercy of the 'predatory male', as Meredith maintains in *Modern Love*, XLVIII:

> Their sense is with their senses all mixed in,
> Destroyed by subtleties these women are!
> More brain, O Lord, more brain! or we shall mar
> Utterly the fair garden we might hope to win.

'Society' on the other hand, is to be led and improved by such women as Diana of the Crossways, although there is more than a hint that Diana herself needs a strong head and hand to guide her. (These, by the way, she finally gets in Mr Redworth.) The conversations at her dinner-table are on a lofty plane — political and literary and social, with an absence of gossip and backbiting, and, of course, her wines are 'trusty'.

Diana herself, we are led to believe, has brains enough to be a leader in this witty, cultivated society. Mrs Mountstuart's epigrams on Clara Middleton — 'a dainty rogue in porcelain' — and on Sir Willoughby Patterne — 'he has a leg' — may, perhaps, be more perfect than any of Diana's, but Diana hit off the relations of the sexes in those times with the remark that 'Men may have rounded Seraglio Point: they have not yet doubled Cape Turk.' Nevertheless there is a decided feeling of strain in all these epigram-studded conversations as well as a considerable amount of attitudinising and preciosity throughout this high social comedy — all of which constitutes a very real weakness both in *Diana of the Crossways* and *The Egoist*. As for Diana, the reader may well agree with Arnold Bennett who, in castigating Mrs Humphrey Ward for her latest 'excruciating heroine, Diana Mallory', exclaims —

> Moreover, in literature, all girls named Diana are insupportable. Look at Diana Vernon, beloved of Mr Andrew Lang, I believe! What a creature! Imagine living with her! You can't! Look at Diana of the Crossways! Why did Diana of the Crossways marry [her first husband]? Nobody can say — unless the answer is that she was a ridiculous ninny. ... Oh, those cultured conversations! That skittishness! ... That impulsiveness! That noxious winsomeness!' [*Books and Persons*]

There can be no question that Meredith is limited by the social conditions which he chooses as the milieu of his novels. It is only occasionally that his descriptions of country house society are diversified, as in *Rhoda Fleming* (1865), by the inclusion of lower types — not quite ladies and gentlemen, not quite cultivated, not quite English, though 'the backbone of Old England' is also to the fore! The result of his concentration on one particular class, of his desiring to write up to what he thinks are the requirements of 'great ladies' is that he is unable to achieve in his comedy that universality which is the mark of all first-class artistic work.

Comedy is, for Meredith, the answer to the demand for more brains, for wit (perhaps the union of the qualities of men and women), for manners and for betterment generally. 'The Femmes Savantes,' he says in *An Essay on Comedy*, 'is a capital instance of the uses of comedy in teaching the world to understand what ails it.' Of the English school of comedy he can say little good in this respect, but 'Shakespeare is a wellspring of characters which are saturated with the comic spirit ... and ... they are of the world enlarged to our embrace by imagination, and by great poetic imagination.' No doubt this 'enlarging by imagination' is to be taken to mean that we are thereby enabled to see more, or to see more deeply into people and situations, but the charge that improvement upon nature is necessary in order to improve us, cannot be ignored — for, among other things, it has an effect on the work of Meredith himself. He tends to give us models of manners, models of conversation, the comedy of comedians, of actors — i.e., 'cultivated' comedy. This claim for comedy as an improver of society at once separates the art dealing with human beings from all the other arts. It is not so that music or painting or architecture will improve the world. And it seems doubtful whether any of the other arts actually does. Do we talk about a comic landscape or a well-mannered piece of music? There is really no such separation of the arts, and no 'idealisation' proper to any one of them; there is only *presentation*, whether the theme be musical or pictorial or human. And all art may be considered as improving delicacy of perception, not because the artist is an improver or because he has 'improvement' or refinement as his theme, but because, in the presentation of his theme, he brings out those 'inner' characteristics that are not easily seen from the outward, everyday point of view. And to accomplish this, he need not, as Meredith does, mix social conditions, i.e., conditions of production and of appreciation of works of art, with the works of art themselves, or introduce himself, as the author, into his novels, in order to 'aesthetise' or to 'improve'.

Certainly in an art dealing with human subjects, there are illusions and there is exposure — the pricking of the bubbles of self-esteem; but is it by manners (or Manner) that self-esteem or the sentimentality that Meredith speaks about is to be exposed? It is to be remembered that the art that deals with 'manners' is one that deals with certain *matters*. Nietzsche sees all comedy and even all drama as dealing with vanity, and nowhere is this notion driven so hard as in *The Egoist*; while the folly Meredith speaks of in the *Essay on Comedy* is an ingredient of all human complications and must be presented by the artist, though not necessarily to the characters in the novels or the plays. And to say as Meredith says, that 'contempt is a sentiment that cannot be entertained by the comic [or, better still, aesthetic] intelligence', is to point to what goes beyond any 'manners' — not in the subject or theme, but in the appreciation of a work of art — namely objectivism, the recognition of a theme and its working out whether it be folly or manners, colour or sound. This recognition may be 'elevating' but only when the author, too, has the objective outlook and eschews didacticism — teaching and learning — except when he is presenting them as ingredients of comedy.

Meredith considers that satire, irony and humour are inferior to wit, the purely comic spirit which of them all is addressed to the intellect alone. With this may be compared the view of Freud (*Wit and Its Relation to the Unconscious*): 'The pleasure of wit originates from an *economy of expenditure in inhibition*, of the comic from an *economy of expenditure in thought*, and of humour from an *economy of expenditure in feeling.*' But the comic is no more economical than the tragic or the plastic or the musical, and, apart from his false distinction between thought and feeling — which is shared by Meredith — Freud is really giving only one condition of the aesthetic object, that of economy, the presentation of the theme in logical order, in contrast to the grotesque. For it is not a question of a difference of attitudes or of different forms of appreciation of different arts. Even if, for example, the distinction between comedy and tragedy is sound, appreciation of both is of the same sort — recognition of the working out of a theme logically and convincingly. Horace Walpole has said that 'Life is a comedy to those who think, a tragedy to those who feel'; but if there *are* tragic and comic situations they are worked out similarly, on the same aesthetic basis. If they seem not to be, then our own attitudes to them may be at fault and need examination, for one of them at least is unaesthetic. In any case, the attention should be given to the work itself, and not to our attitude to it, and then George Meredith's Comic Spirit is seen to be the spirit of objectivity — the spirit that can 'see things as in themselves they really are' (Matthew Arnold). This is indeed partly indicated in the *Ode to the Comic Spirit* which begins:

> Sword of Common Sense!
> Our surest gift;

— an ode which nevertheless continues as a very incoherent, dragging production, mainly because Meredith wishes not merely to present, but to improve.

Meredith's views on comedy appear in his poems as well as in his novels. In *Modern Love* (L) he gives 'tragic hints' — of the fate of those uncomic ones, the sentimentalists, whom he sees as looking back to the brute and as people searching for certainty:

> Ah, what a dusty answer gets the soul
> When hot for certainty in this our life!

And his notion of 'enlargement by imagination' appears again in the introductory poem to Volume I — 'The Promise in Disturbance' — along with his conception of leadership to reach the heights:

> But listen in the thought; so may there come
> Conception of a newly-added chord,
> Commanding space beyond where ear has home.
> In labour of the trouble at its fount,
> Leads life to an intelligible Lord
> The rebel discords up the sacred mount.

One of Meredith's most interesting poems is the 'Hymn to Colour', where the 'colour' of things seems close to the *claritas* or 'radiance' which Stephen Dedalus speaks of in *A Portrait of the Artist as a Young Man:* it is that quality which makes their shape visible. The argument might be that just as dawn gives colour to things and makes them distinct and distinctive, so does the Comic Spirit give illumination and structure to life — 'the newly-added chord' which is indeed creation — and so does aesthetics give appreciation of that structure. Colour also gives permanence to things:

> Dead seasons quicken in one petal-spot
> Of colour unforgot.

Even in its fleetingness it conquers time; by means of it men 'come out of brutishness' and

> With thee, O fount of the Untimed! to lead;
> Drink they of thee, thee eyeing, they unaged
> Shall on through brave wars waged.

Certainly, a love of beauty keeps before the mind the moments that have passed, but aesthetics — or The Comic Spirit — is not for that reason 'untimed' or higher than time. Alexander[1] speaks of Meredith as holding 'the depreciatory view of time' in connection with the stanza:

> Of thee to say behold, has said adieu:
> But love remembers how the sky was green,
> And how the grasses glimmered lightest blue;
> How saint-like grey took fervour: how the screen
> Of cloud grew violet: how thy moment came
> Between a blush and flame.

We can make something of Meredith's attitude to time if we recognise that it is *love* of beauty that enables beauty to abide. There is communication in the love of beauty between one age and another for the love of beauty in one person sustains love of beauty in another, though beauty itself does not communicate. This does not, however, mean that we have to 'believe that our state of society is founded on Commonsense' on pain of being denied comic apprehension, as Meredith declares in the *Essay on Comedy*. A lover of beauty (or truth, or freedom) may have communication with other such lovers and the possibility of further communication in our society still be lapped in folly. Meredith does not take account of the fact that there may be many associations and many possible associations within a social system. His treatment of Lassalle (Alvan) in *The Tragic Comedians* (1880) bears this out. Lassalle may have been a mountebank (or worse) but he did take part in a popular movement whereas Meredith brings social forces down to personal ambition, ill-temper and epigram. In the *Essay on Comedy* he touches further on social questions for he writes: 'A perception of the comic spirit gives high fellowship. You become a citizen of the selecter world. ... Look there for your unchallengeable upper class!' But is there a true 'upper class' (the cultivated) such as Meredith imagines? Is not this an 'uncomic' position for him to take up — an illusion that he has failed to 'master'? Even *The Egoist*, the most complete of all his satires, raises the question of his having more than a residual belief in the gentility, nobility and winsomeness of the English gentry.

The Egoist (1879) is greatly superior to the rest of the novels. There is an element of caricature in the confrontation of the truly noble Vernon and the much cudgelled Sir Willoughby Patterne, but the whole is a great satire on 'country life' and 'country gentlefolk', on public school education and the use of the birch which Dr Middleton so strongly advocates. Meredith here exposes sentimentalism as a pose, bringing out its dishonesty — the trafficking in admiration and the corruption of manners which it involves. It is perhaps a slight weakness on Meredith's part to present such an extreme specimen of egoism as Sir Willoughby is. He would seem to wish to show the height of egoism, egoism at its most intense, but in so doing he rather defeats his own ends, and presents us with a model, (vide supra) a pattern, so that one wonders if there is any significance in Sir Willoughby's surname. Be that as it may, the consequence is that our withers are unwrung, and we do not say, 'This is egoism' but rather 'This is Willoughby Patterne, the man labelled *the egoist*', and there is a partial failure of illumination on this account. This failure appears again in the fact that Meredith makes Clara Middleton and Laetitia Dale *say* at different times that they are egoists, without presenting in more detail their particular form of egoism. Again, is it necessary to talk about egoism in order to exhibit it? It is possibly a defect in the novel that it is Sir Willoughby himself who supplies Clara Middleton with the illuminating word 'egoist'. As a matter of fact, there is really little development of egoism in the work. Its subject would seem to be, not so much egoism, as the unmasking of an egoist.

Nevertheless, Sir Willoughby is allowed to present himself, and this is done with considerable skill. The shattering of the illusion of his greatness is admirably worked out, in spite of a good deal of wit and bright conversation, both boring and absurd, and in spite of the sketchiness of many of the characters, whether the noble and winsome like Vernon and Clara, or the vulgar and interfering like Lady Busshe and Lady Culmer. Indeed, between virtue and vulgarity, egoism is a refreshing change. Sir Willoughby has more stuff in him than any of the rest, and the attitudinising of the egoist, the shattering of the illusions of his greatness, even in the deepest recesses of his own mind, the way in which he digs the grave of his own hopes, defeats his own ends, and exposes himself more and more in his efforts to protect himself — all this is the real substance of the book, the substance of comedy itself.

The Egoist, being a comedy in narrative form, unfortunately gives Meredith scope for constant explanations, 'tragic hints', and references to the brute in man, untamed and uncivilised. Nevertheless there is drama, in spite of all the hints and coincidences and moralising in the unfolding of the situations, and high comedy as Willoughby is confronted with one character after another who *knows* what he has gone to great lengths to keep secret — who, in fact, all through his own efforts, come to see his egoism. In the end he is baited on every side: his 'imps' take flesh and become the world, at once the object of his dread and his uncritical worship. Still, it must be admitted that in spite of so much that is excellent, we cannot help being oppressed by the amount of noble manhood and lovely womanhood with which Willoughby is surrounded, and driven to wishing that Meredith had wielded the 'Sword of Commonsense' to more effect in dealing with Vernon and Whitby, Clara and Laetitia.

While *The Egoist* is Meredith's greatest work, *The Shaving of Shagpat*, early though it was, is possessed of considerable merit. The ordeal here consists of the tribulations of Shibli Bagarag, the barber, in his efforts to 'master the Event', i.e., to cut off the Identical or the Identical of Identicals, the famous hair on the head of Shagpat himself. This he achieves only after he has endured much to gain possession of the sword, Aklis, the flashing blade of wit, the only weapon which can destroy such a powerful fetish. In spite of the fancifulness of the allegory, this is perhaps a greater comedy than *The Egoist*. There are no fashions, no manners — just common humanity in place of 'society', women in place of ladies, and verses in place of epigrams. Incidentally, the poems in *Shagpat* are among Meredith's best. There is less dependence on circumstances and externals, and the real emotional development of the mastering of illusions is presented. The last illusion to be mastered is the objection to the thwackings — the shedding of the belief that we can achieve anything except through suffering, especially the suffering involved in ridding ourselves of the longing to cling to illusions instead of facing facts. This final ordeal we must undergo, and survive, if we are to 'master the Event', and do any worthwhile artistic work.

The Comic Spirit, then, is 'like no other blade in the world for sharpness', but even with its help Meredith has not entirely succeeded in presenting to us 'the real world' and the men and women in it. Yet, in spite of his didacticism, he does succeed in presenting in various forms some fundamental conditions of human life and the importance of art in life, and though he does indulge in a certain amount of idealisation, we see in his work a worthwhile approach to direct presentation, to realism, to the mastery of romantic illusions.

— 22 —

The Enormous Room

Questions beyond the purely aesthetic arise in connection with war literature. In it we are presented not only with the treatment of certain human relations, but with historical events, and recent historical events at that. While it is possible for most of us to consider with equanimity the dramatic histories of Shakespeare, acute controversy is apt to rage round anything connected with the present social struggles and attitudes to war. Since books dealing with these subjects of necessity involve questions of patriotism, and serious personal problems regarding it, they tend to be largely the self-exposure of the writer, and there is the question of the social impact the book might have, and the uses to which it might be put. *Goodbye to All That*, by Robert Graves, is an intensely personal presentation, full of boasting and of the poses of the officer class — a book which it would certainly be difficult for most sections of the public to view with detachment. Even in his preface to *The Enormous Room*, Graves introduces his own personal problems in an intensely personal way. 'As I have never been on the wrong side of the barbed wire,' he writes,

---

Part of a Symposium on War Literature, 4 August 1932, reported in the *Union Recorder*, 11 August 1932.

so neither have I been on the wrong side of the inquisitor's table. And so my sympathy with the victim does not prevent my sympathy with the inquisitor, particularly when he is not a free agent, but bound by orders from above, to disobey which will mean that he himself will find himself in trouble.

In a case which he cites — that of the court-martial of a man 'maddened by an intense bombardment', who threw down his rifle and ran, and who was being charged with cowardice in the field, for which the only punishment was death ('no medical excuses could be accepted') — Graves wonders what Cummings would have done as one of the judges in the matter.

> Possibly what I did, salved his conscience by a mere evasion. I contrived to get a brother officer to take my place, in exchange for some other (to him) disagreeable duty — I think it was supervising the troops in a laborious tactical exercise.

Readers of *The Enormous Room* will form their own opinion of what Cummings would have done in the circumstances, but there is no doubt that Graves weakens the issues by his sympathy with the inquisitors, and especially by dismissing a serious problem with a little personal arrangement. This kind of self-exposure is mainly psychological or personal, one would say, but it is easy to envisage other kinds which would run foul of censorship, and more seriously, of the law of the land.

Aesthetically there is a strong presumption in favour of the man who presents his own experiences, who says 'I' when he means 'I', so that 'I' becomes a character in the story as in all novels of autobiographical form. And even if he does not thereby produce a work of great literary merit, provided that he has faithfully recorded his experiences, his book could be of considerable political and social interest. If, on the other hand, he has falsified or romanticised these experiences, he has not only produced a thoroughly bad piece of work in the aesthetic sense, he has falsified history itself. There is another type of war book which is purely fictional (cf. *The Case of Sergeant Grischa* by Stefan Zweig) in which the experience is generalised, and which has not the force of the autobiographical form because of the muddling of fiction and fact and because the issues raised are so often fictitious.

His own personal feeling with relation to war has been made the theme of [F. A.] Voigt's *Combed Out*. He presents himself as a pacifically minded man, confronted with servile conditions, degrading discipline, work of which the aim is not indicated, and the horrible ordeals of the surgical ward and of the night bombing. Fear might be said to be the prevailing motif of this book, hence Voigt's reactions as a character in it are to something he does not entirely understand. And as he is also the author of the book, this lack of comprehension is responsible for a weakness in its construction. It allows a streak of sentimentality to creep in, especially in Voigt's descriptions of the 'beauties of nature' and the way in which he contrasts these with the miseries of military duties — a natural indulgence which the reader can understand even if he cannot pardon it aesthetically; though he might argue, on the other hand, that it is part of the author's presentation of himself as a character in the book. At any rate, it does not seem so alien to the theme as the conversations between the soldiers speaking soldiers' language (with soldiers' oaths) and the author talking in classroom English. Here the contrast, the incongruity, is so strong that it smacks of the written-up.

Connected with this is the rather contrived situation with which the book ends. Instead of the quiet meditations of a disillusioned, thoughtful man we have, after the Armistice has been declared, a raucous slanging match between two soldiers, one of whom wants to go out and celebrate, while the other upbraids him for showing so little respect for their dead and maimed comrades as to want to go 'shouting and singing and getting drunk'. The conversation would seem to have been introduced to point the moral — 'they never made a soldier of me' — but the book should have been left to speak for itself.

Cummings, like Voigt, presents himself as a character in his book, and the self he presents is a somewhat romantic one. It might be questioned whether he succeeds here in working out a theme in a realistic manner, or whether he romanticises it; but the question could only be settled by a more detailed consideration of the book than the present occasion demands. At least, he has in his book a more definite theme than the will to peace amid the horrors of war — a theme which achieves a high degree of convincingness even if it is not as realistic as one might wish. He is concerned chiefly with spy-mania and with its relations to government and patriotism and honour, and his theme is regimentation as revealed under war conditions, and the reactions to it of the people with whom he is concerned; but incidentally it is an exposure of actual conditions of war and the character of governments. 'Le gouvernement français' is the villain of the piece, hit off humorously early in the book by soldiers waiting at a station for a train that seems never to be going to arrive. 'Quelle heure?' one demands. 'Mon cher, il n'y a plus d'heures, le gouvernement français les défend!' But what the government *permits* is, as Cummings shows, as bewildering, unjust and cruel as what it forbids, and Cummings brings out its villainy by reference to the kind of life suspects had to lead, and the kind of men they were — or became — under duress. Contrasted with the suspicion and spying (characteristic of existing governments during war time) is the humanity, the human decency, to be found in various forms in *The Enormous Room*. It may be claimed that Cummings romanticises some or all of the people who occupy it, but even if he does so, it could be argued that he is showing what kind of outlook would be developed in captivity by a character like himself.

As Graves points out in his preface, the book falls into two parts — the events and the journey that lead to The Enormous Room, and the experiences Cummings undergoes therein. It is a natural enough division of the subject, and one might get over the weakness of construction which it represents if one could regard the book as having two themes — as being two works of art, the first leading to the second but being distinct from it. But there is no real working out of a theme in either part — in the earlier the regimented ones are being moved like pawns across the face of France, and in the later they have come to rest in The Enormous Room at La Ferté Macé. Cummings himself attempts to bridge the gap by references to *Pilgrim's Progress*, actually calling the first section 'A Pilgrim's Progress' which ends when

> into the square blackness I staggered with my paillasse. There was no way of judging the size of the dark room which uttered no sound. In front of me was a pillar. 'Put it down by that post and sleep there for tonight. ... You won't need a blanket,' he [the guard] added; and the doors clanged, the light and fencer disappeared.

But Cummings is unable to keep up the parallel to any extent, and it is only after several chapters that we get back to the notion of *Pilgrim's Progress* when we come to 'The Delectable Mountains' — a group of people so extraordinarily interesting that they alone would have made his sojourn in The Enormous Room an experience which, he claims, he would not have missed for worlds. This rather far-fetched literary allusion is a somewhat sentimental weakness, and in conjunction with the division of the book into two parts, prevents the work from being as great as it might have been.

Yet Cummings has succeeded very well in doing more than recording the horrors of war. A victim of spy-mania (he was arrested because of his great friendship with Brown who had written a letter which the French censors regarded as insufficiently patriotic), he found that his fellow-captives were as innocent of treason as he himself was.

> The majority of these dark criminals who had been caught in nefarious plots against the honour of France were totally unable to speak French. Curious thing. Often I pondered the unutterable and unextinguishable wisdom of the police, who — undeterred by facts which would have deceived less astute intelligences into thinking that these men were either too stupid or too simple to be connoisseurs of the art of betrayal — swooped upon their helpless prey with that indescribable courage which is the prerogative of policemen the world over, and bundled same prey into the La Fertés of that mighty nation upon some, at least, of whose public buildings it seems to me that I remember reading
> LIBERTÉ ÉGALITÉ FRATERNITÉ

The great merit of Cummings is that he has shown the sufferings of civilians under war conditions, and has brought out the senselessness from any point of view of the actions of governments of that time, by the detailed characterisation of the inhabitants of The Enormous Room, and by the close connection he maintains between the development of the characters and their environment. The outstanding figures are 'The Delectable Mountains' — The Wanderer, Surplice, Zooloo, Jean le Nègre; but there are many other memorable portraits, like those of Emile the Bum, and the schoolmaster. Zooloo, in particular, he characterises as an 'IS', for there are certain things in which one is unable to believe for the simple reason that he never ceases to feel them. Things of this sort — things which are always inside of us and in fact are us and which consequently will not be pushed off or away where we can begin thinking of them — are no longer things; they, and the us which they are, equals a verb; an 'IS'. The Zulu, then, I must perforce call an 'IS'.

To the women inmates of La Ferté, separated from the men but in such close proximity as to be an added irritant to prison conditions, Cummings makes his bow for the spirit and endurance they show, in refusing to be cowed by the brutal 'Apollyon' (M. le Directeur) and his plantons (warders) with their 'dry bread' and their dreadful solitary confinement.

It is without doubt due to the fact that Cummings is both a poet and a painter that he shows such acute penetration and gives such vivid descriptions. Here is the arrival of the Washing-machine Man in The Enormous Room:

> In the doorway ... quietly stood a well-dressed, handsomely middle-aged man, with a sensitive face culminating in a groomed Van Dyck beard. I thought for a moment that the Mayor of Orme, or whatever his title is, had dropped in for a formal inspection of The Enormous Room. Thank God, I said to myself, it has never looked so chaotically filthy since I have had the joy of inhabiting it. And sans blague, The Enormous Room was in a state of really supreme disorder; shirts were thrown everywhere, a few twine clothes-lines supported various pants, handkerchiefs and stockings, the poêle was surrounded by a gesticulating crowd of nearly undressed prisoners, the stink was actually sublime.
>
> As the door closed behind him, the handsome man moved slowly and vigorously up The Enormous Room. His eyes were as big as turnips. His neat felt hat rose with the rising of his hair. His mouth opened in a gesture of unutterable astonishment. ... In a deep awestruck resonant voice he exclaimed simply and sincerely,
> 'Nom de nom de nom de nom de nom de Dieu!'

In his description of the snowfall that came to La Ferté at the end of his sojourn there, Cummings gives us another glimpse of The Enormous Room. The three prison commissioners, in their inscrutable wisdom, had transferred his friend, Brown, to the prison at Précigné, and Cummings was depressed and lonely in spite of the efforts of those friends who were left to comfort him. 'One afternoon', he writes,

> I was lying on my couch, thinking of the usual Nothing, when a sharp cry sung through The Enormous Room:
> 'Il tombe de la neige — Noël! Noël!'
> I sat up. The Garde-Champêtre was at the nearest window, dancing a little horribly and crying:
> 'Noël! Noël!'
> I went to another window and looked out. Sure enough. Snow was falling, gradually and wonderfully falling, silently falling through the thick soundless autumn. ... It seemed to me supremely beautiful, the snow. There was about it something unspeakably crisp and exquisite, something perfect and minute and gentle and fatal. ... The Garde-Champêtre's cry began a poem in the back of my head, a poem about the snow, a poem in French, beginning Il tombe de la neige, Noël, Noël. I watched the snow. After a long time I returned to my bunk and I lay down, closing my eyes, feeling the snow's minute and crisp touch falling gently and exquisitely, falling perfectly and suddenly, through the thick soundless autumn of my imagination. ... The Enormous Room is filled with a new and beautiful darkness, the darkness of the snow outside, falling and falling and falling with the silent and actual gesture which has touched the soundless country of my mind as a child touches a toy it loves.

And when he at last leaves La Ferté, Cummings by a skilful use of language conveys unforgettably the sensation of confusion and excitement at his departure, and the sense of the unreality of the world to which he is returning — feelings which accompany him on the train journey, in Paris and on the sea; culminating in his first glimpse of his homeland with its wonderful space and sunlight —

the tall, incomparably tall city, shouldering upward into hard sunlight leaned a little through the octaves of its parallel edges, leaningly strode upward into firm, hard, snowy sunlight; the noises of America nearingly throbbed with smokes and hurrying dots which are men and which are women and which are things new and curious and hard and strange and vibrant and immense, lifting with a great ondulous stride into immortal sunlight.

– 23 –

H. G. Wells

Wells is mainly a novelist, his social theories and his historical works being less important than his works of fiction; but since we find his social theories almost invariably present in his novels, both in the stories of contemporary life and in the scientific and 'futuristic' romances that pour from his pen, they cannot be entirely separated from his work as a novelist. They are embodied, for instance, in *A Modern Utopia* and in *The Time Machine*, in *Possible Worlds* and *New Worlds for Old*. Indeed, in the creating and ordering of worlds, Wells might be said to be playing the part of God, and in *A Vision of Judgment* he actually tries to think what God would do! Not only so, he sees future man as a bigger and better edition of man as we know him now; he sees him drawing nearer to God, so to speak, in such books as *The Food of the Gods* and *Men Like Gods*. He makes it very clear also, in *The New Machiavelli*, that he has no time for all the muddle and mess that characterise the society in which he finds himself, and he envisages in many of his novels a kind of life in which the discoveries of science will be used to bring about a greater efficiency in the business of living; for Wells, like Shaw, is a good Fabian, with a passionate desire for order and method — and comfort! — in the organisation of society.

Address to the Literary Society, 6 July 1933, reported in the *Union Recorder*, 20 July 1933.

In spite of this seemingly practical and scientific approach to things, an element of dreaming pervades much of the work of Wells, especially, as might be expected, that which deals with the future — with the worlds that are to come. He confronts us with a great many visions which might have some basis of fact and a great superstructure of fantasy, embodying many nebulous schemes for the Utopias he is so fond of imagining. Thus there is not always very clear thinking to be found in the expression of his ideas, and this is true not only of his imaginary worlds but of his novels of contemporary life as well. In *The Food of the Gods*, for instance, bigness — mere growth — is confused with greatness. Young Redwood, addressing the giants in their fight against the little people, exclaims,

> Even if they should destroy us every one, what then? Would it save them? No! For greatness is abroad, not only in us ... but in the purpose of all things. ... To grow, and still to grow, from first to last, that is Being, that is the law of life. What other law can there be?

And in *Marriage* the writing of criticism is confused with a search for God. We find the scientist, Trafford, setting out to discover a new religion (which Wells himself thinks is a necessity for a new world) and saying to his wife, 'Since we don't know God, since we don't know His will with us, isn't it plain that all our lives should be a search for Him and it? ... I believe', he adds, 'that I shall write criticism.'

Yet Wells is considered a realist in spite of all this dreaming and confusion because he comments on the existing social fabric, directly in his ordinary novels and indirectly in his dream worlds. His descriptions are always wide and all-embracing — slap-dash might be a better word for them; at least they are never so meticulous as those of Henry James and those of Arnold Bennett. And this is true whether he is talking of his Utopias or of the Sacco and Vanzetti case, as he does in *Mr Blettsworthy on Rampole Island* or the General Strike of 1926 which is dealt with in *Meanwhile*. The former is dismissed with the consolatory words of Lyulph Graves: 'After all you are not so certain that these men were entirely innocent. And all mankind was not against them. ... If you knew more of history and nature, Blettsworthy, you would be less distressed by current things.' But the latter puts the rich Mr Philip

Rylands into a fighting mood. In the course of a long, garrulous and far from careful account of the struggle written to his wife, he declares that for 'the great revolution of the whole world' he is prepared to work 'like hell'. It may be argued that the contradictions we find in these two attitudes can be explained by the fact that they belong to different characters in two different novels; but it is remarkable that both have echoes of much that the reader will find elsewhere in the works of H. G. Wells, and it is at least a possibility that the contradictions are to be found in the mind of Wells himself.

Whatever we may think of the way he has dealt with these and other social questions, it must be emphasised that realism does not consist in social commentary or in reproductions of 'slices of life' with easily recognisable details, for these are quite compatible with an absence of theme — an absence of structure, and with the romantic treatment of psychological facts, both of which are exemplified in the two novels mentioned above. Realism consists in having a theme and in working it out logically, and the excellence of *Tono Bungay* and *The New Machiavelli* is not due to the characterisation of social conditions which Wells gives in them, but comes from the coherent presentation of character in the story, from the development of states of mind. In so far as Wells succeeds in treating the social views of people as part of their character he may achieve realism, but no amount of description of social beliefs and conditions without straightforward presentation of psychological facts will save him from the charge of representationism and even of romanticism.

And Wells, though he talks so much about science, is fundamentally a romanticist! He creates his dream-worlds by starting with a slight basis of actuality, on which he builds by dragging in material of all kinds without considering whether it belongs to that particular work or not. Unhampered by the logic of events, he can give his fancy full play, trusting to his plausibility to bridge the gap between reality and his imaginings. Indeed, if he achieves coherent structure in any of his works, it must be by inadvertence, for in *Boon* he attacks the notion that this is a requisite for the novel. Referring to Henry James, Boon remarks,

But James has never discovered that a novel isn't a picture. ... He wants a novel to be simply and completely *done*. He wants it to have a unity, he demands homogeneity. Why *should* a book have that? For a picture it's reasonable, because you have to see it all at once.

In his *Aspects of the Novel*, E. M. Forster, talking of the question of the rigid pattern, asks,

> Can it be combined with the immense richness of material which life provides? Wells and James would agree it cannot. Wells would go on to say that life should be given the preference, and must not be whittled down or distended for a pattern's sake. My own prejudices are with Wells. ... That then is the disadvantage of a rigid pattern. It may externalise the atmosphere, spring naturally from the plot, but it shuts the doors on life and leaves the novelist doing exercises, generally in the drawing room.

But the diversity of life is taken care of by the diversity of *themes* possible in literature, and without unity, without a coherent structure, a book cannot be a single work of art. It might, in reality, be several works of art, each of which can be appreciated separately; but if the author presents the activities of the same people as a continuous and single story, his work must have coherence and structure or it will be bad artistically. And if a book cannot be comprehended at one sitting, neither can a picture with one glance. It takes frequent viewing and lengthy study to arrive at comprehension of any worthwhile picture or piece of sculpture, or even any worthwhile book.

Connected, perhaps, with his dislike of homogeneity and coherent structure in art, is Wells' praise of versatility and his attack on specialisation. He satirises the latter in *The First Men in the Moon*, describing how the Selenites are raised for their special functions from birth and how their lives are, in consequence, narrowed down to the exercise of these particular functions with the consequent atrophy of all other mental and physical powers. Yet alongside this satire of science, he sets up *scientific* thinking as something especially to be desired — not simply as being contrasted with superstition, but as something higher than ordinary thinking. Wells, of course, is himself a scientist, and he himself has been praised for his versatility. Very often, however, this versatility has meant simply incompetence such as we see in his weak treatment of psycho-analysis in *Christina Alberta's Father*; while his own thinking involves him in a great deal of dreaming and arranging of things as *he* would like them to be — a position which has nothing to do with the objectivity of science. Nevertheless, his versatility has enabled him to cover a great deal of ground in his works, without producing anything that could be described as 'great'. He has dealt with religion in *The Soul of a Bishop*, in *Mr Britling Sees it Through* and in *Marriage*; with sex in *Tono Bungay* and *Ann Veronica* and with politics in *The New Machiavelli*. He has constructed ordinary romances in *Kipps*, *The History of Mr Polly* and *Love and Mr Lewisham* (to mention only a few of his many novels); and besides his innumerable scientific and dream-world romances, there are his *Outline of History* and other historical and critical works that are not being discussed here. So that he *has* attempted to cover 'all life' in one way or another, even if he has needed more than one book in which to do it! In *Books and Persons*, Arnold Bennett sees *Tono Bungay* as a magnificent failure to do just that. 'I do not think,' he says, 'that any novelist ever more audaciously tried, or failed with more honour, to render in the limits of one book the enormous and confusing complexity of a nation's racial existence. The measure of success attained is marvellous. Complete success was, of course, impossible.'

Wells, in his writing, entertains the idea of the development of a collective mind, but he shows himself more or less indefinite about how such a mind is to be brought into existence. His suggestions range from 'great educational campaigns' to 'love and fine thinking' and 'understanding spreading like the dawn'; but whatever they are, they all make it clear that he considers education a peaceful process; whereas it is, in fact, a struggle to come to grips with subjects, whether in the purely educational, the political or the social field, a struggle that may be physical as well as mental. In *A Modern Utopia*, for instance, everything proceeds by dream and delusion, but in *Mr Blettsworthy on Rampole Island* we see how, where there is no struggle, the result is a yielding to Ardam, the reactionary and superstitious despot; worse, it actually leads to playing Ardam's game. Wells, however, cannot be more specific or coherent because he is really against learning, against classicism. Perhaps it is as a defence of his own lack of literacy that he makes so many of his heroes uneducated men, and expects us, for instance, to find the moralisings of Mr Polly, at the conclusion of the novel that bears his name, fraught with deep meaning. And whether educated or not, his hero is always the inspired amateur, like Philip Rylands, seeking for some 'meaning' in things, some higher significance, some task that mankind has not yet grasped. Amateurish, too, is the scientist Trafford, in *Marriage*, who gives up his research work for

> the great work — the Reality. I want to become a part of this stuttering attempt to express, I want at least to resonate even if I do not help ... And you with me, Marjorie, you with me! Everything I write I want you to read and think about. I want you to read as I read.

All this 'love and fine thinking' sounds very well, but it is really quite empty of content even for Wells himself. Apart from the fact that it leads to the downfall of the hero in *The New Machiavelli*, Wells does not seem to think that it conflicts with his advocacy of eugenics — one of the ways by which a well-ordered universe is to be achieved, with men in it like gods. He is really as great a sophist as Shaw; and, indeed, his 'mind of the race' is comparable with Shaw's 'evolution of the life-force'. Neither is quite clear as to what he means by these great thoughts, but they can both talk as if they are saying something real.

In the short story Wells often succeeds in presenting a point satisfactorily, his tendency to moralise and romanticise having less chance to show itself when he is writing on the smaller scale. The best of his satires is, perhaps, *A Vision of Judgment*; there is some good work in it, though it is a great way after the work of Swift. Best of his novels are *Tono Bungay* and *The New Machiavelli*. Though they are not entirely free from weaknesses, and though the two types are hard to define, we do find in each the coherent development of a certain character. Remington, in *The New Machiavelli*, is the study of the rise and fall of a politician, with interesting sidelights on Beatrice and Sidney Webb in the persons of Oscar and Altiora Bailey. *Tono Bungay* is perhaps the better book. Of Ponderevo, Arnold Bennett says in *Books and Persons*:

His fine detachment and his sublime common sense, never desert him in the hour when he judges. Naturally his chief weapon ... is just common sense; it is at the impact of mere common sense that the current system crumbles. It is simply unanswerable common sense which will infuriate those who do not like the book (cf. Meredith's 'Sword of Commonsense').

There is a striking section where the poetic Ewart discourses on the value of advertisement. To be fully appreciated it would have to be read in its entirety, and it is too long to quote here. But a few excerpts can be given from his dissertation on Grundy who, he alleges, is a man, while Mrs Grundy is merely an instrument and has borne all the blame! —

Grundy in a sexual panic ... Every boy and girl to be sewn up in a sack and sealed ... until twenty-one. Music abolished, calico garments for the lower animals! Sparrows to be suppressed — ab-so-lutely ... Grundy meanwhile is in a state of complete whirlabout ... 'They're still thinking of things — thinking of things! It's dreadful! They get it out of books' ... Grundy in another mood. Ever caught him nosing, Ponderevo! Mad with the idea of mysterious, unknown, wicked, delicious things ... Grundy with a large greasy smile — like an accident to a butter tub — all over his face, being Liberal Minded — Grundy in his Anti-Puritan moments, 'trying not to see Harm in it' ... He makes you sick with the Harm he's trying not to see in it ...

One other book is also worthy of mention — *Mr Britling Sees It Through*. Here Wells has presented by quite artistic means the case for freedom and the case against spying. But Wells as a peacemonger, a pseudo-progressive, can be judged by this extract from *Mr Blettsworthy on Rampole Island*. The words are put into the mouth of Lyulph Graves, but there is no doubt that they express the ideas of H. G. Wells. It is an artistic fault of which Shaw, too, has been accused — that of creating characters and of putting them into situations, no matter how unreal or contrived, in order to provide them with an opportunity for expressing the author's opinions. *Mr Blettsworthy on Rampole Island* was published in 1928, and Lyulph Graves says:

'The war *was* a war to end war and it will end war. There will never be a war so huge and silly as that last war again. We just carry on with the old things for a time, the old governments, the old arrangements. The war exposed and damned them all, but we carry on. The real reconstruction of human affairs isn't to be done in a hurry. No need to worry about trial reconstructions and transitory failures. The *real* reconstruction is afoot. It's launched now just as certainly as progressive experimental science was launched in the seventeenth century. We must begin with promotion companies — exploratory operations. Naturally. Everything begins with sketches and incomplete suggestions. No hurry, but no delay. To alter all this we want expenditure on a scale far beyond the scale of the Great War; and the job may take a few lifetimes. Great propaganda campaigns. Great educational campaigns. They will gather and come. Watch what happens now. First the statesmen have to get the courage to ask for the outlawry of war. A phrase, you say, but is it only a phrase? When they are used to that idea, and when they have accustomed people to that idea, then, first timidly and then boldly they will begin to discuss the next stage towards that international control of the collective interests of mankind, without which this blessed outlawry is obviously absurd. These steps *are being taken* — now.'

Wells' prophecies of an 'adult' world show that he himself has not an adult mind; he is baby Wells, always looking for new worlds to play with.[1] The supposition of ideal worlds (i.e., 'dream' worlds) is a definite example of infantile thought (as are, of course, the day dream and the night dream). That is to say, in imagining these systems we can give free play to our *wishes*; we can alter facts as much as we like. Wells' imaginings show that he has no grasp of human nature and history, in the study of which the first thing to be learned is that we can't do what we like, and the second that we don't know what we are doing. After that we can go on to give an account of them as they are, and that knowledge helps us to bring about those of our aims and objects that are possible. It might be 'very nice' if we could all get rid of childishness, but that is only a pious hope; the real problem is to estimate the force of childish tendencies in our grown-up nature; to see in what respects the child is the man and the man is the child.

23 H. G. Wells

Granted that 'co-operative association' is a good thing (or, more exactly, a condition of all good things), the fact remains that we could only have discovered this by observing actual instances of 'co-operative association' within the existing system. To suppose a system founded on it is to think quite unhistorically, and to base a forecast of such a system either on the fact that 'man must change' or on the development of scientific industry or world finance is sheer guesswork. Obviously, without a certain amount of co-operative association neither science nor industry nor any other human undertaking could go on; equally obviously any such undertaking embodies strongly dissociative tendencies as well, and not in any way the less because the undertaking in question may (like industry) have world-wide ramifications. Real co-operation will only be extended by the operation of our associative tendencies themselves and not by any abstract 'will to associate' or the trivial fact that we could now co-operate with almost anybody in the world if we wanted to.

Wells' future world is just the newest brand of heaven, got up with all the latest scientific falderals, and gulped down by the good old credulous public, always wanting something for nothing. He is not a good prophet (there are no good prophets) but merely a bad artist — one who has come to think more of his public than of his work. The same may be said of Shaw in his mawkish *Saint Joan* or his platitudinous *Back to Methuselah*. But Shaw has done work which stands by its own merits and in relation to which the question 'What effect will this have?' is clearly out of place. This distinction is important, for the association of the artist and the appreciator is only co-operative if it is the work itself that is in question — if they can both make something of it as a real thing. Otherwise the artist is only a vendor of dreams — *New Worlds for Old*.

— 24 —
Thomas Love Peacock

In this address I shall restrict myself almost entirely to Peacock's novels, or to what are generally described as his novels, greatly though they differ from the type to which we are accustomed. Like Melville and Meredith, Peacock did not confine himself entirely to prose, and his poetry merits at least a passing reference. His first volume, *Palmyra and Other Poems*, was written in 1806, *The Genius of the Thames* in 1810, and his *Paper Money Lyrics* in 1825, though the latter were not published until 1837. None of his poems can be described as great, but though a number of them are in the conventional manner of his day and some display that sentimentality which also appears in his novels, they are never didactic. Often vigorous and racy, they accord well with the liveliness of the tales in which the best of them appear. This is particularly true of 'The War Song of Dinas Vawr' in *Melincourt*, the chorus, 'Hail to the Headlong' in *Headlong Hall*, and the ballads in *Maid Marian*; and there are many others that give delight to the readers of the novels.

His first novel, *Headlong Hall*, was written in 1817, and his last *Gryll Grange* which, although inferior to his others in many respects, was a remarkable product for a man in his seventy-sixth year, appeared

---

Address to the Literary Society, 12 April 1934, reported in the *Union Recorder*, 19 April 1934.

in 1860. The very names of the novels, with their alliterative titles, suggest that they were conceived in a comic and even jocular spirit, and this supposition is borne out of the names given to most of the characters and the remarkable derivations of them which the author sometimes supplies. This jocular style is least apparent in *Nightmare Abbey* and in *Melincourt* or *Sir Oran Haut-ton*, though the latter has as its motto 'Vocem Comoedia Tollit'; but this is not to be taken to mean that there is not a considerable amount of comedy in both of these works. Understandably enough, while the earlier novels are all more or less lively, there is a certain 'mellowness' in *Gryll Grange* — a quality which is felt from the very beginning of the story in the quotation from the *Satyricon* of Petronius at the head of the first chapter: 'Always and everywhere I have so lived, that I might consume the passing light as if it were not to return.'

Apart from *Maid Marian* and *The Misfortunes of Elphin*, the novels deal with Peacock's own times, and real contemporary characters are sometimes introduced. In *Nightmare Abbey*, for example, we have Shelley, Coleridge, Godwin and Byron presented under the names of Scythrop Glowry, Flosky, Toobad and Cypress while Southey is referred to as Roderick Sackbut, Esquire. *Maid Marian*, however, is concerned with the Robin Hood story and the reign of Richard I, while *The Misfortunes of Elphin* has, as its historical setting, the legendary times of King Arthur. In the latter tale, we find that interest in Wales and Welsh history and literature which has been notable in many nineteenth-century writers — in Meredith, whose first wife was Peacock's daughter; in Borrow, and in Watts-Dunton. Peacock's own wife, incidentally, belonged to North Wales. The Welsh influence appears also in *Headlong Hall*, and there is a Welsh excursion in *Crotchet Castle*. Peacock's treatment of Wales is interesting although he does not give a very thorough account of Welsh customs. His description of Welsh scenery, which indeed lends itself well to descriptive work, is lively and vigorous and he finds much to interest him in an alien people with an alien literature and with definite literary traditions.

Conversation bulks large in all the novels, and *Headlong Hall*, *Crotchet Castle* and a good deal of *Gryll Grange* are primarily conversational — that is, there is very little incident in them, but much commentary on men and affairs through the conversations of characters who have a definite outlook on men and affairs and are interested to dispute actively about them. While it is quite possible to work out in a novel the ramifications of a theme by means of conversation among the characters, this is not the task which Peacock has set himself. Rather does he deal in his novels with certain main topics which are discussed by the characters, not worked out in or by them. In *Headlong Hall* the main topic is whether so-called human progress is deterioration or improvement; in *Melincourt* it is whether reform is not really reaction — though the whole of this tale is really an advocacy of the simple life and contains a great deal more of description and action than the other conversational novels; in *Crotchet Castle* the topic is the march of mind; and in *Gryll Grange* the whole question of 'progress' is well to the fore. While these may be said to be the main topics in the various novels, all sorts of other social, political, literary and financial questions are touched upon so that there is no monotony but much variety in the discussions. Even in *The Misfortunes of Elphin* and in *Maid Marian*, which are more after the style of novel to which we are accustomed, Peacock finds opportunity for touching on his favourite topics, and his account of the education of Taliesin in *The Misfortunes of Elphin* very cleverly attacks both Arthurian and contemporary customs by comparing what Taliesin got with what he missed by living in the 'good old days'.

It is in *The Misfortunes of Elphin* that Peacock makes much use of the educational Welsh Triads, which are collections of historic facts, legendary lore and moral maxims arranged in groups of three for mnemonic purposes. They are to be found mainly as headings of various chapters, but some are incorporated in the body of the story itself like 'the kiss of Taliesin to the daughter of Elphin, which is celebrated in an inedited Triad as one of "the Three Chaste Kisses" of the island of Britain'. More resounding was the slap delivered by Gwenivar to Gwenvach, the wife of Modred when, on her return to Arthur's court, she deemed herself to have been insulted by the latter.

> This slap is recorded in the Bardic Triads as one of the Three Fatal Slaps of the Island of Britain. A terrible effect is ascribed to this small cause; for it is said to have been the basis of the enmity between Arthur

and Modred, which terminated in the Battle of Camlan, wherein all the flower of Britain perished on both sides.

Nevertheless the conversational style of novel is not suited for every kind of situation. In the description of the hunt for the missing heroine in *Melincourt*, 'Mr Forester determined not to rest night or day till he had discovered Anthelia'; but it was many pages and several weighty conversations later that he and Mr Fax and Sir Oran Haut-ton discovered her in Alga Castle by the sea. There was neither excitement nor urgency in the account of the chase, and the discovery, when it was made, had very little dramatic force. Anthelia's welcome to her hero was quite in keeping with it all, for when he finally reached the door of the room in which she was imprisoned, her greeting to him was:

> 'Oh, Forester! ... you have realised all my wishes. I have found you the friend of the poor, the enthusiast of truth, the disinterested cultivator of the rural virtues, the active promoter of the cause of human liberty. It only remained that you should emancipate a captive damsel, who, however, will but change the mode of her durance, and become your captive for life.'

Much livelier, however, is the account of the fracas at Chainmail Hall (*Crotchet Castle*) when the attacking labourers are beaten off by arms of the twelfth century in the hands of Mr Chainmail and his guests, who simply had neither time nor opportunity for discussion during the mêlée.

As the names of the characters suggest, there is not in these works of Peacock that examination and development of states of mind which we have claimed to be the mark of great literature; but that other function of the literary art — the exposure of the character of institutions and people — is quite well done. Generally speaking, we call that art comic which concerns itself with the exposure of pretension and humbug, and Peacock has succeeded so well in doing this by means of the conversations of rather 'stock' characters that R. Brimley Johnson, in his preface to the volume of Peacock's *Poems*, calls him 'the laughing philosopher'. But unless a character is nothing but a mouthpiece he has to suffer exposure like everyone else in the story and, unfortunately, Peacock does not expose his leading characters, who are so often the agents of the exposure of others, to the same extent as he does most of the others. He tends to idealise them — to attribute to them the noble feelings and the lofty thoughts which are the marks of romantic heroes and heroines; and though there is at times some ironical contemplation of these high-minded creatures — the 'perfectionists' who are working towards 'the golden age' — they are for the most part presented seriously and their virtuous sentiments are taken at face value. Escot, in *Headlong Hall*, exposes the critics writing for contemporary reviews, but he himself is insufficiently exposed; while there is the even more noticeable case of Mr Forester in *Melincourt*, who is as consistently noble and high-minded as Anthelia describes him in her speech of welcome. In passing, we might add that there is a further weakness in Peacock's work. Even when characters are not being worked out in great detail, it is still necessary for them to be presented in relation to the things said, and we do sometimes find in the novels the least intelligent of the characters uttering the most intelligent social criticism.

Throughout all his work, Peacock's general attitude is the same — a strong preference for the natural life, and the exposure of the corruption, humbug and greed of contemporary conventional society. Its vaunted progress he satirises in *Headlong Hall* as 'so many links in the great chain of corruption, which will soon fetter the whole human race in irreparable slavery and incurable wretchedness', and when Mr Foster is rejoicing at the facility with which one can be transported through the heart of the country, Mr Escot replies:

'... what is the advantage of locomotion? The wildman is happy in one spot, and there he remains: the civilised man is wretched in every place he happens to be in, and then congratulates himself on being accommodated with a machine that will whirl him to another, where he will be just as miserable as ever.'

Since Peacock, in the preface to *Melincourt*, remarks *in propria persona*: 'The art of enjoying life ... is in the regulation of the mind and not in the whisking about of the body', it is quite evident that he himself has little sympathy with what was regarded as the progress of the age, and much to say against it.

At the same time, while advocating the simple life and extolling 'the good old days', he is capable of satirising both. He often points out the ignorant and squalid aspects of the Middle Ages, even while he admires the age of chivalry, and this he does not inartistically so long as the characters in his stories are each putting forward a definite point of view; but in the lively tale of the noble band of Robin Hood in *Maid Marian*, he admits that the men are robbers, though he idealises them as jolly foresters. There is thus a certain opposition or lack of coherence in the work because of these two lines of presentation, for the confusion in the author's mind is reflected in the structure of the tale. Peacock, in fact, not only idealises his leading characters; he tends to idealise all those characters who portray the life and utter the sentiments with which he is sympathetic. Because of this, he fails to achieve an out-and-out comedy though he certainly presents a considerable amount of comic material which we can always enjoy along with some of the other sentimentalised material, although as far as the latter is concerned not in the way that Peacock would have expected. We might here note that in the episode entitled 'The Drunkenness of Seithenyn' (*The Misfortunes of Elphin*), we have an example of true comedy, pure and universal, embedded in the good-natured satire with which he usually describes the idiosyncracies of his characters.

In *Headlong Hall* the champions of the various theories are rather caricatured as 'deteriorationists' and 'perfectibilians', but up to a point Peacock does give a positive account of human deterioration and improvement. For a more full-length presentation of his times with less caricature, we have to go to *Melincourt*; and while his main theme there is the advocacy of the simple life and the dubiousness of the benefits of reform, he touches on a wide variety of topics in the many discussions with which the book abounds. It is here that Sir Oran Haut-ton appears, a sort of eighteenth-century Tarzan, but very well-mannered and politely silent, and one of the two candidates for Parliament in the city of One-vote which had a right to return two members to the Honourable House! It is in *Melincourt*, too, that we find a lengthy criticism of *Auld Robin Gray* given to Mr Derrydown to illustrate what he means by 'the truth of things', which, in his opinion, makes *Chevy Chase* a finer poem than *Paradise Lost*; and a visit paid to Mr Moly Mystic of Cimmerian Lodge by Mr Forester and his friends when searching for the heroine, gives Peacock ample scope to deal with Kantian philosophy.

That he is dealing with the actual conditions and questions of his time is made clear in his preface to the Second Edition of *Melincourt* where he casts his eye over his earlier writing and compares it with the contemporary scene. 'Many of the questions discussed in the dialogues,' he says, 'have more of general than of temporary application, and have still their advocates on both sides.' And while this is true of most of them even today, we must admit that Peacock takes up a rather simple-minded attitude to the evils in society when he believes that paper-money and bad parliamentary representation are far and away the worst that he is faced with. Much is said in *Melincourt* and in *Crotchet Castle* about financial bubbles, Scotch pound-notes and Jewish financiers. Indeed, the two races, separately and together, come in for a good deal of attention from Peacock on account of their monetary transactions. Mr Crotchet of Crotchet Castle unites the two in his own person, he being the son of Ebenezer Mac Crotchet whom poverty drove south to England where he proceeded to make his fortune, changing his name to E. M. Crotchet in the process. Peacock wrote various poems on the Scotch economists and 'kite-fliers' and several on Jewish financiers, one of which on 'A New Order of Chivalry' begins:

> Sir Moses, Sir Aaron, Sir Jamramajee,
> Two stock-jobbing Jews, and a shroffing Parsee,
> Have girt on the armour of old Chivalrie,
> And instead of the Red Cross, have hoisted Balls Three.

Though his verse, as the above shows, is often supremely quotable, his exposure of society is more effective in the conversations in his novels than in his poetry.

In the educational activities of his day Peacock found much to satirise. As a classicist, he could not but deplore the prevailing theories about continual intellectual progress and the belief that 'scientific organisation for teaching everybody everything, would cure all the evils of society' (*Gryll Grange*).

'God bless my soul, sir!' exclaimed the Reverend Doctor Folliott, bursting one fine May morning, into the breakfast room at Crotchet Castle, 'I am out of all patience with this march of mind. Here has my house been nearly burnt down, by my cook taking it into her head to study hydrostatics in a sixpenny tract, published by the Steam Intellect Society, and written by a learned friend who is for doing all the world's business as well as his own, and is equally well qualified to handle every branch of human knowledge. I have a great abomination of the learned friend.'

When Mr Firedamp accuses him of making very light of science, he retorts: '"Yes, sir, such science as the learned friend deals in: everything for everybody, science for all, schools for all, rhetoric for all, law for all, physic for all, words for all, and sense for none."' The 'learned friend' was Lord Brougham, whose educational experiments, if the reader does not already know them, may be imagined from the above quotation, and whom Peacock further satirised in a poem called 'The Fate of a Broom'.

In *Gryll Grange* he was in mellower mood and poked gentle fun at all this fever for learning in the character of Lord Curryfin who

> when lecturing became a mania, had taken to lecturing; and looking about for an unoccupied subject, he had lighted on the natural history of fish, in which he soon became sufficiently proficient to amuse the ladies, and astonish the fishermen in any seaside place of fashionable resort.

It must, however, be admitted that Peacock had little to say in favour of universities either, referring to them as places where young men lose whatever little learning they have acquired at school. Peacock himself had very little formal education. In his later years he wrote: 'I did not go to any university or public school. I was six years at a private school at Englefield Green. I left it before I was thirteen.' At sixteen he took his education into his own hands, according to R. Brimley Johnson, and chose the British Museum for his schoolmaster. There he must have made good use of his time, for one of the delights of his novels is the multitude of quotations from widely different sources of which he makes use. He has long quotations from Lord Monboddo, the eccentric Scottish Law Lord, as well as from the naturalist Buffon, mostly in footnotes. A great many of the quotations are from the classical languages, but French, Italian and English are well represented. The only language of any standing which does not find a place is German, but Peacock may be of the same opinion as Mr Falconer in *Gryll Grange* who, in speaking of the languages he has acquired, says:

> 'I think any scholar fortunate whose acquisition extends so far. These languages [Greek and Latin, French and Italian] and our own comprise, I believe, with a few rare exceptions, all the best books in the world. I may add Spanish for the sake of Cervantes, Lope de Vega and Calderon ... but there is nothing in it [German] to compensate for the portion of life bestowed on its acquirement, however little that may be.'

Kantian philosophy, which is satirised in the visit to Cimmerian Lodge (*Melincourt*) would certainly be no inducement for him to learn the German language.

Peacock also attacks the reactionary literary men of his time, especially those whom he considers to have sacrificed principle for profit as Wordsworth and Southey had done. He deals more lightly with Coleridge and Shelley, the former of whom he satirises as a sort of 'poetical philosopher who settled everything by sentiment and intuition', while the latter, a close friend of Peacock, has his difficulties in the realms of art and love presented in a very comic way in *Nightmare Abbey*. In all his criticism of literary men, Peacock confined his remarks to their public utterances, claiming in his preface to *Melincourt*, that he never trespassed on private life. And in his fierce attacks on *The Quarterly Review* for its favouritism, its irresponsible criticism, its reactionary anti-Jacobin sentiments, he gives examples of actual passages to show that he is not exaggerating the arguments he is satirising (Mainchance Villa in *Melincourt*).

Two outstanding types of character occur in the conversational novels — that of a Scottish political economist and that of an epicurean clergyman. The former, of a reputedly argumentative race, is a particularly suitable member of a party where discussion is the chief form of amusement; and the latter, urbane and knowledgeable, provides a very necessary makeweight with his love of the classics and the pleasures of the table. Perhaps Lady Clarinda's description of Dr Folliott in *Crotchet Castle* will give some idea of the best of these worthy divines:

> He is said to be an excellent scholar, and is fonder of books than the majority of his cloth; he is very fond, also, of the good things of this world. He is of an admirable temper, and says rude things in a pleasant half-earnest manner that nobody can take offence with.

It is the Rev. Dr Folliott who questions Mr Crotchet about the propriety of the latter's displaying the Sleeping Venus in his home in full view of his daughter and his guests; and it is the doughty Dr Folliott also, who ends an argument about the march of mind and the claims of Edinburgh as a literary centre with a well-turned quip. Mr MacQuedy has been maintaining that "'laughter is an involuntary action of certain muscles, developed in the human species by the progress of civilisation. The savage never laughs.'" "'No sir'", retorts Dr Folliott, "'he has nothing to laugh at. Give him Modern Athens, the 'learned friend', and the Steam Intellect Society. They will develop his muscles.'"

Before finishing, one might mention the chapter called 'Theories', in *Crotchet Castle*, where Mr Crotchet junior, remarking that 'there is one point on which philosophers of all classes seem to be agreed; that they only want money to regenerate the world', offers to 'put into the hands of this company a large sum for the purpose'. The ensuing amusing wrangle is prognosticated by the chapter-heading from Butler:

> But when they came to shape the model,
> Not one could fit the other's noddle

and terminated by a song from Mr Trillo which might almost have been written by Gilbert:

> After careful meditation
> And profound deliberation,
> On the various petty projects which have just been shown,

> Not a scheme in agitation
> For the world's amelioration
> Has a grain of commonsense in it, except my own.

It is perhaps little wonder that when Miss Brindlemew learns that her niece, Miss Caprioletta Headlong, is to marry Mr Foster, she exclaims: 'Oh that a daughter of our ancient family should marry a philosopher!' But while it may be objected that in the novels the characters confuse the philosopher with the progressive, the same cannot be said of the quatrain with which Peacock prefaces the whole collection of his novels:

> All philosophers who find
> Some favourite system to their mind,
> In every point to make it fit,
> Will force all nature to submit.

In conclusion, then, it can be said that Thomas Love Peacock is an exposer of pretensions and a foe to humbug, and that, without rancour and with many an interesting sidelight on human thought, he presents his criticisms to us. That he does not succeed in producing a thoroughly worked-out comedy, is due mainly to the fact that he has too much of the eighteenth century addiction to 'higher sentiments' to allow his sympathetic characters to suffer the same exposure as the others do; and this leads to a certain incoherence — or imbalance — in the structure of his works. But the conversations in his novels are illuminating, often brilliantly so. His comic material is there, but his comic work is not completed while the gap between sentimentalised and satirised characters remains.

Janet Anderson with son Alexander (Sandy), 1926.

– 25 –
Herman Melville

Until recently, Herman Melville was not well known in literary circles. In fact, it could be said that, having attained a certain amount of notoriety through his very early works, he faded into obscurity during his own lifetime; and it is only of late years that he has been rescued from that obscurity, and given the position to which he is entitled. The authors of the main recent studies of Melville are most enthusiastic about him, with a tendency to overestimate, in particular, the importance of his later works. It might be argued that these writers are not objective enough, but literary criticism *can* benefit from the work of critics like them, because they bring into the light of day many things that have been, or tend to be, passed over. Their work is of value as a preliminary account of Melville's writing, although it is to be remembered that it is not the enthusiast alone who is a good critic. Thoroughgoing criticism must bring out the defects as well as the merits of a work, and must not, for preference, be the production of a disciple — though even that may be of value in leading the way to balanced criticism.

Melville's main works were written about 1850, his magnum opus, *Moby Dick*, being completed by the time he was thirty; and although

---

Address to the Literary Society, 5 July 1934, reported in the *Union Recorder*, 19 July 1934.

he continued writing until he died at the age of seventy-two, he never again received the public acclaim that had been his at the publication of his first two novels. *Typee* appeared in 1846, and *Omoo* in 1847. Both of these works give a straightforward account of Melville's own experiences in the Marquesas. In the former he describes four months spent as a solitary white man among the Typees, whose very name, according to Mumford, meant eaters of men. In their secluded valley, we are told, 'there were none of those thousand sources of irritation that the ingenuity of civilised man has created to mar his own felicity ... to sum up all in one word — no Money! That root of all evil' was not to be found there, and all was 'mirth, fun and high good humour'. *Typee*, Lewis Mumford remarks, 'belongs to the morning of the imagination. ... It is direct, fresh, free from self-consciousness'. These qualities were not so evident in *Omoo*, a continuation of Melville's adventures in the South Seas; nevertheless, it won almost equal commendation from the public that had welcomed *Typee* so warmly.

Such was not the fate of *Mardi* which followed them closely. It too, for about a quarter of its length, is a straightforward tale of South Sea adventures, but thereafter it takes a mystical turn, very puzzling in some ways and full of symbolism. Much more easily understood is the social satire, which seems to be at least part of Melville's purpose in writing the book. Mardi, itself, is a fanciful archipelago, the background of the adventures of the hero and his companions. But it also represents the world where Dominora, standing for England, is ruled over by hump-backed King Bello, whose hump symbolises the national debt. Although a few precise political issues are dealt with, the satire is very vague and general, the points made are rather obvious, and the whole serves for the most part to provide material for Melville in developing his critical attitude to society in general. But Yillah, Azzageddi and the Three Brothers with their symbolism, puzzling enough for twentieth-century readers, were too puzzling for Melville's nineteenth-century readers, and *Mardi* had a most unfavourable reception.

Following *Mardi*, came the pot-boiler, *Redburn*. Here, again, Melville relates a voyage of his own — one he undertook when a mere boy, from New York to Liverpool and back. This work has no fanciful elements. It is straightforward — rather pedestrian, indeed, but it has flashes of something better, and its descriptive passages are, at least, interesting. On the journey out from New York, Melville held converse with a whaleman — the first he ever met — with whom he must have felt a certain kinship, and who taught him the word 'snivelisation'. 'And what's the use of bein' *snivelised*?' the whaleman used to say. '... Snivelised chaps only learns the way to take on 'bout life, and snivel. You don't see any Methodist chaps feelin' dreadful about their souls; you don't see any darned beggars and pesky constables in *Madagasky*. ... Blast Ameriky, I say.' Melville found plenty of beggars in the city of Liverpool, which presented him with such squalor and misery, such depths of poverty with their attendant horrors, that he was utterly appalled. It is in this work that we find emerging his concern, amounting to an obsession, with the problem of evil. It was a force that he found difficult to understand, corrupting the world and seeming to accompany civilisation, and his whole suggestion is of innocence facing society and being unable to stand up to it. Already in his soul, he feels 'the emptiness of all the sweet professions of civilisation' (Mumford), and he finds in this journey of his, how his innocence and simplicity leave him vulnerable and friendless in the world of men. Melville is not alone in thinking of civilisation as a corrupting agency. A similar notion is expressed in the works of Peacock, in a more light-hearted manner. It is the intensity with which Melville describes the conflict between simplicity and civilised society and the effect of the conflict on the mind of man that gives such vigour to his work.

White Jacket, published in 1850, is also an account of Melville's own adventures — this time, in the American Navy. This, as might be surmised, is mainly a study of oppression and tyranny, which reach their peak, in the book, in the practice of flogging. His descriptions of the barbarity of the surgeon and the arbitrariness of the orders are convincing and horrifying, and again we are conscious of the intensity with which Melville feels these things, especially the degradation of flogging, the degradation of both flogger and flogged. Indeed, he expresses himself with such forcefulness that we can understand how the book could well have led, as has been claimed, to the abolition of flogging in the American Navy.

But neither *Redburn* nor *White Jacket* helped him to regain the popularity he had lost with *Mardi*. The themes of oppression and tyranny were obviously much in his mind, and these were not themes that found favour with the public of his day. It is interesting to note that, after the first edition, passages in *Typee* criticising missionary endeavours in the South Seas (as well as passages considered 'broad') were excised. Melville's serious account of the exploitation and extermination of the natives at the hands of the missionaries was cut out as being unsuitable for publication, and *Typee* was made simply into a traveller's tale. Melville had stated the real situation quite accurately and definitely, but he was very young and unsure of himself and he finally submitted to the pressure of relatives and others and allowed the excisions to be made. After the failure of *Moby Dick*, he complained that he was regarded merely as a spectacle — as a man who had lived among cannibals and come back to tell the tale. From all of this, it may be gathered that Melville was essentially in opposition to his epoch. He spoke on behalf of the oppressed in general, showing himself as an artist whose art, explicitly and implicitly, was a form of social protest; for he attempted to deal with things as they were and not as the readers of that period, the 'nice-minded' Victorian public, liked to think that they were.

Moby Dick; or, The Whale (1851) seems to gather together many different strands in his preceding work. In form it is autobiographical like all the others, but it is not an account of any actual voyage. It combines simple description with imaginative material in the account of the struggle of the Captain of the *Pequod* to meet and overcome the white whale and to win the crew to his purpose; and it exhibits the states of mind of the Captain and the other participants of this struggle with a certain suggestion of symbolism. But this work, too, was badly received, and Melville fell still further into obscurity.

After *Moby Dick* he could not make a living with his pen, yet he continued to write. His following book, *Pierre*, written in 1852, completed the ruin of his reputation. It certainly is of less merit than *Moby Dick*, and shows considerable decline in power which may, in some measure, be accounted for by the state of Melville's health. In addition to the depression engendered by the heartbreaking reception of his books, the privations of his early years at sea were making themselves felt and the writing of *Moby Dick* had taken a tremendous toll on him, for the questions he grappled with there stirred up much that had been repressed within him. In none of his earlier books does he touch on sex (the idyll with Fayaway in *Typee*, interesting though it is in some respects, hardly counts). But in *Moby Dick*, although he is dealing with a world composed only of men, with whales and with the struggle of Ahab and the white whale, there is much conscious and unconscious sexual symbolism, in the expression of which Melville must have experienced great mental turmoil. Be that as it may, it was in *Pierre* that he, for the first time, dealt directly with the question of sex, and while the work is somewhat fantastic and melodramatic, it is neither a mere adventure story, nor a sentimental one, but treats of human doubts and difficulties, of states of mind. Mainly, Melville is concerned with Pierre's feelings towards a girl whom he believes to be his half-sister. From the very beginning of the novel, when Pierre calls his *mother* 'sister', we are prepared to believe that there is something unusual about him, and it is the confused relationships in Pierre's mind and the working out of half-stated conflicts that are the real theme of the book. This was not the kind of work to win popularity in 1852, when literary oppression existed in a very active form. Thackeray and Dickens, Melville's contemporaries, bowed to the prevailing tastes and, through fear of their public, hardly treated sex at all in their books and spinelessly covered it up. When the comparatively harmless *Oliver Twist* was published in America, there was an outcry against the immoral picture of Bill Sykes and Nancy, and Melville himself had already suffered from Victorian prudery and sentimentalism in connection with *Typee*; but, as Mumford remarks, 'the clothed and carpeted world of convention' was not for him, and he turned aside from it to face 'the nakedness of life'. Although Melville was indeed writing in a different world from that of Smollett, it was not only oppression from outside with regard to sex which overcame him; his own suppressions were too much for him, and he never dealt with the matter openly again, though he came close to it in *Clarel*.

In 1855, he wrote *Israel Potter*, a straightforward piece of work based on Potter's autobiography, and in 1856, there followed *Piazza Tales*, the most interesting of which is 'Bartleby'. Here again, as in almost all his work, Melville presents his own conflicts. Like Bartleby, he would 'prefer not to' accept the conditions of civilisation, and Bartleby's final statement in prison, 'I know where I am', would be quite in harmony with the thoughts of Melville, who always felt a stranger in society and who also would have found some relief in being in a place which was what it purported to be.

The Confidence Man, which appeared in 1857, is the best work published after *Moby Dick*. It is social satire consisting simply of a description of the passengers aboard a Mississippi ferry boat. In the situations and conversations, which turn mainly on the theme of trust and distrust, and exhibit the manifest varieties of human credulity, Melville attempts to bring out the contradictions of the morality — or the professed morality — of Christendom, and once more we have a presentation of the opposition between the individual looking always for something in which he can trust and the civilisation which deceives and finally overcomes him. This book evokes comparison with Mark Twain, a much less vigorous but more romantic, and thus more acceptable, satirist than Melville.

In 1860, Melville published a collection of poems, entitled *Battle Pieces*, followed in 1876 by *Clarel*, a long poem concerned with his pilgrimage to the Holy Land; by *John Mann and Other Sailors* in 1888, and finally by *Timoleon* in 1891. The story of *Billy Budd, Foretopman* was published posthumously. According to Mumford, this last work of Melville presents his reconciliation with society, with civilisation. He suggests that in the end Melville has come to the conclusion that evil means *have* to be used by those responsible for the maintenance of order in the world, that innocence may thereby suffer, but that we can be reconciled to the suffering through a recognition of the necessity of the evil means. It might rather be said that Melville here is actually admitting defeat — an admission which may be responsible for a greater intrusion of sentimentality than is usually found in his novels.

Billy Budd, like Oliver Twist, is thoroughly romantic — too good to be true. He was found in a silk-lined basket, hanging 'from the knocker of a good man's door in Bristol', and with his evident noble blood, his good looks and his innocence, he survived unscathed until he met Claggart on the *Indomitable*. 'The Handsome Sailor' had brought peace to the forecastle of the *Rights of Man*, according to the Captain of that vessel, 'not that he preached to them or said or did anything in particular; but a virtue went out of him sugaring the sour ones'. He had also, though this is mentioned only in passing, given in his early days on the ship 'a terrible drubbing to the bluffer of the gang'. This sentimental characterisation leads also to a noticeable lack of detail in the presentation of the all-important final interview between Billy and the Captain of the *Indomitable*; yet it was such as to make Billy cry, as his last words on earth: 'God bless Captain Vere!' If this be reconciliation, as Mumford claims, there is little to distinguish it from defeat, and it had a bad effect on Melville's art. On the whole, it might be said that Melville realised he was fighting a losing battle after the failure of *Moby Dick*. He attempted poetry only because he could not succeed as a prose writer, and he presented themes in poetical form which would probably have been better treated in prose. At any rate, his struggle was considerably watered down in his poetry, and in his later prose work he has lost much of his force. In *Billy Budd* he gave up the struggle, and having given up the struggle, he died.

We have seen that in spite of his insight and his descriptive power, Melville could not gain recognition either for the straightforward tales of *Redburn* and *White Jacket*, the phantasy of *Mardi* or the symbolism of *Moby Dick*. *Mardi*, indeed, is rather scraps and announcements than an actual performance, though Melville's ironic treatment of contemporaries, especially the more scholastic of them, is amusing. But *Moby Dick* is great literature; the whole story hangs together well and definitely works out a theme by means of the struggle of Ahab, the Captain of the whaler, with the white whale, Moby Dick. One of the most remarkable things in the book is the contrast between the wild unruly hearts of the crew, and the orderly, scientific account of the kinds and parts of whales, and the way in which, in the working out of this contrast, all the characters of the novel come to be clearly distinguished. Mumford thinks that Moby Dick represents the Universe, and not merely a particular whale, but this interpretation takes away much of the dramatic force of the struggle. While men may fight against necessity, it is always some particular necessity that is weighing on them, and not necessity in general, against which no one can struggle (cf. 'Bartleby'). It is true that Shakespeare makes Hamlet speak of the 'cursed spite' of his being born to set the world right, but it was no such general task — it was a particular duty that was pressing on his mind.

Similar dramatic considerations apply to the notion of the Sea as a character. It is not even a living combatant, like the whale which is Ahab's special antagonist. Rather it provides the background — the conditions — for the more general struggle against which the particular struggle of Ahab and the Whale takes place — the struggle of all aboard the *Pequod* against conditions of life which are intolerable. It is not a question of the Sea being a character, any more than it is a question of the Whale being the Universe. It is a question of the kind of life sailors had to lead in those days, when whaling ships, in particular, were often at sea for a number of years, and of the way in which human feelings developed in these long absences from land. And woven into all these struggles is the phallic symbol of the great white whale, by which each member of the crew becomes obsessed, whose very whiteness adds to the terrors of the dark waste of waters surrounding it, for 'there lurks an elusive something in the innermost idea of that hue which strikes more of panic in the soul than that redness which affrights the blood.' It comes to be hated by the men, because unconsciously it represents their sexual deprivation, a great part of the intolerable life they have to lead.

But to Ahab it is especially intolerable — it is a special object of hatred. Having been wounded earlier by the whale, he now finds it unbearable that he should have to live at the caprice of a creature which could destroy him. The knowledge of its very existence oppresses and tortures him, for he cannot admit that anything could be more powerful than he. Therefore he must seek it out in order to put an end to this intolerable situation; he must show who is master. All this is the very stuff of tragedy. The tragic hero, with his illusions of power, tries to be master of destiny, and finds destiny to be stronger than he: and the essential unreasonableness in the drama, of Ahab's making an enemy of the whale, brings out more strongly than is usual, the tragic delusion of power.

Moby Dick is so massive and important that it is difficult to quote from it. It must be read in its entirety. It sums up the different strands in Melville's work, and it brings out the character of tragedy. It is not always explicit concerning oppression, especially sexual oppression, but oppressions of various kinds emerge in the rich symbolism of the book. It is significant that the first words of the narrator of the tale are 'Call me Ishmael' — words which prepare the reader for a story of loneliness and struggle. Melville, like Ishmael, found himself alone in the world and at odds with the world, akin not only to the hero, Ahab, but also to the white whale — another solitary being fighting alone. Indeed, just as the theme of *Ulysses* is exile, so that of *Moby Dick* might be described as loneliness — loneliness as seen in the narrator, in Ahab, in Moby Dick itself, developed against the background of a solitary whaler, a speck on the vastness of the sea, carrying a body of men cut off and apart from all the activities that go on where men and women congregate. There are so many complex strands woven into the story of Moby Dick; so much and such penetrating psychological insight into the characters of the tale; such unconscious symbolism — and conscious symbolism too — embedded in it, that it is one of the great books of the world.

– 26 –
Feodor Dostoevsky

The nineteenth century was the great age of Russian literature. Up until that time there had been no writers of any importance in the country, but then there appeared in quick succession Pushkin (1799–1837), Turgenev (1815–1883), Dostoevsky (1821–1881) and Tolstoi (1828–1910), giants not only in Russian literature, but great novelists in the literature of the world.

As is always the case, this great artistic activity was connected with culture-contacts. These are responsible also for the well-known periods in Scottish history during the fourteenth and eighteenth centuries, the age of Shakespeare, and the upsurge of 'Byronism' in the nineteenth century. Of the Russian writers, it is significant that Dostoevsky was a Lithuanian, while Pushkin had in him a strain of negro blood. But the great and stirring force was the impingement of Western culture on a backward Eastern country. Dostoevsky was affected by the movement, only to be violently opposed to it, and very critical of the doctrine of Progress and of Western Liberalism in general. In his novels, he satirises Russian Liberals and their Europeanism, and when any of his characters utter anti-Western sentiments, we know from internal evidence, and from other sources as well, that these are the opinions

---

Address to the Literary Society, 2 April 1936, reported in the *Union Recorder*, 16 April 1936.

of Dostoevsky himself. He thought Russia should repel all Western influences and remain entirely Slav; especially should it retain its ancient faith, for, to Dostoevsky, the important thing for a country was not so much politics as religion, and he believed that all the Western Churches had succumbed to utilitarianism, and that only the Orthodox Church was truly religious.

In addition to this tremendous ferment of opinion of an international character, there was, within Russia itself, the struggle against bureaucracy, in which the claims of culture had a large place; and the 'epoch of reform' had a great deal to do with the revival of literature after 1855.

If literature flourishes in periods of social agitation, does it follow that it consists in giving a 'picture of the times' or a message for the times? It would appear that this is the view that has largely been taken for granted in Russia where the Western doctrine of *pure art* has never penetrated deeply; and it is one reason why the Marxist theory of art as a 'reflection of social conditions' has found such wide-spread acceptance in the present period, and that literature has come to mean the expression of a social attitude. It was perhaps inevitable that these nineteenth-century Russian novelists should have their minds on the state of society and that, in consequence, there should arise the theory of a necessary relation of literature to social conditions. Tolstoi and Dostoevsky were particularly vulnerable in this respect. Of Tolstoi, who had a definite theory of the didactic function of art, Lenin wrote:[1]

> Tolstoi not only produced works of art which will be valued always and read by the masses after the latter have created for themselves humane conditions of living, after they have overthrown the yoke of feudal landlords and the capitalists: he was able to transmit with remarkable force the mood of the broad masses oppressed by the modern system, to depict their plight and give voice to their elemental urge of protest and indignation. ... Tolstoi's books reflect both the strength and the weakness, both the sweep and the limitation of precisely a peasant movement.

And again,

The contradictions in Tolstoi's *views* are not the contradictions arising solely from his own mentality, but are the reflections of those most complex, contradictory conditions, social influences and historical traditions which determined the psychology of the various classes and estates in Russian society during the reformist but pre-revolutionary epoch.

(i.e., *views* are assumed to be the same as what determined them — the effect the same as the cause, and mind practically non-existent.) The logical outcome of all this is a denial, not only of literature which is the art of presenting states of mind, but also of psychology which studies the mind, for both are reduced to, and muddled with, history, the function of which is to deal with states of society.

It can be freely admitted that Dostoevsky does take up a social attitude in his books. He presents a criticism of Western progressivism; he supports a religious as against a secular view of life; and he exhibits the upheavals and general misery in the Russian life of his day. Nevertheless, his main themes (crime, punishment, humiliation, redemption and murder) are not peculiarly nineteenth-century themes — they are as old as man himself. While they are all social phenomena, Dostoevsky presents them, above all, as *states of mind*, as forces operating in the souls of his characters; and thus his work is not history but literature. There are, of course, connections between states of mind and states of society; but, as has been suggested above, it is, for literature, a matter of 'universal' themes. Dostoevsky's preoccupation with religion (or theology) makes him treat these themes in a supremely personal way. It is his opinion that until we get back to the state of the individual soul, we are not seeing crime, punishment and so on, as they really are. Thus he comes nearer to human (i.e., emotional) themes than any progressive can who has, as Dostoevsky thinks, lost all sense of the relation of human thoughts and actions to God. From the theological point of view, there is really no history; there is only the rebellion or the redemption of individuals. It is all a question of personal relations, relations among men and the relations of men to God; and this outlook, though it is not a true one and ignores all other social relations, is important since it means that Dostoevsky will treat states of mind as such, and not in the light of social conditions. The epoch to which Lenin refers in his remarks on Tolstoi (vide supra) was the epoch of Dostoevsky himself, and the extent to which his theological attitude enabled him to get away from the sociological view of literature, gave him the opportunity to produce something solidly literary.

There is the further question of the influence of an author's personal history on his work. In an interesting book by his daughter, Aimée Dostoevsky [*Fyodor Dostoevsky: A Study*, 1921] persons and places in Dostoevsky's life are related to characters and scenes in his novels. This is, of course, of no real *literary* importance. For aesthetics, it is not a question of the *origin* of the characters we find in Dostoevsky's works — it is a question of the characters themselves; but we may, by means of such information, find an explanation of certain deficiencies or peculiarities in his books. For instance, in Aimée Dostoevsky's study of her father, there is a reference to a certain Pauline N. ... with whom Dostoevsky lived in various parts of Europe after his separation from his first wife. This part of his history

> explains the characters of many of Dostoevsky's capricious and fantastic heroines. Aglaia in *The Idiot*, Lisa in *The Possessed*, Grushenka in *The Brothers Karamazov* and several others, are more or less Paulines. It is in this love-story of my father's, I think, that we shall find the explanation of the strange hatred-love of Rogozhin for Nastasya Filippovna.

There is certainly a great resemblance between Nastasya and Grushenka — both 'deceived' in early life; both tempestuous and revengeful characters. On the other hand, Aglaia seems rather to resemble Katerina, a well brought up, proud, impulsive girl, going to extremes of emotion, high-spirited, risking social opprobrium and demanding recognition of her 'individuality'. Among the male characters also, there is a certain amount of repetition. Marmeladov, General Ivolgin and Captain Snegiryov are all weak and disreputable fathers who, in spite of their good-tempered and kindly dispositions, bring shame and poverty on their family. And a still more interesting recurrence is that of epilepsy in Prince Myshkin and in Smerdyakov, since this was Dostoevsky's own ailment. Indeed, taking epilepsy itself

26 Feodor Dostoevsky

to be a manifestation of a compulsion to repetition, the whole set of recurrences could be regarded as symptomatic.

It is natural enough that his personal history and peculiarities, as well as the general conditions of his time, should influence Dostoevsky's themes and characters; but this gives no ground for a special 'interpretation' of his work. One must reject all such 'interpretations' of literature, for literature is not good or important because it is Russian literature, or Australian literature, religious literature or proletarian literature. There is no literature but literature, and literature deals with states of mind. As regards Dostoevsky, the general position might be put as follows: a background of social misery supports a theological interpretation of human life as a vale of tears, with probation and redemption through suffering; and this, in conjunction with the author's personal peculiarities induces an interest in psycho-pathology — in general unbalancedness and scenemaking, in roguery and the vileness of human life (i.e., the meanness and depravity of what Dostoevsky calls 'secular' man). These interests leave the author much freer to deal with psychological phenomena, to expose men (i.e., to bring out their mental entanglements), than any kind of progressivism could do, with its humanitarianism and its romantic theories of the 'good' in human nature. Nor is Dostoevsky constrained by being a revolutionist. In her short preface to *The Brothers Karamazov*, Constance Garnett remarks that he was 'neither by temperament nor conviction a revolutionist'. He was, in fact, a Slavophile and a Populist, as his daughter shows in her study of her father. 'Not by servile repetitions of the Utopias of the Europeans which lead them to their own destruction will you serve humanity, but by preparing together with your people the new Orthodox idea,' he said in a speech to the Society of Letters in 1880, at the inauguration of Pushkin's monument. Indeed, Dostoevsky's theocratic views have more kinship with anarchy than with revolutionary Socialism, for the anarchist, too, 'believes' in humanity. But these views, interesting though they are, are not particularly important, except in so far as Dostoevsky's opposition to revolutionary Socialism and Western Liberalism kept the way clear for him to examine the human soul. And literature is such an examination, resolving itself into a presentation of human pretensions and the clash of ideals with reality. Nevertheless, it is to be noted that the theological

245

outlook, with its emphasis on redemption, also leads to a confusing of the facts, though it is always possible to have a presentation of the theologically minded, with *their* illusions and *their* clash with reality.

The influence of the belief in redemption is particularly noticeable in the working-out of *Crime and Punishment* (1866). To most of us, these are simply legal terms, but Dostoevsky regards them principally as states of mind. Consequently, for him, the punishment meted out by society is unimportant and irrelevant in comparison with the punishment (and suffering) in the mind of the criminal. In the course of the novel, we are also confronted with the notion of crime as 'social protest'. In the interesting first interview with Porfiry, Razumikhin lashes out at the Socialists, crying 'Everything with them is "the influence of environment". ... From which it follows that, if society is normally organised, all crime will cease at once, since there will be nothing to protest against and all men will become righteous in one instant.' At this same interview, there emerges still another theory about crime. Raskolnikov, the man who is being questioned in connection with the murder, is confronted with an article he had written on the subject, wherein he dealt with the case of the 'extraordinary' man, who is permitted to overstep legal obstacles and even to murder in the name of conscience. In this man, he had argued, crime is really an expression of 'good intentions'; he sees himself as a benefactor, a hero, a saviour. It is only if he fails before he has achieved his end that he finds himself in the hands of the law. In the case of Raskolnikov himself, Dostoevsky shows that *his* crime is a protest of the ego against the law, an exhibition of an inferiority complex, a desire to master circumstances, a refusal to accept reality. Raskolnikov was determined to demonstrate that he was as great as Napoleon, by murdering someone ('a louse') with calmness and resolution, after which he would be able to go on and be truly philanthropic. His punishment begins when he *recognises* his inferiority — when he realises that (in the commission of the crime) he has again, and as usual, acted in a weak and feeble manner.

The completion of the mental punishment lies in his getting beyond egoism — in his getting reconciled with God, which he can accomplish only by shedding his illusions and achieving a state of humility. It is his realisation of these first steps in his punishment that leads him to an acceptance of social punishment — to his giving himself up. And his moral regeneration is completed, *not* through official (humane or inhumane) punishment, but through love — love in the broadest sense — loving-kindness as we might put it. This is achieved through the influence of Sonia, a woman who, because she has 'sinned' for good purposes, has kept, through all the degradation that followed, her innocence of heart whereby she is enabled to save Raskolnikov. It is feasible enough that a prostitute might not be so mentally degraded as some women in the social round, but the retention of a fundamental innocence is a false conception, and is responsible for the fact that in Sonia's character there is no development. In the novel she is just the idea of innocence — a person whose basic reason for entering on a life of prostitution was a sacrificial one. This contrast of the 'inner' and the 'outer' reminds us of Ibsen's *Emperor and Galilean*, and of Socrates in *The Apology* saying, not truly, that the Athenians could not injure him but only themselves; and the use that is made of this idea is a decided weakness of *Crime and Punishment*. The whole notion of redemption by innocent love is a falsification of the facts, and leads to the sentimentality of Svidrigailov's repentance and death, and to the forced pathos of the conclusion — the recognition by Sonia and Raskolnikov of their love and mutual redemption.

Among the many remarkable features of the book, is the early scene with Marmeladov. In depicting Sonia's father in his drunkenness telling how Sonia was driven to 'shame', as it is called, Dostoevsky brings out well the internal character of shame — how it must always be reaching out for, and seizing upon, things that one can be *openly* ashamed of, in order to hide what one is secretly ashamed of, and what one cannot bear, consciously or unconsciously, to bring into the light of day. There is more than a suggestion that Marmeladov is, in the depths of his heart, ashamed of his relations with his wife, but it is of his shame at Sonia's shame (which everyone knows about) that he babbles when he is drunk. And even getting drunk is one of the things that one can be ashamed of openly, with the added advantage that it provides an outlet for, and some relief from, the guilty feelings that oppress and shame. This is a remarkable dramatic presentation of a psychological state, and here Dostoevsky is definitely carrying out the work of the literary artist. Throughout his novels, he always tries to show the psychological roots of ordinary actions, and his characters are a criticism of the attempt to reduce all human activities to the effect of environment — a pursuit which would finally annihilate literature.

On the whole, *Crime and Punishment* is a great book, weakened though it is by the notions of redemption and innocence which are part of Dostoevsky's beliefs. Its strength lies in its psychological analysis, penetrating even in the less important characters of Svidrigailov and Luzhin. Much of the criminal's mentality comes out in Raskolnikov's confessions to Sonia — his longing to be exposed and his struggles between self-assertion and abasement. In his case there is no contrast of the inner and the outer; there is simply a presentation of what criminality is in the mind of the criminal. While Dostoevsky shows him as having an inferiority complex and as possessing, in general, a megalomaniac character, there is no mention of his having a feeling of persecution (persecution mania), and this may actually not be very great in a criminal. If, as might well be the case, the criminal does not experience the mental punishment that Raskolnikov does, it could be because he is convinced that he *is* being persecuted by society. However, as Dostoevsky sees it, the apparatus of social punishment is largely external to the struggle in the criminal's own mind. Finally, we must note that the three interviews with Porfiry, the police official who is trying to bring Raskolnikov to betray himself, are on a very high level, comparable to those between Ivan and Smerdyakov in *The Brothers Karamazov*, where there is the same searching psychological analysis, and, it is interesting to observe, the same succession of interviews.

There does not seem to be anything remarkable in saying that idiocy is a state of mind, but in *The Idiot* (1868) it is not a question of imbecility, only one of simplicity — of the child-like mind as contrasted with the sophisticated. Prince Myshkin, the 'idiot' hero and an epileptic, has the faculty of exposing people, of making them show their true character by his own freedom from pretences; in which notion of exposure, we see the kind of work the literary artist, himself, does — the bringing out of the hidden characteristics and relations among people. Maurice Baring, in his *Outlines of Russian Literature*, tells us that Prince Myshkin represents a type of person often to be found in Russia — a person whom he describes as 'God's fool' — a man who is really wiser in some ways than the more sophisticated members of the community.

This strain of simplicity, by the way, is well-marked in Dostoevsky himself. But Baring was wrong in believing that Prince Myshkin was unharmed by the 'worthless lot' surrounding him. He suffered great wrongs, and he learned that he could neither influence people as he wished, nor get what he himself wanted, although Dostoevsky sees him as defeating his own purposes by his manner of doing things, by his excitability and rushing to extremes. The little influence that Myshkin had was on people of low character, and it might be argued that thoroughly respectable people, in their conventionality, are beyond influence. It is interesting to compare him with Frank Guiseley in *None Other Gods* by R. H. Benson, who also, just by being what he was, showed up people as they really were, and who also, like Myshkin, attempted to redeem them and perished in the attempt.

The failure of both lies in their having some pretensions left, particularly those of rescuing the suffering and of saving society. This function of the redeemer came out especially in Myshkin's relations with Nastasya, whom from the beginning he recognised as having suffered from man's exploitation. As a result of his preoccupation with Nastasya's sufferings, he lost Aglaia whom he loved and would have liked to marry; and though he was quite prepared to marry Nastasya, she ran away with his friend, Rogozhin, who murdered her. Prince Myshkin stood by his friend, but the strain on his mind was too great, and he relapsed into complete idiocy in the ordinary sense — a catastrophe which arose, we might say, from his not being simple enough.

The Idiot has a less convincing theme than *Crime and Punishment*, because the 'simple' state of mind is largely illusory, whereas the criminal mind is not. But, on the whole, it is more coherently presented — or, rather, Myshkin's function as touchstone enables Dostoevsky to give sketches of characters which, whether they cohere in the work itself, or whether Myshkin is well-conceived or not, are valuable in themselves. We have, for example, a study of worldliness with its hollowness and its vanity brought out, as R. H. Benson brings it out also, by contrast with an unworldly character, who is greater in his 'failure' than the worldly are in their 'success'. It is possible that Dostoevsky realised that a man putting himself forward as a redeemer was bound to come to grief. In *Haveth Childers Everywhere*, James Joyce hints at the impossibility of vicarious atonement, and it is true that though development can come only through suffering, there is nothing in that to support the notion that it can be brought about by vicarious suffering — a notion which is the basis of Christianity. The Prince, with all his simplicity, his suffering and his sympathy with suffering, cannot save either Aglaia or Nastasya, and, in the end, they, as well as he himself, are destroyed.

The Brothers Karamazov (1880) is Dostoevsky's last and, though it is unfinished, his greatest work. In it appears Alyosha, 'the great sinner' — a remarkable description of him in view of the fact that he resembles Myshkin in his simplicity and in his ability to make everybody love him. But Alyosha recognises that he is not only a 'natural' sinful man; he is 'also a Karamazov', one of a family outstanding for its sensuality, its vileness and meanness, for its secular human baseness, the denial of which is what is called pride. It is only by the rejection of self, by love and submission to God, all of which Alyosha strives to achieve, that this baseness can be overcome. Against a background of ideas such as these, the story unfolds, the characters in various degrees and in various ways exhibiting this sin of pride, this lack of love and of humility.

Connected with these ideas are the scenes between the schoolboys and Alyosha — scenes which, however, seem to be dragged into the book instead of occurring naturally in the working-out of the theme. The suggestion would appear to be that these children are not proud and sinful, and that if they encounter love and humility in their early life, they will not become so degraded and secularist as they would be if allowed to develop 'sensually'. The main point here is that Dostoevsky is trying to force on the story a notion of innocence in contrast with the guilt of humanity, much as he did in the character of Sonia. The believer in sin also believes in innocence and seeks for it — a characteristic which is possessed by Dostoevsky himself, according to his daughter's study of her father. She relates how

> the African love of Maria Dimitrievna [Dostoevsky's first wife] and the somewhat Oriental passion of Pauline N— had left no very pleasant memories, and in his maturity my father returned to the Lithuanian ideals of his forefathers. He began to seek for a pure and chaste young girl, a virtuous woman, who would be a faithful life companion.

It is this characteristic which is responsible for the introduction into the work of a certain amount of romantic sentimentality, of which the episodes with the schoolboys are an example.

The theme of *The Brothers Karamazov* is again murder, and here the murderous mentality is dealt with more fully than in *Crime and Punishment* for this murder is a parricide, and all the members of the family feel murderous towards their father. The actual murderer is the valet, Smerdyakov, supposed to be a natural son of old Karamazov, though the point is never cleared up. But Smerdyakov is able to show in discussions with Ivan, the second son, that the latter had, in effect, put into his head the idea of the murder. Alyosha, also, has contributed to the deed, because he failed to visit Dimitri, his oldest brother, but for whose arrival on the scene that evening, the murder would not have taken place. Though it is Dimitri who is charged with the crime, the suggestion is that all the Karamazovs are guilty of their father's death, and more than that, that *we* are all Karamazovs. At the trial of Dimitri, Ivan bursts forth:

'... Who doesn't desire his father's death?'
'Are you in your right mind?' broke involuntarily from the President.
'I should think I am in my right mind ... the same nasty mind as all of you ... as all these ... ugly faces.'
He turned suddenly to the audience. 'My father has been murdered and they pretend they are horrified,' he snarled, with furious contempt. 'They keep up the sham with one another. Liars! They all desire the death of their fathers. One reptile devours another. ... It's a spectacle they want! Panem et circenses! Though I am one to talk!'

The whole section dealing with the trial is full of remarkably good examples of Freudian psychology. In Ivan's outburst we have a striking parallel with Freud's *Totem and Taboo*. The original sin, according to Freud, was parricide, social organisation (i.e., morality and religion) arising among the sons of the slain father as penance for the sin, and protection against any repetition of it. At the same time, the guilty feeling finds some symbolic satisfaction, some outlet, in the totem feast. All society is thus based on the fear of parricide, and religion provides the only safety-valve, parricide remaining in symbols on ceremonial occasions. Freud himself questions the possibility of establishing a purely secular civilisation, and certainly for Dostoevsky, the only protection against crime is religion. It is interesting to note, in connection with the totem feast, that he regards the outcome of the secular view of life as nothing less than cannibalism. In *The Brothers Karamazov*, Ivan Feodorovitch says, 'If you were to destroy in mankind the belief in immortality, not only love but every living force maintaining the life of the world, would at once be dried up. Moreover, nothing would then be immoral, everything would be lawful, even cannibalism.' The liberal notion of 'the brotherhood of man' is, for Dostoevsky, a brotherhood in vileness; justice (cf. Freud) is simply the punishment meted out to those who remind men of their evil nature, and at the same time, by punishing criminals, men 'expiate' (vicariously atone for) their sins. Since from the secular point of view, everything is lawful, it follows that the stronger, or more cunning, man can break the bonds and sin with impunity (cf. Raskolnikov's argument), while the weaker is punished for being found out, for betraying the secret. Only by acknowledging the Fatherhood of god, is it possible to keep society from collapsing. When we tie this in with Dostoevsky's monarchism, we see that his belief could be phrased: 'No God, no hierarchy, no order', and in *The Possessed* we have his view of Socialism with special reference to Nihilism, as pure destruction, as the forces of disorder themselves; while one of the characters remarks: 'If there's no God, how can I be a captain, then?'[2]

Even if we think Dostoevsky's theology confuses certain issues, we can still accept his criticism of 'liberals' who imagine that justice can be set up on a basis of pure reason — that there is a mathematical solution, 'a square deal', for all social problems. It is to some such 'liberal', Bernard, a French scientist, that Dimitri contemptuously refers on several occasions. And what is more important, we can also recognise that he has presented parricide as a state of mind. The parricidal state of mind is worked out most fully in the case of Ivan, who, as was shown at the trial, was prepared to accept his brother's guilt rather than expiate his own. In him we have the struggle between religion and sensuality, between humility and pride, carried to the highest pitch — he seems to be a stronger and more refined edition of Raskolnikov. He can discover no sure foundation (no 'rationality') either in God or in 'Reason' (freedom from law); he struggles with his salvation. Dimitri is a simpler character than Ivan though just as stormy, and he is less intellectual. In the speeches of the defending and of the prosecuting counsel at his trial, the clever ideas of the Westerners are introduced, with the purpose of showing not only that the peasants on the jury are unaffected by this cleverness, but that the essential nobility of Dimitri (in spite of his vulgarity) shines forth against the meanness of the village student, Rakitin, who has been influenced by Bernard and affects Western ideas. Even the gentle Alyosha has base and sensual characteristics, though these are not brought out so clearly, except in the reference to his forgetting to visit Dimitri on the night of the murder and in the suggestion that he, too, had allowed himself, if only momentarily, to believe in Dimitri's guilt. His great sin would seem to have resided in the fact that he took pride in his humility, that he was conscious of his 'saintliness'. There is something very naive about Dostoevsky's account of how Alyosha entered upon his chosen path. Although no student or thinker, 'as soon as he reflected seriously, he was convinced of the existence of God, and at once he instinctively said to himself: "I want to live for immortality and I will accept no compromise".' In the same way, if he had decided that God and immortality did not exist, he would have become an atheist and a Socialist. It is to be noted, too, that while Dimitri, Ivan and Alyosha are content to remain Russians, Smerdyakov had turned away, like that other murderer, Raskolnikov, from the Russian way of life, and had set his mind on going to Paris, to be free and Western.

Secular virtue, then, is nothing but pride — a point which Dostoevsky drives home in the character of Katerina Ivanovna, Dimitri's betrothed who is in love with Ivan. She is a much more developed character than the corresponding Aglaia in *The Idiot*, and with her pride and nobility, is generally considered a type of virtue and high-mindedness; but Dostoevsky shows that her 'righteousness' is only a form of sensuality, and that it breaks down as soon as her egoism (pride) is attacked. In one of the earlier chapters of the book, Katerina goes through an elaborate scene of humbling herself to Grushenka, joining with her for the salvation of Dimitri; but when Grushenka plays a trick on her, showing mockery at her high-minded sacrifice, Katerina turns upon her immediately with voluble abuse — behaviour which is repeated on a greater scale at Dimitri's trial. Katerina at first gives evidence favourable to Dimitri, perhaps decisively so; and then, when Ivan has endangered himself by his evidence (though it is not believed), she gives further evidence, producing a letter that ensures Dimitri's condemnation. The legal procedure seems strange here, but the important point here is that we are presented with 'virtue' prepared to undergo humiliation before the world so long as *it* can feel great, so long as things go the right or flattering way for it. Katerina elects at first to be Dimitri's saviour, but she thinks she is equally free to damn him when things are not going her way.

Dostoevsky's attitude to women alternates between idealisation and contempt. He over-praises their intelligence and high-mindedness, only to cause them to fall into all the deeper baseness. The exceptions are the innocent victims like Sonia, and the simple comic characters like Madame Epanchin in *The Idiot* and Madame Hohlakov in *The Brothers Karamazov* — though there may be some contempt even there, for their secularism. At any rate, we have the important demonstration that high and mighty virtue is a form of sensuality; in trying to be self-sufficient, it fails to meet moral (religious) requirements. It is 'all too human' as with secular virtue in general, and reminds one of Shaw's pungent remarks in *Back to Methuselah*: 'I come to call not sinners but the righteous to repentance'.

In our final judgement of *The Brothers Karamazov* we must agree with Bennett's verdict.[3] There are magnificent scenes but the construction is imperfect, partly, it must be admitted, because the book is unfinished. We have to remember, too, the speed with which Dostoevsky had to work to make a living by his pen, not only for himself but for 'unfortunate' relatives and friends. There is, on any judgement, much irrelevant material due to the intrusion of a non-literary purpose — the justifying of the ways of God to man, instead of the presentation of themes with their own secular development; though the religious state of mind is eminently presentable, and is, in fact, presented very well by Dostoevsky. This book is especially great in its exposure of righteousness as sensuality and pride.

All things considered, Dostoevsky stands the aesthetic test. His theological or teleological point of view, while it induces him to bring in alien material and miraculously to bridge gaps in his structure, has freed him from the sociological interpretation of literature and has not prevented him from dealing in a solid literary way with persons and circumstances. Thus, *in spite of himself*, Dostoevsky appears as a Westerner, not as embodying 'enlightenment', 'reason' or the mathematical solution of social difficulties, but as presenting pure literary art with its human conflicts, its psychological studies. For him, people's merit is in their personal character — a belief which, however, weakens his treatment of redemption. Here a stronger social line might have brought out the problem more clearly, for no redemption is, in fact, possible except through movements; still, there is no doubt that Dostoevsky has strongly presented the psychological side.

Aesthetics is part of our heritage from the Greeks whose works have shown that the aesthetic is the unhistorical, in the sense that it is not concerned with the conditions of the production of a work of art; it is historical only in the way in which it shows how one phase of a work passes into another. Literature is not romantic uplift, with its Utopias and phantasies, its humanitarianism and belief in the unsullied goodness of the human heart. It is not a picture of social conditions, and it is not, as it was for Tolstoi, a means of improving men and women. A better life is measured by its achievements in art and science, not art and science by their achievements in social betterment. With all Dostoevsky's confusions, he follows in the footsteps of the Greeks and remains the greatest writer of his period — great in spite of his theology, great because of his psychological insight — indeed, one of the great writers of the world.

Farewelling friends, 1939.

– 27 –

R. H. Benson

It is the Roman Catholic position which R. H. Benson sets forth in his novels, and while his presentation of it is a fairly coherent one, the question that arises and is never far from the mind of his readers is whether art should ever be used as propaganda to the extent that Benson uses it. In his writings, an author cannot help giving evidence of the quality of his mind — a quality which is at its highest for the artist (and the scientist) when he can consider his subject with the greatest objectivity. His prejudices, his limitations, his general outlook will come through unconsciously, as we might say is the case with Kipling; but there are writers like Meredith, Shaw and Wells who, in addition, consciously endeavour to bring the reader to their theories of art or to their outlook on the world. Generally speaking, the more an author colours his work with his own prejudices, consciously or unconsciously, and the more he tries to *persuade* his readers to his way of thinking, the less aesthetically satisfying the work is. It is true that Dostoevsky, in spite of his fierce anti-Westernism and his strong religious beliefs, did achieve greatness, but these attitudes of his, although they had some drawbacks, actually helped him to the deeply penetrating studies of the human mind that made him outstanding.

Address to the Literary Society, 11 July 1935, reported in the *Union Recorder*, 18 July 1935.

R. H. Benson has been more hindered than helped by his Roman Catholicism. There is hardly a moment in his novels when the reader can forget that Benson is a Roman Catholic, with the result that his work has something of the flavour of a religious tract.

Benson's theme is much the same in all his novels. There is invariably a clash between the worldly (those who, whatever their religion, are tied to the things of this world) and the unworldly (not just those who care little for material possessions or for position, but those who, in some way, come into contact with the other — the supernatural world). Benson presents quite well the conventional outlook of the usual English county family, and there are some excellent satirical analyses of them in most of his novels; but in dealing with the 'otherworldly' outlook, he is not so successful in the accounts he gives of various mystical experiences. These are, for him, the means by which men may arrive at what is highest, for mysticism, he holds, is the highest common sense and gives knowledge of the world as it really is.

Like Meredith, though from a different point of view, he treats life as an ordeal, and curiously enough, he deals with the same stratum of society. But the difficulties of Meredith's characters are for the most part intellectual ones — the cultivation and appreciation of the Comic Spirit whereby they may be enabled to shed their illusions and see things as they really are. Those of Benson's characters are religious — the arriving at the reality of things by mystical experiences, by the overcoming of many crises and the enduring of many ordeals.

These characteristics are very well illustrated by *The Conventionalists* which is the best of Benson's novels. Here the conventionalism of an English county family is in conflict with the conversion to Roman Catholicism of one of its sons. It is only their conventionalism which is involved, for Benson shows that the religion of the family — that of the Church of England — is simply a part of their worldly life; that it consists merely in observances, and has nothing to do with the things of the spirit. The ordeal which faces the converted son is that of breaking, first of all, with his family; and then, later, of leaving ordinary life altogether to take up the life of a religious. This, after a struggle, he finally does; he has found his vocation.

It is in this work that we have, from the mouth of Christopher Dell, the important conception of vocation — the idea that the problem for everyone is to find his vocation and follow it. There will be various ordeals in finding it, but, having found it, one's main problems will be solved. And there are many kinds of vocation; there is the spiritual which leads men to embrace the religious life; there is the ministering vocation; and there is the ordinary layman's vocation. Since Almighty God has arranged all things, no man should judge his neighbour, for no vocation is better than another, and all men, whatever their vocation, have contact with higher forces, though the 'contemplative' or religious man has, as might be expected, a closer connection with them.

It seems to be the vocation of men like Christopher Dell and his predecessor, John Rolls, to help others to find their vocation, a work which we see in progress in *The Sentimentalists*. Mrs Hamilton has been consulting John Rolls upon the unsuitable attachment which has sprung up between her daughter, Annie, and Christopher Dell, who was, at that time, very far from realising *his* vocation.

Mr Rolls is speaking:

'We must not expect people to do what they cannot, neither Mr Dell nor your daughter.'
It was said so quietly that she did not understand.
'Nor yourself, nor myself, Mrs Hamilton,' he ended.
She was completely bewildered. But it was a comfort that he had included himself.
'Then — then what happens to responsibility?'
'We are responsible for doing what we can,' he said gravely.
This was very odd conversation; it was either the deadliest platitude, or the most startling novelty; and she was not sure which.
'Then — then what is the proper treatment?' she asked vaguely, hoping that she was making the right shot.
It seemed that she had; for the melancholy eyes instantly turned upon her full, and the drooping eyelids lifted. There was a new ring in his voice too.
'Ah! One must be nurtured and encouraged; the other must be broken to pieces. One is weak and the other deformed.'
'And how are we to know? And — and what am I?' she added on a sudden impulse.

She felt that she was being intelligent, but the feeling waned a little as he turned full on her.
'Do you wish me to answer, Mrs Hamilton?'
'Why, yes, of course.'

And here the conversation ends, while the rest of the book contains an account of how Christopher Dell was broken and mended, and we are told much later that John Rolls had informed Mrs Hamilton, to her great discomfiture, that she was a thoroughly conventional woman.

Benson's belief in vocation is one of the anti-aesthetic tendencies in his books. He goes beyond the facts of human life, straining them to fit his theories, arbitrarily assuming 'higher' ends and forcing them on the facts. Consider the difficulties of finding out, or of demonstrating, what a person's vocation is! For one thing, we are forced to assume the infinite God-like wisdom of a Mr Rolls or a Christopher Dell; for another, we see the results aesthetically of such a belief, in the weak pretentiousness of the excerpt quoted above. And if we say that a person shirks his vocation, what then! Could not the answer be that shirking his vocation *is* his vocation?

Now, in considering Benson's novels, we find it possible, so long as people actually have the beliefs he says they have, for them to clash with other people and things. But our view of the working out of the theme will be greatly influenced by our experience or non-experience of those spiritual (in the sense of supernatural) forces which to Benson are so important. If we do not recognise them as existing, we can only think of those parts of the novel in which they occur as not belonging to the working out of the theme, but as simply superfluous. What we have is the introduction of a part of the author's mentality. When, in *The Necromancers*, the cats are described as reacting to the evil forces called up by the séance, we not only have a false picture — we have something that interferes with the story as a direct presentation of experience. Benson is introducing into it himself, *his* mind, *his* beliefs, without making himself a definite character in the work (although he does this in a quite legitimate way in some of his other stories), and in doing so he breaks the logical development of his theme, and introduces incoherence.

Our difficulty in approaching Benson's work involves more than this; we simply cannot accept certain of his beliefs. When he deals with the questions of spiritualism in *The Necromancers*, the impression left with us is that Benson not only believes that the spiritual forces conjured up are more potent on animals than on men, but that these phenomena are the work of actual devils. He seems to believe in the 'possession' theory, of insanity, and in exorcism as a cure — a belief which, as we have pointed out with regard to Kipling's work, is a denial of learning, of the knowledge we have acquired that the bases of obsessions are in a person's own history, and are not imposed from without. In *A Winnowing*, we actually have supernatural happenings influencing the story — not just being believed in by some of the characters or interpolated for effect like the episode of the cats. Here it is related that the husband goes to Africa and dies there; and that, before his death, all sorts of weird things occur at his home in England, culminating in the news that he is dead. There is no organic connection between these events and the death of the husband, though we are asked to believe that there is; and the effect is entirely unaesthetic. Benson is a mystic, and will not let things develop naturally; he has to force on them supernatural connections which are simply not there.

Although *The Conventionalists* and *The Sentimentalists* are the best of Benson's novels, *None Other Gods* contains a great deal of interesting material. The story here is somewhat hampered by the mystical experiences of purgation and illumination through which the hero has to pass to final union in death. He is a complete failure from the worldly points of view, though from the spiritual, he has fulfilled his vocation. For it was Frank Guiseley's vocation to bring out people's true character — to show that the girl he was engaged to was thoroughly mercenary, that another character was really conventional in spite of appearances, and that a third was murderous. Here we have a more coherent picture of a person with a 'vocation' than in any of the other novels, for there do exist people who seem naturally, and without any special merit, to draw other people out. Prince Myshkin, in *The Idiot* by Dostoevsky, was such another, and though *None Other Gods* is very weak in detail, it is this fact of experience which makes it more credible than the rest of Benson's novels — so much so that the purgation, illumination and mystical union, the hearing of beautiful singing and the visions (all alleged experiences of Frank) do not affect us so very much and rather tend to pass over us.

These unreal elements that have been mentioned are a serious defect in Benson's stories, but some of his work is definitely good. There actually are such conflicts of belief as he depicts, and such social cleavages. Although he does, like Galsworthy, over-emphasise the English middle-class without reason (they are not of such social importance as he suggests), they are perfectly legitimate literary material. But he intrudes his own character and beliefs far too much into the stories, and affects at times an attitude of mock humility that is extremely irritating. His situations, too, often develop rather crudely and obviously. In spite of these defects, however, we can still appreciate his two virtues, his analysis of the worldly character and his presentation of various clashes in social life.

John and Janet Anderson, Sydney, late 1930s.

– 28 –

The Detective Story

The late nineteenth century and the early twentieth saw the greatness of the English novel which culminated in the *Ulysses* of James Joyce. After that came an abyss and there is no reason to expect anything good in this field for a long time to come. Like much of the reading matter of the present day, the detective story is not at a high literary level; yet that alone does not explain its great popularity. It appeals to many classes of readers from those who devour it for its adventurist qualities to those who look upon it as an absorbing literary puzzle. The aesthetic reader will be more likely to appreciate in it a sense of structure, a working out of a pattern — very external, it must be admitted, but something which he does not get from most of the literature of the period. There is a certain satisfaction to be derived from reading something that has a beginning, a middle and an end, like the detective story, instead of the formless 'slices of life' or the interminable family sagas which so often pass for literature at the present time. And beyond any attraction even of form, there are psychological considerations which give the detective story an unusual appeal. As will be seen, it is not, and it cannot be, concerned with the exposure of illusions, which is the function of all good literature, for there can be no deep psychological treatment of the characters involved. The detective story is really a type of escapist

---

The date of this address is uncertain: probably about 1947.

literature, which can provide a greater or less amount of catharsis for those who read it.

This catharsis comes about through an identification of ourselves with the protagonists in the presentation and the working out of the problems connected with the crime. If we take the Id as representing the 'unconscious' of all of us with its deep-seated feelings of guilt, these feelings find some relief, some outlet, in our identification of ourselves with the criminal.[1] But there is usually much more identification of ourselves with the detective and, generally speaking, the cleverer he is, the greater is his identification with our Ego — our conscious self. We may even try to beat him to a solution of the crime! In addition, we very often find in the detective stories a distinction between the private detective and the police — the representatives of the law — and it is with the police that our Superego, or conscience, is identified. So that it is not just by chance that a private detective and a police detective so often figure in the same story; they, as well as the criminal, arise from, and give satisfaction to, psychological trends in all of us.

Bearing these psychological trends in mind, we cannot help noticing that the private detective is usually made to 'show up' the representative of the law, by solving the case brilliantly while the latter is still plodding along like Inspector Japp in Agatha Christie's 'Poirot' stories; or demonstrating pig-headed authority like Major Smythe in H. C. Bailey's short story, 'The Quiet Lady'. Some stories do have a police detective as the main figure, but he very often exhibits clumsiness or slowness, as is the case with Inspector French. Occasionally there are eccentric police, more like private detectives, and their creators usually make it easy for us to identify ourselves with them, by insisting on their 'human' characteristics rather than their official ones — by presenting them to us as cultured gentlemen, with or without aristocratic connections. Such as Josephine Tey's Inspector Grant and Ngaio Marsh's Inspector Alleyne. One detective story-writer, G. R. Malloch, actually calls his police detective 'Inspector Ego', and the result is rather interesting. In his short story entitled 'In Confidence', the detective behaves in a very cavalier fashion to his superior officer, for which he is not reprimanded; he deceives the criminal by posing as a confidence man and being taken into partnership with him; and he brings everything to a successful conclusion. Here we have the satisfaction of every possible identification — the Id has a chance of an outlet, the Superego is tame enough to be understanding and tolerant and the Ego shows that *it* can outwit the criminal, manifest its independence and please its 'conscience' at the same time. This particular story is a humorous one and, of course, it is not concerned with murder.

Again, since the days of Sherlock Holmes, most detectives have had a 'fidus Achates' with them in their work. He is not always made use of in the mechanics of the plot, but he has a psychological function all the same. If the reader is halting far behind the detective in the solution of the crime, he need not despair, for he could hardly be more stupid or 'slow in the uptake' than a Watson or a Hastings, and so the Ego is not too much bruised. Dorothy Sayers, tiring perhaps of the plodding Inspector Sugg, has created an interesting friend for Lord Peter Wimsey in Detective Inspector Parker. The latter is neither stupid nor plodding, but methodical and thorough; and he works co-operatively with the private detective — he even marries his sister! Parker's very definite identification with the Superego — the conscience — emerges in the strictness of his personal life, and the fact that he has a mind 'blank to art and literature and exercising itself in spare moments, with Evangelical theology'. There are many other variations to be noted with regard to the Id, Ego and Superego (cf. the Queens, father and son), but whatever differences there may be between one detective story and another, there is always for the reader, more identification of himself with the criminal than with authority, and more identification still with the private detective than with either.

The difference between the various methods of detection also makes it easier for us to identify ourselves with the private detective. Not for him the taking of fingerprints or the lifting of footprints, the measurement of bullets and all the other procedures which require a laboratory and its apparatus! These are at the disposal of the police, though Austen Freeman's Dr Thorndyke is a private detective who not only possesses a laboratory but a laboratory attendant as well. The methods of Father Brown and Philo Vance are based almost entirely on considerations of personality and social type — what might be called the psychological methods of detection in contrast to the mathematically scientific treatment of material clues — methods which are more imaginative and less rigid than those of the authoritarian side.

In *The Benson Murder Case* there is a dissertation by Philo Vance on methods of detection where the use of material clues is deprecated and shown to be misleading — considerations whose value is demonstrated in *The Benson Murder Case* itself and in *The 'Canary' Murder Case* which follows it.* The purely cerebral method of solution is typified by Rex Stout's Nero Wolfe, and some way after, by Agatha Christie's Hercule Poirot with his 'little grey cells'. Common sense might be said to be the keyword for a story like *The Castle Rock Mystery* by George Gibbs with his 'folksy' detective, and particularly for *The Man Who Didn't Answer*, by Inez Oellrichs, where the murder is solved by a friend of the victim, neither a private detective nor a police officer.

The private detective, too, has less of an attitude of condemnation than the police detective. He can, and often does, let the murderer off, as Perry Mason does in *The Case of the Howling Dog*. Father Brown, as a priest, is concerned almost entirely to bring the guilt home to the criminal, and like Dostoevsky, evidently considers legal punishment more or less irrelevant, while S. S. Van Dine nearly always allows his criminals to commit suicide rather than face the extreme penalty of the law. There are not many detective-story writers like W. Stanley Sykes, who, in *The Missing Moneylender*, takes his readers to the gates of the prisons (there were two murderers) 'at eight o'clock one autumn morning where the assembled crowds were so great that the warders could scarcely get to the boards to pin up the final notices'. But this is made possible because the story, from first to last, is a police case — and much better than the usual type where a police detective is in charge alone.

It is when the writers of detective stories are on the side opposed to authority and the full rigours of the law, that there is a danger of their getting too human, of their bringing out the human situation too much. Dorothy Sayers has broken down the detective story by trying to

---

* Vance explains to his police friend, Markham:
  'Circumstantial evidence, Markham, is the utterest tommyrot imaginable. Its theory is not unlike that of our present day democracy. The democratic theory is that if you accumulate enough ignorance at the polls, you produce intelligence; and the theory of circumstantial evidence is that if you accumulate a sufficient number of weak links, you produce a strong chain.'

make her characters real, and thus doing away with the escapist nature of the work. For her, it is dangerous to take her characters right to the condemned cell to say nothing of the morning of the execution. In doing so, she exposes too much the social actualities and shows that detection by the private investigator is a rather mean thing. There is a serious breakdown in *Busman's Honeymoon* where the reality of things comes through with terrifying force. Lord Peter's man is reporting to Lord Peter's wife:

> 'If the condemned man is able to display a friendly spirit, the reaction is less painful for all concerned. ... they [the prison authorities] told me there that he continued to be a sullen and intractable prisoner. His lordship came away much distressed. It is his custom under such circumstances to ask the condemned man's forgiveness. From his demeanour, I do not think he had it.'

On the other hand, Erle Stanley Gardner has decidedly realistic elements in his stories. He exposes the law and the judicial authorities, and his fantastic criminal lawyer operates in the way of social satire and exposure. Here there is no breakdown because he does not probe too deeply into the human heart. His thumbnail sketches of characters and circumstances are brief but vivid, and his stories all have something of the fascination of the kaleidoscope — one shake at a particular time, and the clues form the pattern that Perry Mason has worked out in his mind.

Is there any good literature that could be substituted for the detective story? If we go back to Dostoevsky we find the unravelling of a crime in several of his novels. Like G. K. Chesterton and S. S. Van Dine, he is interested almost entirely in the ways of living of those concerned. Here, there is no private detective; legal mechanism does come in but it is not very important, though the various interrogations of the accused are presented with great skill and psychological insight. In the exchanges between Raskolnikov and Porfiry in *Crime and Punishment*, for instance, the whole sordid murder is unravelled. But the essential thing for Dostoevsky is to bring out the nature of crime and punishment as states of mind. In *The Brothers Karamazov* we find guilt and murderous states of mind throughout the whole family; and in

The Idiot, Prince Myshkin, the touchstone character, 'detected' murder before it occurred and sensed the fate of certain other people, for he identified himself with all mankind and felt their guilt within himself. Ivan Karamazov also identified himself with all men, for he knew their hearts were just as murderously inclined as his own.

So there would seem to be considerable identification taking place in connection with crime, an identification that is brought out in the mental states of characters conceived by a writer of the stature of Dostoevsky, an identification that takes place, whether we know it or not, when we ourselves are reading detective stories. Our Ego finds it easy to identify itself with the detective, who is generally made to appear a prepossessing person as well as a clever one. Our feelings of guilt are less obvious to us, but they are there nevertheless, and in order that the identification of the Id with the criminal should not become so strong that it breaks through and destroys the escapist character of the story, the author has to give the criminal sufficient unpleasant characteristics to keep us from sympathising too much with him.[2] Nevertheless we occasionally do find the 'sympathetic' criminal, particularly one who shows the same cleverness as the private detective, like the murderer in *The 'Canary' Murder Case*. And there is still another and very interesting identification possible, as can be seen in Lord Peter Wimsey's attempt to get forgiveness from the condemned man — he, Lord Peter, is the criminal, *he* is murdering the other, and because we identify ourselves so much with the private detective, we are all by inference murderers together (cf. Ivan Karamazov).

By and large, the human race must have spent a great deal of its time thinking about murder and concocting plans for discovering the murderer. According to biblical history, a murder took place in the second generation of mankind, when one of the sons of Adam murdered his brother. And Theodor Reik tells us that many primitive peoples (he mentions, in particular, the now extinct Abipones of South America and the natives of Madagascar) held the belief that no man died a natural death; he was always murdered.[3] In Madagascar, the usual greeting to relatives of the dead man was: 'Cursed be the magician who killed him!' Even when a man was a victim of a wild animal, his death was due to the magician who had entered into the beast, for the animal itself was considered harmless. Then followed rites and ceremonies calculated to discover the murder-magician, to find 'clues' that would lead the tribe to him. At first these 'clues' were magical, external to all the human beings concerned, and seemingly quite arbitrary. The murderer was to be found, for instance, by watching the direction taken by the first ant that walked over the dead man's grave. At a different stage of development, the 'clues', though still magical and arbitrary, were to be discovered by an examination of the personal belongings of the dead man, by considering the disposition of his limbs in death and the 'behaviour' of the dead body when the various members of his family or of the tribe approached the corpse. Closely connected with this last notion is the trial by ordeal which persisted until well into the Middle Ages, and which retained many magical and arbitrary elements even at that late date. The interesting thing, as Reik points out, is that the 'clues' of these primitive people were not so arbitrary as they seemed, but were really based on an 'unconscious realisation of repressed enmity' between the dead man and the man that they accused. This state of affairs, he contends, is not confined to primitive peoples; and he shows by various examples 'how many judicial errors of our time have no stronger reason than that a person was thought capable of the crime', and that this 'mistake of *psychological* reality for *material* reality connects the judges of London, Paris and Berlin with their black unlettered colleagues in spite of the difference in their cultural level'.

But this mistaking of psychological reality for material reality works in another fashion also. In some of the modern cases which Reik quotes, we find the accused, because he *has* harboured murderous thoughts against the murdered person, behaving as if he were guilty, and making few protestations of innocence because he knows that he wanted the man to be killed, because he is not at all sure that his murderous thoughts did not somehow lead to the murder and because in a confused way, he feels he deserves punishment for his evil thoughts. This belief in the omnipotence of thought links man with his primitive ancestors who in various ways (e.g., pointing the bone) believed a man's death could be encompassed by someone wishing it.

In connection with the need for punishment, Reik contends that the evidence for the condemnation of the criminal comes from the criminal himself. In primitive times, he was supposed to bear stigmata that could be easily seen — the brand of Cain, as it were, was upon his brow. In modern thought this is transformed into the view that the criminal always makes mistakes; though intelligent, he will stupidly give himself away, thus showing to the analyst an unconscious desire for punishment, for expiation. This is also part of the motivation for revisiting the scene of the crime, though here there seems to be a certain amount of excitement, of defiance — seeing if he can 'get away with it' — feelings which are at their strongest where the criminal offers help to the police, well knowing that he is needlessly risking exposure, and giving the police every chance to discover his guilt, but experiencing a wonderful feeling of superiority because he knows all about the crime — he knows better than the police!

Here we are reminded of the well-known procedure of the police and of the detective — that of reconstructing the crime, and of the question whether the detective, in running the criminal to earth, is repeating the crime. Some such notion is suggested at the end of *Busman's Honeymoon* when Lord Peter Wimsey asks the forgiveness of the man he has been instrumental in putting into the condemned cell. Reik contends that, in the psycho-analytical history of crime and punishment, there is no expiation possible without repetition of the crime. This is the basis of what he calls the 'oral ordeal', which consisted in its earliest form in the accused having to eat the flesh of the murdered man — a practice which had its roots in past history when killing was synonymous with eating. Under this ordeal, the guilty man falls ill or dies, while the innocent is quite unharmed. In the Middle Ages, it was believed that a guilty man would die if he took Holy Communion, while an innocent one might receive the Host without any ill effects.

An even more remarkable persistence of these primitive beliefs appears in some religious practices today.

> The oral ordeal ... reminds us in many respects of an element in primitive religion — the solemn killing and eating of the totem animal. ... in the totem meal, all commit the crime once more; but the community sanctions it and so the crime becomes a duty. Like war, it is a crime ordered by society, and it probably awakened the same feelings in our ancestors as the order by the state for mass murder does in us. By participating in the killing and eating of the flesh and blood of the

totem animal all have repeated the old deed and satisfied the instincts which come to expression in the act. This satisfaction ... unites the participants with the totem and among themselves, and guarantees future abstinence. This collective ordeal ... is without a doubt a sacred repetition of an otherwise forbidden deed. This characteristic still appears in the Christian Eucharist.[4] [Cf. Freud in *Totem and Taboo*, Dostoevsky's belief that religion is the only protection against crime, and Stephen Dedalus's wild cry of 'The Corpsechewer!' when his dead mother appears to him in the night-gown scene.]

Reik also draws attention to the misleading character of clues — not only the material ones which Philo Vance deplores, and the scientific, almost 'magical' ones of modern science, but the psychological ones as well. Referring to the difference between deed and intent, he quotes Dostoevsky, who says in *The Brothers Karamazov*: 'Psychology is a stick with two ends', and thus we are not surprised to find that he is opposed to the view that psycho-analysts should be called in to assist judicial procedure if this means that they are to help determine guilt. Unsatisfactory as all clues are, this psychological material has not even the certainty of such clues. Freud says: 'It does not matter who has really done the deed; it only matters to psychology who has willed it emotionally and welcomed it when it was done.' 'These words,' adds Reik, 'not only determine the extent of psychological interest, but also the limits of its competency. The solution of guilt lies beyond its scope.' But he is in favour of judges and magistrates studying the science of psychiatry, so that they may realise how unreliable are the data on which they base their judgements.

Finally (the last of a series of references to Reik which have necessarily been incomplete and fragmentary), it has to be pointed out that murder has *always* been regarded as the most serious of crimes, and that, even today, an unexplained murder has for many people an uncanny quality which no other unexplained crime has. 'The special feeling connected with the deed is one of pronounced psychological uncertainty, as if we ourselves and those dear to us were exposed to unknown dangers.' It is as if we were back to the old belief in the omnipotence of thought — in the possibility of murder by thought. And as most of us at some time or other have wished the death of someone, so now we fear that any or all of us may be killed at any moment by the unknown murderer who may be among those we know; and, what is worse, that we ourselves may even be the murderer. When, however, he is caught, we return comforted (according to Reik), to our sensible, sober world, convinced for the time being that no murder can be accomplished by thought alone; and what is more comforting still, that not we 'but somebody else is the murderer'.

– 29 –
Orage and the *New Age* Circle

Admirers of the *New Age* in its palmy days (of at least a decade preceding 1919, when it became infected by the Douglas blight) would naturally look with interest to these 'reminiscences and reflections' by a regular contributor from 1911 onwards, but any expectations they had formed of some fresh insight into what must be one of the most amazing performances in the history of journalism would be disappointed. Despite Selver's claim that he is 'jotting down a strict minimum of personalia', his story is largely a record of his own productions, interests, antipathies and attachments; and his devotion to Orage in particular has not enabled him to convey any clear notion of the character and achievement of that interesting figure.[1]

Thus, while indicating how much he himself was repelled by Major Douglas, Selver is confessedly baffled by the favourable view Orage took both of Douglas's personality and of his doctrine and makes no attempt to show from what *weakness* of character or intellect his hero's conversion to the 'scheme' arose. He is puzzled again on the question of religion; he says, with reference to certain pronouncements of Orage in his later years on the 'search for God', that it would never have occurred to him that the man he had known would be seriously concerned

---

This article was originally titled 'Amazing Journalists' and appeared as a review of Paul Selver's book, *Orage and the New Age Circle*, in the *Observer*, V, 3, 1960.

with this — though discussion of the literature of Indian religion in particular had been a regular (and to some of us rather irksome) feature of the *New Age*, and especially of Orage's own contributions, for most of its 'classic' period.

That Orage did not take a conventional or institutional view of religion is clear enough from his remarks, quoted by Selver at the end of the book, on the general question of culture and the special problem of 'disinterestedness'. 'No word in the English language,' says Orage,

> is more difficult to define or better worth attempting to define. Somewhere or other in its capacious folds it contains all the ideas of ethics and even, I should say, of religion. The *Bhagavad Gita* (to name only one classic) can be summed up in the word. Duty is only a pale equivalent of it. I venture to say that whoever has understood the meaning of 'disinterestedness' is not far off understanding the goal of human culture.

But while this position could be described as fundamentally secularist, there is no doubt that Orage combined it at all stages with dabblings in mysticism.

The main point, however, is that in his 'Weekly Review of Politics, Literature and Art' Orage was upholding the unity of culture; and this is a point that Selver entirely misses when, observing that he regarded many of Orage's followers as bores and cranks, he says that he ought to have borne in mind that literature was only one of the paper's *sideshows*. Certainly, there were many who read the *New Age* only for its politics, as others concentrated on its aesthetics; but those of us who read it from cover to cover, while we could hardly swallow Orage's statement that each issue was as carefully composed as a sonnet, emphatically did not regard it as a thing of bits and pieces. Any readers who could not appreciate Hobson on National Guilds or Penty (not mentioned in this book) on medieval history were thereby shown to have no conception of the *New Age* view of literature as a vital part of a general culture; and the propagandists of the National Guilds League, with the opposite emphasis, equally failed to grasp the interlocking of economico-political and literary-aesthetic criticism.

Undoubtedly, there was a certain propagandism in the attitude of the *New Age* itself — as is illustrated above in Orage's reference to the goal, instead of to the character, of human culture. But, just as what gave its cultural character to 'the Socialist movement' was Socialism as a form of social criticism and not as an object of social advocacy, so the positive content of the doctrine of the Guilds was the place of craft in industry or, more generally, of 'the producer' in society; it rested on a view of *history*, a general standpoint of cultural criticism. In this respect, it is to be strongly contrasted both with the State Socialism it attacked and with Douglasism which, apart from its theoretical confusions, merely put up a 'scheme' and had nothing to contribute to the understanding of the major departments of social life. It is precisely in such cultural terms that the catastrophic descent to Douglasism from the previous *New Age* level calls for discussion. But, even at this late date, Selver's personal enthusiasm debars him from the critical appraisement of Orage and his work which this would involve.

It was the standpoint of universal criticism that made Orage (while he retained it) a great editor — even if he was not a great thinker or, apart from the forceful 'Notes of the Week' which put him in a class by himself as a political commentator, a specially distinguished contributor to his own paper. In this connection Selver compares unfavourably Arnold Bennett's column of literary comment, 'Books and Persons', with Orage's 'Readers and Writers' which succeeded it; Orage, it seems, though not so knowing, 'was deeper and subtler. Wittier too. Thus, to take only a trifling example, Jacob Tonson [i.e., Arnold Bennett] could never have written this: "Apropos of the *New Age*, I must have told somebody ... that its career is that of a rocking-horse, all ups and downs, but never getting any forward."' Presumably Orage said 'forrader', but the 'wit' is unremarkable, and those who have read the selection from 'Books and Persons' which Bennett brought out in book form will readily see the much greater vigour and ease of his style than of Orage's in the samples that Selver offers.

It is interesting to compare what Selver says here with Orage's own comment on Bennett's remark that his 'Jacob Tonson' articles *enlivened* the *New Age* during the years 1908–11; it was that the relation was reciprocal, that Bennett was stimulated by the *New Age* environment to express himself in an altogether freer and livelier manner than he could have done in contributions to more commercial publications. And this brings up Orage's conception of a 'free press' — a press not tied to the requirements of any vested interest and thus not 'respecting persons' but following the argument wherever it led. The right, provided by the *New Age*, of unfettered and disinterested comment had a stimulating effect even on the correspondence columns, which (allowing for a few 'bores and cranks') attracted many first-rate minds and illuminated, often through quite lengthy controversies, many fields of theory. But interesting as this was, the work of regular contributors to the paper was more important and here, while severe comment on loose thinking (and, in reviews particularly, 'letting daylight into downright rubbish') was common, it was not a question of mere slating, but the work was dominated by that conception of systematic and autonomous culture which Orage upheld. Criticism of that sort is lamentably rare today, when spurious productions like *The Catcher in the Rye* are given general credit for high originality.

It was his recognition and encouragement of a critical power which became creative that made Orage a great editor, his personal contributions being of much less value, though detailed examination of some of them (e.g., his 'Tales for Men Only') might be illuminating. Selver, however, backs his vague laudations of Orage by depreciation of other contributors. A. E. Randall, for example, Orage's lieutenant in the production of the paper, is described by Selver as having a cantankerous outlook which was 'peculiarly suited to the needs of the *New Age* and which enabled him to ring the changes, with a caustic effectiveness on his rather scanty stock of ideas'. But in fact, even apart from Randall's informed comments on plays and players in his 'Drama' notes (signed John Francis Hope), any serious student of his 'Views and Reviews' could recognise him to have, in addition to his critical power, a wide range of knowledge, illustrated in his treatment of legal and constitutional questions — of questions of politics, medicine, psychology — of the major subjects of strong public interest and weak public criticism. He was the first *New Age* writer to show an appreciation of the work of Freud, and his detailed textual account of Jones's theory of *Hamlet* contrasted notably with Orage's feeble rejoinders in terms of the vague conception of 'spiritual shock'. And though naturally, in contributing to a paper with standards, he

29 Orage and the *New Age* Circle

condemned more than he commended, he praised certain books, plays and actors just as decisively as he 'slated' or 'trounced' others.

Another main contributor to the New Age to whom Selver does much less than justice is Beatrice Hastings. His resentment at her attack on Orage in a pamphlet published in 1936 is understandable enough, though some of her contentions are certainly not refuted; but any weakness in her later writings that he is able to bring out in this penultimate section of his book does not entitle him to brush aside her work for the New Age as merely 'clever' or as exhibiting 'hit-or-miss' methods of criticism. His only other reference to her is the remark on an early page that she 'sometimes made her appearance' in the Chancery Lane ABC where the New Age circle foregathered. It would never appear from this that she wrote regularly and copiously for the paper throughout the time of which Selver is speaking. He commits himself to the statement that 'at a rough estimate' Orage, Randall and J. M. Kennedy (principal writer on Foreign Affairs) 'between them wrote more than half the contents of the New Age each week' — a claim which probably could not be substantiated for *any* week and which, for a good many issues, can be shown up by reference to the real signatures (not pseudonyms) attached to most of the contributions. But there were, in particular, many weeks when the contributions of Mrs Hastings (taking pseudonyms into account) were fully as extensive as those of more than one of Selver's triumvirate; essays, in general literary criticism as well as in its special form of parody, poems and stories distinctly more forceful on the whole than the 'Impressions of Paris' which Selver singles out for lukewarm commendation. She also took a leading part in the presentation of the *New Age*'s anti-feminist case and, in this connection, was the protagonist in its campaign against the 'White Slave' legislation ('flog the brutes,' etc.) of late 1912. Discounting so prominent a figure is no way in which to tell the story of the New Age.

Comment may finally be made on Selver's treatment of Ezra Pound. Though he made extensive, if somewhat irregular, contributions over a long period, Pound could not be classed as one of the *New Age* writers, but his position was sufficiently close to theirs to give it a useful impact on the paper's general contents. It is interesting to learn from Selver that, as some of us had strongly suspected, the 'Music' notes signed William Atheling — a particularly stimulating feature of the paper for several years — were by Pound; but it is astonishing to find Selver saying that they were signed 'Edgar Aethling', and the impression created by this and other errors is that he did not, in writing this book, refer to a New Age file. Besides this, the version of such musical criticism which Selver digs up from his novel *Schooling* is crude caricature, and the same may be said of the representations given there (but not quoted here) of the work of Randall and of Orage himself; they give the impression that the leading characteristic of New Age writing was cheap smartness and convey no sense of its *content*. (Incidentally, it is also misrepresentation to say that 'Ezra much disliked the piano'; Atheling's line was that the piano was a percussion instrument and was misused as a substitute for orchestra and badly played by many executants of considerable reputation, but he gave high praise to a number of performers who realised its possibilities as well as its limitations.)

It is mainly on poetry, however, that Selver is at odds with Pound and here, while his main quotation is of a passage he thinks ridiculous from Pound's later work, he makes no reference at all to the large body of writing in which Pound discusses the poet's craft and defends the standpoint of certain schools. There is no such discussion from Selver, but, while saying that this has not warped his literary judgement, he goes out of his way to condemn Pound's Italian broadcasts on the typically egotistical ground that 'I am bound to consider what would have happened to myself and to others like me, if the cause which he served had proved triumphant.' It is rather curious that he should speak of Pound as approving of the translations from a Czech poet which were Selver's first contributions to the *New Age*, since these differ little in poetic character from his translation of a poem by a Polish writer which, he says, was badly received by Pound's circle. What Pound upheld was direct treatment of the object, as against mere narration or the issuing of manifestos like that of the 'rebellious coal-miner' who, in the work of the Czech poet, predicted a 'day of reckoning' for his masters. To call this 'revolutionary' poetry, as Selver does, is to show oneself limited to *prose* content. And it would seem that Beatrice Hastings was so far right, in taking Orage to be opposed to creative work, that he also had this prosaic outlook and expected poetry to have 'lessons'.

However, in emphasising Selver's inability to bring out Orage's weaknesses, I would affirm just as strongly that he has little sense of the *New Age*'s solid achievements under Orage's guidance, of its great contributions to politics and aesthetics and to the critical treatment of human problems generally. The *New Age* in its great period remains a source of stimulation for the student of culture, a mine from which material of the greatest value to scholarship can still be extracted. It is unfortunate that Selver's 'reminiscences' should be discouraging rather than encouraging to such potentially fruitful labours.

— 30 —
Music and Emotion

Inaugurating a series of Study Groups in connection with the Musical Society, Professor John Anderson gave an address on Friday, 15 July [1932], on 'Music and Emotion'. The meeting, which was open to all interested (as all future meetings will be) was well attended, and the address most interesting. The address was followed by discussion.[1]

Professor Anderson said that, rather than offer criticism of any particular musical work, he wished to indicate the conditions under which sound musical criticism is possible. We criticise music, and describe some music as being good and some as being bad. In criticising music, then, we have to determine as far as possible what the characteristics of good and bad music are. Prior to any criticism, of course, there are various technical considerations which refer especially to the various instruments (just as in painting, for instance, we have the technical consideration of pigments, brushes and canvas) — and after we know what a particular instrument can do, we may produce a work for that instrument; but those technical considerations do not determine the aesthetic value of the music.

As aesthetic criticism in music is part of aesthetic criticism in general, the same general aesthetic conditions have to be recognised in music as in any other art. We have differences of material and subject-

---

Holograph by Anderson, summarising his address of 15 July 1932

matter in music just as in any other art; and, to continue the analogy of music and painting, whereas in music we have a range of notes as our material, in painting we have a range of colours. Having, then, as our materials in music a number of notes or sounds which we may arrange in various ways, we have the treatment of these notes or musical materials as the object of our criticism.

There are certain views of art which endeavour to bring the arts together and identify their respective subject-matters. Expressionism, for instance, would maintain that in music we are concerned with the expression of a composer's feelings or some part of his mentality. The expressionist claims that what we are appreciating when we hear a musical work is just how the composer had managed to give expression to his feelings or his spiritual state. Thus, on expressionist's showing we would have, in the arts, merely different ways of expressing feelings, and the arts would be concerned with expressing certain spiritual states. In that case we could translate a piece of music into poetry or painting, for example, and in general have an expression of the same feelings or the same spiritual state.

The question arises: why don't we consider simply feelings, and not the works themselves? The answer to this is that, in the case of music for example, musical art is definitely concerned with musical sound, just as painting is concerned with colours; and if there were not these distinctions (i.e., in materials) we could not critically distinguish the arts at all.

The emotional interpretation of music is common. We say of this music that it is cheerful, and of that music that it is sad. Yet the sounds themselves are not cheerful or sad. We are referring rather to the feelings that the sounds occasion, or maybe we are referring to the emotional state of the composer's mind. However, such a criticism of music from the emotional point of view must be arbitrary because the same kind of music or the same composition may occasion different feelings in different persons; it may occasion ecstasy in one person and sadness or boredom in another. Characterisation by effects, then, is purely arbitrary and of no sound critical value.

It may be said with reference to a musical work that the person in whom it occasions the right kind of feeling is the one who is really appreciating it. But this again would obviously be arbitrary, involving as it does the question of what kind of feeling a composition *should* occasion and the setting up of ideals which, coming (as they may) from different persons holding different viewpoints, may be quite opposed.

There must be definite characteristics in the music itself (i.e., the way in which the materials, notes and sounds, are treated). It is these characteristics that we want to determine if we are to have progress in the musical art and if we are to have any sort of musical criticism. Supposing that it is said that we do have certain spiritual conditions stimulated by a work of art, there are still works that we enjoy, and works that we do not enjoy; and we would still have to go further back and see why we do or do not enjoy the respective spiritual states.

We can have an aesthetic theory in art only by discussing the various works of art themselves. There are, of course, some people who would say that to criticise a work of art is to take all the joy out of it, just as explaining a joke takes away its enjoyment. This is not so. The analysis need not be cold — the critic may indeed be quite emotionally stirred in his criticism. The point is that if we do recognise that musical compositions have certain characteristics, we can go on and criticise them simply as working with certain sounds and show how the subject or theme is built up. With certain forms of music (e.g., the Preludes and Fugues of Bach, and the Sonatas of Beethoven), we have a definite plan of construction; and certain themes are taken and treated quite definitely. In other musical works, also, criticism must take the form of a search for the theme and a consideration of its working out. Moreover, considerations of this kind are not confined to music, but are common to all the arts.

In the appreciation of a picture we have an entirely different view of the picture according to which part of it we focus our eyes upon. Usually there is some central subject or theme which we can concentrate upon, and around which the whole is built up. We find the same conditions in music. It is the work of the critic both in music and in painting to bring out that central subject or theme and to make it as clear as possible. If he cannot do so (i.e., find a central subject or theme), the work, be it a musical composition or a painting, is a mere jumble and our fundamental criticism of it would, in effect, be that it was bad.

There is the romantic conception of art whereby a work is estimated by its uplifting effect. This suggestion of ideals, however, would only serve to take away critical attention from the details of the work itself. The suggestion of a meaning outside the work itself is made plausible by the fact that we have works in which music is combined with other material, as in songs and operas. But the contention that in these cases the music *means* the words or the action makes criticism too easy, and does not show why the different materials should be combined at all. It may be that the additional material puts us in a better condition to appreciate the music, but this does not make it part of the work of art. And it is more commonly the case that the mixture of art weakens critical attention to each. An outstanding example is the badness of the dramatic part of the operas, which would command no attention as dramas.

John and Janet Anderson, Sydney, 1941.

– 31 –
Art and Morals

Broadly speaking, there are two main positions adopted by those who seek to discern the relation between art and morals; the first is that art should be moral, or that it should support the conventional morality of its society — the other, that art can find its subject anywhere and should treat the moral and the immoral equally objectively. The second view, which has found reactionary expression in the development of a school of 'immoralism', involves the contention that the artist cannot be expected to concern himself with the possible results of his theme.

The moralising of art has been supported on a false theory of the 'expression', in the work, of the psychical states of its author or appreciator. In a piece of music, for instance, one would not expect to find moral qualities, and indeed they are simply not there, despite the fact that many would attribute the results of a musical performance to the music itself. They would say that a particular work encourages looseness, and that, therefore, it itself is loose and immoral. The tendency is carried to even greater extremes when psychoanalysts and others profess to discover sexual characteristics even in works of architecture. Combination of this Freudian view with the common

---

A report from the *Union Recorder*, 29 April 1937. This is Anderson's own summary of a paper which has been lost.

moral condemnation of sexuality takes one right up to the Puritan contention that art is something lustful and degraded.

But even if it could be established that the symbolism of art could be immoral, this has no bearing on the aesthetic question. Plainly impressions vary from one person to another, yet we cannot argue that because certain persons are affected badly by a given work of art, that the work itself is bad, still less immoral. Persons who are so adversely affected are simply lacking in education, so that art, by pointing to such deficiencies, may even be valuable as a social criticism.

The question is, then, whether we are going to allow the fact that certain people are unable to maintain an objective point of view to restrict our own appreciation and activities.

We may discuss as well the desirability of the artistic way of life. George Moore, for instance, in the *Confessions of a Young Man*, supports the advancement of art even at the expense of virtue. He is here simply reversing the view that good art encourages conventional virtue. The more important point, however, is that the artistic life is itself a good or 'virtuous' one. An artist cannot be held to be immoral simply because he presents a point of view not in accordance with convention; he is under no obligation to teach or even conform to what is nominally accepted.

The artistic life, then, needs no external justification but can be supported for its own sake. But if such a justification were required, it could at least be argued that artistic appreciation does refine one's senses and perceptions. It is only through these perceptions that we can judge life, so that the study of art may be said to help good living by making towards a finer estimate of things as they are.

In discussion, Mr Passmore raised the point that pornography was not essentially opposed to the moral code, that it might even be said to support conventionally accepted practices.[1] Professor Anderson indicated that this was not in any sense opposed to his own position, elaborating and extending his point by reference to *The Picture of Dorian Gray*. Among other points raised by Mr Partridge was the contention that the 'moral' critic often hedges by stating that an artist had stated *a* truth but not *the* truth; for example, Gould's criticism of Joyce. Mr Partridge and later Mr Passmore had something to say of 'poetic' justice and the popularity of 'moral' works. Mr Ward stated a view (disclaiming either authority or belief) to the effect that Shakespearian tragedy had a moral effect, insofar as it witnessed a 'refining fire' at worth or deficiencies of character. So it was that Othello was a very much better person at the end of the play than he was at the beginning. Professor Anderson doubted whether our inability to meet certain demands made on us was either tragic or moral.

– 32 –
Australian Culture

Mr P. R. Stephensen represents a certain trend in the outlook on Australian culture.[1] Of course many points he makes represent his special prejudices. For example, he says Christopher Brennan has not yet got recognition. This is a debatable point, for if Brennan represents anything it is European culture, as his studies in German and classic Greek show, so we cannot appeal to him.

There is a tendency for people's minds to be bounded by British traditions, and this is a definite limitation on culture. But if one substitutes some nascent Australian culture, one goes from bad to worse. The best way would be to substitute as a basis European culture.

The problem we meet with is that this is a community without local tradition of any great extent. Those of us who are not immigrants are descended one or two generations back from immigrants. Only in recent years has there been any cultural development. An attempt has been made to get a fake aboriginal touch about local culture, but it is obviously artificial. It is impossible to get British descendants to attach themselves to aboriginal tradition. There are naturally problems in which aborigines come in, but these could never be important in the culture of a British or European community.

Report from the *Union Recorder*, 14 October 1937

People breaking off from a culture in which they themselves formed a part cannot just transplant a new culture to a new country. And the difficulty is increased when the immigrants come from different places at different times. To have a developing culture you must have a traditional background. In a new community there are retrogressive tendencies, a habit of going back to primitive forms. It is not merely a question of transplanting British institutions. Time must pass before a new and settled form of life will develop.

There are peculiar facts leading to a more primitive character in literature and culture. The gold rushes, *et cetera*, tend to a development of a literature like that of Western America in the course of the last century. We get a literature similar to Bret Harte's, which tends to be sentimental and melodramatic, because of the rough and ready ways of life. That has influenced American literature generally in, for example, a group of humorists of the end of last century, of which Mark Twain is the best known. He is a good example of a provincial attitude. *Huckleberry Finn* shows that he has literary ability, but in his attitude to European culture in *Innocents Abroad* he exhibits a raw, would-be humorous attitude.

In an early culture the best kind of work will not be of a satirical character. But parody will be prominent even though there is no basis for good independent work. Harte's parodies of other men's writings are more forceful than his more original writings.

There is a good deal of Australian literature of the camp, but we cannot recognise that as a permanent feature of Australian life, and it would be artificial to make it especially Australian, since America had that kind of life as well and it has already disappeared.

What productions like Stephensen's are trying to do is to praise works simply because they are local products, even when there are European works much more worth our study. The proposal of an Australian literature course misses the point.

The study of literature is to give people a grasp of literary criticism and enable them to judge for themselves in any literature they may like to read, including that of Australian writers. There is no more an Australian literature than an Australian philosophy or mathematics. There is a world literature to which Australians contribute. We should not take up the attitude that we must praise even the best of Australian writers more than foreign writers simply because they are Australian.

We cannot always be feeling the pulse of cultural development. If good Australian writers come to the fore, it will be because of their contributions to literature as such and not because they are Australians. A writer must have a background. But the essential thing is to deal with men and women. It does not matter if they are Australians or Eskimos.

There is no question, then, of artificial stimulation or setting apart Australian literature for special studies, but if we in Australia develop cultural studies we will develop culture in Australia, because we are interested in those things.

— 33 —
Literature and Life

Professor John Anderson began by pointing out that discussion of literature was complicated by the fact that the subject-matter was presented not concretely as in sculpture or music, but solely through the medium of words.[1] Accordingly, it was quite commonly held that the words themselves had an aesthetic character independently of their meaning. He did not propose to go into that question but would treat literature as being what the words meant.

From that point of view it was a mistake to regard literature as 'imitating' life and as having its value in the exactitude of the resemblance. The fictional character of a great deal of literature lent colour to this view, but fiction could be appreciated only as presenting the same order of events of a certain type. It was thus in the same position as the science of psychology, the study of which involved a direct knowledge of the workings of mentality (or some species of mentality) itself, and not a mere imitation of it. It followed that biography was also literature; for, while it had to present facts which could be strictly dated, they were such as to constitute the development of some human character or the working out of some human situation. The appreciation of literature, then, was appreciation of human life — or, if we liked to put it so, literature *was* life.

As in the *Union Recorder*, 20 April 1939.

This did not imply the romantic view that all literature had a single theme, life, or 'the Meaning of Life'. It implied on the contrary, that literary themes had the same diversity as human situations had. Moreover, the single theme of the romantics was one that could not be presented but only symbolised. In painting we were presented with a flat surface and had to think of the three-dimensional structure which the surface might be said to 'represent' or, at any rate, which it brought before our mind. This was possible because we were independently acquainted with such structures. But the romantic 'meaning' was something we were unacquainted with apart from the 'slices of life' which were said to symbolise it, so that there is no standard by which the adequacy of the representation could be determined. Thus, in judging literature, the romantic had to fall back on the feeling of satisfaction or the spiritual exaltation that a particular work induced in him; in other words, his judgement was arbitrary and uncritical.

If anything could be said to be the leading theme of literature, it was criticism itself. The clash of human agencies presented in a literary work involved a clash between men's illusions and reality, and such illusions, or, at least the more abiding illusions, were of the romantic type — the finding of a 'meaning' which transcended mere facts. On this view, it was impossible to regard romantic literature (or the literature of 'escape') and classical or realistic literature as species of a common genus. The classicist had to say that romantic works were not literature at all, or, at the very least, that they were *bad* literature, since they did not work out a human theme in its own terms.

There was another current 'interpretation' of literature, which purported to be directly opposed to the attitude of 'escape', but which might be found itself to contain romantic elements. This was the view that literature was a form of social activity, in which a writer took part in and reflected the struggles of his time. Though it was actually maintained that all arts, even music, had not merely a social influence but a social content, such a view could not plausibly be maintained except in regard to literature, which did appear capable of dealing with social affairs and in which we certainly did encounter social comment. But, even in regard to literature, the view was false. The working out of a social theme was *history*, and should not be confused with the working out of a psychological theme, whatever connections there might be between the two. It might be true that special psychological types were thrown up by particular social conditions, and the literature of the period would tend to deal with such types. And it was certainly true that, in exposing human illusions, the writer would find himself opposed to prevalent social assumptions; and he might be subjected to censorship on that account. But this would still not imply that his work was of a social character — the literary artist should still be distinguished from the pamphleteer.

The treatment of literature as exposing illusions implied that it had an influence on life; if a reader came to see through his previous illusions, he would presumably live differently. In this connection literature would have a function not definitely distinguishable from that of psychoanalysis. It would, in any case, induce a refinement of perceptions such as Meredith referred to. It should be noted that the appreciation of good literature did not involve 'disillusionment' in the sense of disappointment, since that implied that the retention of the illusion would have been preferred; whereas the thorough rejection of illusion and embracing of reality would involve more vigorous activity. It might be supposed that the treatment of the writer as an exposer of human illusions meant the assimilation of his function to that of the critic. It was certainly the case that, in order to show whether or not a theme was worked out, the critic had himself to be acquainted with the subject-matter. Nevertheless, the working out of a criticism of a novel was not the same as the working out of a novel itself. But the fact that the artist was himself a critic (of illusions) and the critic himself an artist (in criticism) would permit of a close co-operation between the two; in fact, the establishment of schools of strict criticism would make for improvement in literature, just as literature made for improvement in ways of living.

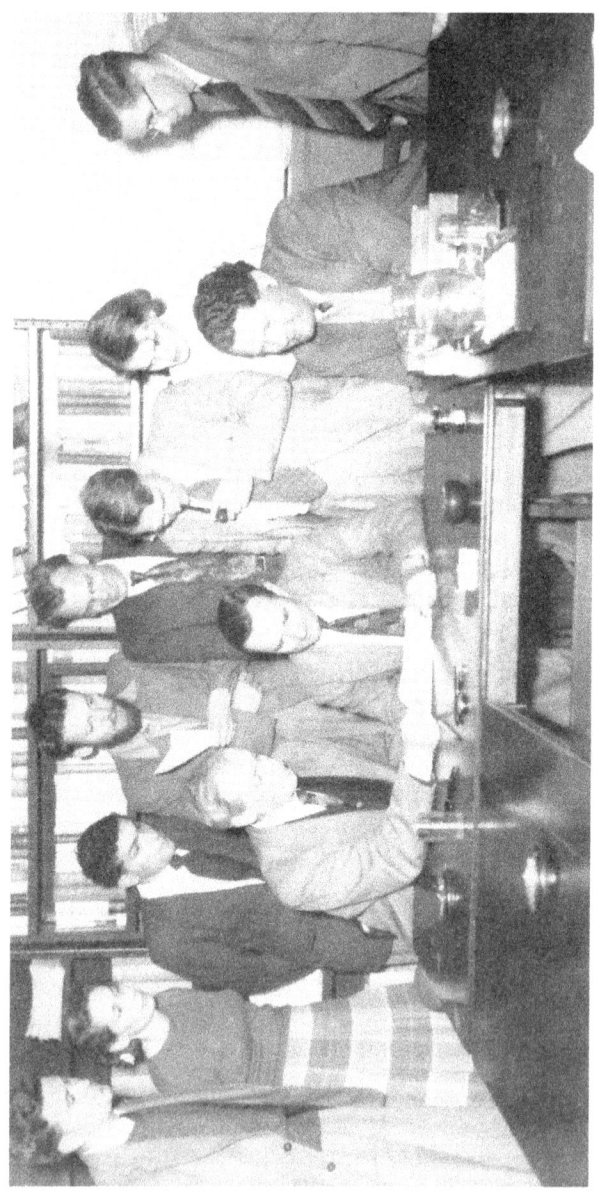

At a conference of Sydney philosophers, Newcastle, 1954. The formation of an alternative Australasian Association of Philosophy was under consideration. Anderson is seated at left beside A. Bussell. Standing left to right: R. Walters, Ruth Walker, M. Roxon, Sandy Anderson, W. H. Eddy, D. H. Munro, Barbara Roxon, J. L. Mackie. Seated at right is T. A. Rose. (Photograph: The Newcastle Herald)

– 34 –
Literary Criticism

On July 2, 1952, Professor John Anderson, M.A., of the Chair of Philosophy in the University, addressed a largely-attended meeting of the English Association on 'Literary Criticism'.[1] The address, which led to a lively discussion, has been summarised by the speaker as follows:

A major question concerning literary criticism is whether it is a branch of aesthetics, an exemplification, in a particular field, of quite general critical principles or is a special subject with its own special principles, differing from those of musical or of pictorial criticism, even though they are called 'criticism'. Professor John Passmore, in his article 'The Dreariness of Aesthetics' (*Mind*, July 1951) comes down on the latter side; for, while he says that *perhaps* the truth is that there is no aesthetics and yet there are principles of literary criticism, principles of musical criticism, etc., his conclusion is that the alternative to the 'dreary and pretentious nonsense' talked by aestheticians is not subjectivism ('it's all a matter of personal preference') but 'an intensive special study of the separate arts, carried out with no undue respect to anyone's "aesthetic experiences", but much more respect for real differences between the works of art themselves'.

A summary of an address, from the *Union Recorder*, 30 April 1953.

The view that in criticism we are concerned with a diversity of subject is, of course, supported by the consideration that the arts have diverse subject-matters, that in particular they do not all have a human content. Acceptance of 'expressionism', the doctrine that the understanding of a work is an understanding of the spiritual condition that gave rise to and is embodied in it, involves amalgamation of the arts; on that view, we should be able, by finding the 'spiritual equivalent', to translate any art into any other art. And the attempt to find what a painting or a piece of music is *saying* certainly results in a great deal of 'pretentious nonsense', and more particularly, in the substitution of accidental associations ('that reminds me') for actual content. This sort of view, then, gives no account of the work of art itself; and it likewise can make nothing of 'beauty in Nature', unless Nature is taken as also the work of an artificer. But such attribution of meanings is always arbitrary, and, in point of fact, what is appreciated in a landscape is not a set of interrelated mental activities but a set of interrelated shapes and colours.

Passmore is unjustifiably critical of the conception of beauty which he regards as having something 'phoney' about it. It cannot be denied that a great deal of vague and rhapsodical talk is passed off as aesthetics, but the same applies to ethics or politics and that is no reason for saying that there cannot be exact doctrine in each case. To deny that there is a common subject-matter of the arts is not to deny that there are common aesthetic principles (principles of beauty), and, failing such a basis, there would be no ground for speaking of principles of literary *criticism* — there would only be particular observations on particular works, observations little if at all removed from the 'that reminds me' procedure. Also there would be no ground for Passmore's distinction between formal and technical considerations in the arts; in default of a general theory, we should not know what 'formal' meant.

However, when we do know what it means, we have also to be acquainted with the material. We may speak, in literary as in other criticism, of 'the working out of a theme', but without knowledge of human beings we could not recognise a literary theme or distinguish what was from what was not its working out. It is true that literature heightens our understanding of human nature, but we could not appreciate literature at all unless we had some independent knowledge of human beings to begin with. Thus, in criticism generally, questions of content and questions of form (aesthetic principle) go together; but the principles are still principles of all art and of all beauty. In Joyce's *A Portrait of the Artist as a Young Man* Stephen Dedalus elucidates the aesthetic doctrine of Aquinas that three things are required for beauty, 'wholeness, harmony, and radiance' (*integritas, consonantia, claritas*). Dedalus finds these principles, indeed, to be involved in all disinterested perception, all recognition of things as they are in themselves independently of our purposes. We perceive the object as *one* thing, as a *thing*, and as the thing that it is. There is some difficulty about distinguishing the second and third principles; it may be argued, at any rate, that they are closely connected in our apprehension — that it is only when we apprehend a thing's structure that we apprehend its quality (*quidditas*) and vice versa. But the fact remains that there can be general questions of structure (or working out), however much qualities may vary.

Such questions would not arise if the principle of *unity* were rejected in the first place. This is the position taken up in Wells's fantasy, *Boon*. Boon accuses Henry James of having taken over from painting the conception of unity and imposed it on the novel. Why, he asks, since life is heterogeneous, should not a work of art be heterogeneous too? The answer is that we cannot make a theme of heterogeneity, and that, unless a production has unity, it is not *one* work of art. On the other hand, it is in the interests of unity that Poe demands brevity. But, in maintaining that a work in order to be good cannot be long, Poe is thinking more of the appreciator, of the conditions under which he can get a single impact from the work, than of the character of the work itself. And this seems to be just as unaesthetic a position as that which demands that a picture may be such that it cannot be appreciated at first sight or a piece of music at first hearing. There is an immense amount of aesthetic experience in support of the view that it takes time to arrive at appreciation.

This is connected with the quite real problem of presentation, of the artist's *bringing* the spectator to apprehension of the theme. Poe maintains that, in the work of the literary artist, 'there should be no word written, of which the tendency, direct or indirect, is not to the pre-established design'; even the first sentence, he says, should contribute to the effect aimed at. (It may be said, in illustration, that the first sentence of Joyce's *Ulysses* gives the effect of fantasy or unreality which is an aspect of the theme, estrangement from self, or, in its other formulation, 'hell'.) But, although the point is presented by Poe in terms of the relationship of writers to readers it is apparent that a directly aesthetic question, a question of the unity of the work itself, is also being raised.

Similar considerations apply to the question of *style*. It may at first appear as a question of impact on the reader, but if in fact the style (manner) is separable from the matter, if the rhythm of presentation is not the rhythm of the subject itself, then it is an obstacle to the bringing out of the subject and the work is a bad one. A rhythm which does not vary with the material but is externally imposed upon it is frequently to be found in Wordsworth, and is one of the conditions of the commonplace or pedestrian character of much of his work and of the 'unconsciously funny lines' which, according to Arnold Bennett, he constantly perpetrated. Bennett's example is

> Yea, his first word of greeting was,
> 'All right ...';

and a parallel instance is

> Why art thou silent? Is thy love a
> plant ...

That the four-three couplet also tends towards the commonplace and lends itself to parody may be illustrated, at the expense of Wordsworth and Browning, by the juxtaposition of the lines

> You know, we French stormed Ratisbon:
> She was eight years old, she said.

These criticisms, whether they precisely hit the mark or not, at least illustrate the point that it is by reference to general principles of criticism (here, the rejection of the importation of what is alien to the theme) that any particular literary criticism has force.

Further developments of aesthetics would take the form of showing more fully what is meant by structure or harmony. In my view the question is similar to that of definition in logic, to the setting out of the 'essential features' of anything. A theme is grasped when we recognise characteristics which together constitute it. Thus, if we took the conventional view of the theme of the *Iliad* as 'the wrath of Achilles', we should say that the goodness of the work depended on its exhibiting the 'moments' or leading features of wrath. It is to be understood that these features are not simply juxtaposed, that there is *development* from one to another or that (leaving aside the question of temporal sequence and taking a formula that would apply to any art) they form together an articulated structure.

But there is a special feature of the art whose subject-matter is human beings, in that a human being is not merely an aesthetic object but is also an aesthetic 'subject', that he not only illustrates principles but professes principles. It is for this reason that I have argued in my article 'The Comic' (*Hermes*, Lent Term, 1936) that, whereas in other arts the question is simply of exposition, in literature it is rather a question of exposure — since no dynamic account of human beings can be given without bringing out the contrast between their professions and their performances, between their imaginings and their actual situations. But this special feature of literary material does not imply that it is governed by any other principles than those which govern the rest of the arts.

– 35 –
Further Questions in Aesthetics: Beauty

We apply the term beautiful — or not-beautiful — to things whether they are made by men or not. Works of art belong to the class of things made by men, and we distinguish these from other things made by men by the fact that they are made within one of the traditional artistic fields, manufactured articles of any kind being considered outside these traditional artistic fields. And though it is not a question of drawing an absolute line of distinction between arts and crafts, nevertheless there are socially recognisable arts, and it is to works within those fields that we apply the term 'work of art'. Craft works, then, may be beautiful, but they are not works of art. And a work of art is not always beautiful; it could be *bad*, i.e., not beautiful, but still a work of art — still something made within those traditional artistic fields (literature, painting, sculpture, etc.).

Is beauty, then, a quality like red, directly recognised, so that no question need arise about what is required for beauty? Even Samuel Alexander does not look on beauty as a character of an object, and indeed, a realist position in this connection is very rare.[2] Of course, judgements of the type 'x is beautiful' are themselves rare — rare, that is, when 'beautiful' is taken in any strict sense. In talking of a work of art, more often we find the judgement expressed as 'x is good', a practice

---

Reconstructed from notes of lectures and discussions.[1]

that leads to confusion — to treating aesthetics as ethical. Strictly one should always say that a work of art is *beautiful* — or *not beautiful* — as the case may be.

One view that is often expressed is that those things are beautiful which are pleasing to us; it is simply, as it were, a question of liking, of taste. This, it is obvious, means variation in standards of judgement, and leaves no sort of distinction between the kind of liking we have for beautiful objects, for certain lines of conduct or for certain commodities. If we try to distinguish these likings, it can only be done in terms of what we find aesthetically pleasing, what ethically pleasing and what economically pleasing, so that, in spite of the adverbs, we are no nearer to an understanding of 'the beautiful' — the aesthetically pleasing.

In dealing with a literary work of art, the question of what we mean by beauty is obscured by various *personal* interpretations of the work — expressionism, romanticism, etc. (cf. *Some Questions in Aesthetics*). Although a musical work does not lend itself so readily to such treatment, there *are* people who admire *The Pastoral Symphony* because it 'reminds' them of lambs frisking in a meadow; and even a man like Shaw ascribes excellence to a musical work because of the 'meaning' he can read into it (cf. *The Perfect Wagnerite*). He has, however, to admit the existence of 'pure' music, which is a working out of a pattern of different sounds and rhythms. Literature also, it is contended (cf. *George Bernard Shaw*), consists of such a pattern which, by means of a sequence of phases or situations, presents in a particular work of art a particular psychological study. Judgement of the plastic arts has its own special pitfalls — in the main, that of representationism, which, in addition to expressionism and romanticism, etc., it shares with literature and music; but it is more difficult to get away from this outlook in the matter of painting and sculpture. A picture, a bust, a portrait are said to be beautiful or pleasing because they are 'so like' something or someone we know or recognise. But what merit is there in resemblance, however accurate? Do we really admire works of art on account of it? If so, we are making an aesthetic mistake.

For if this were the case, how could we judge a portrait if we had never seen the original? How could we judge the beauty of a landscape if we had never seen it or the flowers and trees and grasses that figure in it? *Any* photograph, on the grounds of its being an exact reproduction of a scene or a person, would be considered beautiful — which is simply not the case. Moreover, not every scene in nature itself is considered beautiful. Following our arguments in connection with music and literature, it might be said that appreciation of the plastic arts was concerned with the balance of the various masses which we find in any picture, and it is unimportant whether these masses are found in human material or in any other space-filling material. Can we say that a portrait is an exhibition of some subject in human nature (which would be representationism)? Or is it an exercise in form and colour, so that knowing that the subject is a man or a woman would help us to know what the structure of the work is? For instance, in a portrait, can a certain human complex be developed and worked out? Does it compose? Is it a human structure as in drama? Or is it a balance of masses so that if we know him we can say, 'That is John Anderson', though the excellence of the work will depend not on the accuracy of the resemblance to the subject but on the balance of these masses? My photo has made some people say, 'That is an idealist'; but idealism is not presented or worked out in it. If they were nearer the mark and said, 'That is a philosopher', we could still reply that even by looking at a bust of Socrates, we could not get a grasp of philosophy.

So just as in music we have an arrangement of sounds in time, we have in the plastic arts an arrangement of shapes in space, and it is the merit of the abstract school of painting that it emphasises this fact. But many abstract painters fail because they present us with a *flat* picture only — much like a pattern on a carpet, and do not achieve the presentation of *objects in space,* i.e., the presentation of three-dimensional material on a two-dimensional surface. It follows from this that a photograph may be a work of art (in spite of its origin), for the photographer can skilfully produce photos that enable us to observe a beautiful structure, the excellence of which will depend on the balance of masses, the arrangement of shapes — on the presentation of three-dimensional material on a two-dimensional surface.

In all art, then, we find some kind of arrangement; in literature, an arrangement of situations among human beings; in music an arrangement of sounds in time; in painting and sculpture an arrangement of masses in space. But all these arrangements must go to make a single work if it is to be beautiful; it must not be simply a collection of bits and pieces. It must be built round some *theme* forming what I have called the structure of the work. In the case of literature and music this theme is often enunciated quite early in the work by a significant phrase of words or of notes; in the plastic arts by a significant shape, or mass by focusing on which we get the structure which has been built up around it.

This is not to say that the artist always started with these significant phrases or shapes — he may be vague about it all. He may not even be concerned with the beauty of his work; he may be concerned with its saleability or he may just feel like doing something. But he knows roughly what a poem, a picture or a novel is (perhaps this is why he is not always the best critic of his own or of other people's works) and his most striking ideas may come to him as he goes along so that he finally produces something of an excellence that he had never envisaged.

Sometimes, however, the significant phrase or shape is not to be easily perceived; sometimes as in dreams (*Hamlet*, for instance, is not all incest) there are themes below themes in a complex work of art; and it is here that the discerning critic can help us, so long as he is as free as possible from the vices that beset so many people concerned with the arts, e.g., sentimentalism, romanticism, representationism and so on (cf. *Some Questions in Aesthetics*).

And having come to the position that structure is necessary in a work of art, i.e., that a subject must be 'seized', consciously or unconsciously, and everything in the work built up around it, we might argue that everything that holds together has structure. Even if we take the aesthetic view put forward by Joyce (following Aquinas) that all works of art must have *wholeness* (being one thing), *harmony* (being a thing), *radiance* (being a thing of a certain sort — a what), we could say that all things fulfil these three conditions. Are all things beautiful, then?

We have, for instance, the presentation of A who is a man. A is exhibited *qua* man, and the more the 'whatness' (x or manhood) is brought out, the more beautiful aesthetically is the presentation of A. For A is many things besides a man; A falling on one's head, for example, is appreciated not as a man but as a mass; but the more we're impelled to say 'That's a man' (and not to say anything else) the more we are appreciating *manhood* in him — the more we find him to be *beautifully* human. Here beauty would seem to be the typical or the characteristic (cf. De Quincey and a 'beautiful' ulcer). But there is here also a suggestion of *natural kinds* or of degrees of repetition of 'essence' (vain endeavours to get beyond the hampering of the particular); an attempt to find the eternal in the particular and in *Ulysses*, Joyce himself speaks of 'the beautiful or pure hell', referring to the hopelessness of the artist's task, for nothing is ever 'pure', or if we like to put it so, nothing in life or art is ever entirely 'typical'. Inessentials necessarily appear, but in art the question would always seem to be how far the work allows the appreciator to separate the essential from the inessential — how well the theme (x) stands out or is worked out; how well it is illumined — in a word, what 'radiance' it possesses. Thus aesthetic contemplation might be considered as the finding in the instance A what is involved in xness (whatness) where A is also Y and Z, etc.

It is interesting to note the way in which radiance implies the other two: i.e., (to avoid 'individuality' and 'natural kinds') it must be the wholeness and harmony of a *certain sort of thing* (as *one* thing and as having certain *phases* — order or structure).

So, although A has any number of characters, we apprehend his x or whatness as a certain sort of thing. And we know various things of that sort, and various characters they may have in common; we can even recognise a thing of that sort without having the group of common characters presented *in their interrelation and balance* (in which case we have 'that sort of thing' incompletely presented). In the address on Meredith, it was argued that *The Egoist* was thrown out of balance by the fact that Meredith seemed to be concerned to make him the 'perfect egoist', the model of an egoist, and had not introduced the necessary 'repetition with variation' (vide supra) which I have argued for in any work of art, by presenting egoism as it would appear in Laetitia Dale and Clara Middleton, both of whom lay claim to being egoists. Compare with this the various repetitions of loneliness in *Moby Dick*, of exile in *The Odyssey* or of wrath in *The Iliad*. And a perception of this would bring our appreciation of literature into line with our appreciation of music and sculpture, allowing for the difference of the material in which the artists work. The significant phrase in music is repeated with variations in pitch, in volume, in rhythms, etc., just as the significant shape in the plastic arts (the square, the oblong, etc.) is repeated in various ways, sometimes with the aid of colour, yet all working together to form an articulated structure of 'wholeness, harmony and radiance' (cf. *Literary Criticism*).

The excellence of a work of art* will then depend on how well the enunciated theme (or shape) has been worked out, how well it has been presented to us, no matter whether its creator has chosen novel or drama, etching or painting, sonata or fugue for 'putting it across'. The more we know of a certain sort of thing, the less we may be pleased with its presentation of it. Thus for a full appreciation of the arts, learning and study are required. Those artists who are 'not for an age but for all time' have nothing to fear from an increase of knowledge. This is particularly obvious in the case of literature, since all the latest discoveries of psychoanalysis have but served to show how truly the great writers built their structures, and how the Greek dramatists take their place with Shakespeare, Dostoevsky, Melville and Joyce in the examination and understanding of the human mind. No matter how many techniques may be developed with the advance of the sciences, the question for any work of art is the 'seizing' and working out of a theme.

People often ask how one does come to appreciate the beautiful and how one can come to judge the aesthetic value of a work of art. Just as there are people who have a natural aptitude for mathematics, for languages, for painting, etc., so there are people who have a natural aptitude for criticism, for appreciating beauty in the arts, in crafts, in nature. This is not to say that they do not require further training in the subject of aesthetics, or that others who have no natural aptitude may not improve with training also. Here the advice of Matthew Arnold is perhaps as good as can be given — to get 'to know the best that has been known and thought in the world'; and one can do this by

---

* While these remarks refer chiefly to works of art, it is to be remembered that the same principles of beauty govern the aesthetic judgement of craftworks and of works of nature. Thus the appreciation of a beautiful room is like the appreciation of a beautiful scene in nature. Neither is a work of art, but both can be beautiful if the arrangement of the masses is balanced — or harmonious. Our appreciation of a chair, table, etc. is akin to our appreciation of a piece of sculpture. They are the work of a craftsman, not of an artist in the traditional sense of the term, but they may be beautiful.

studying what has been considered beautiful throughout the ages, what has stood the test of time; by heeding such discerning critics as one can come upon and by eschewing what has been referred to as romanticism, sentimentalism, didactism *et hoc genus omne* (cf. 'Some Questions').

Nevertheless it must not be forgotten that it is, in the long run, by observation and experiment that we come to know aesthetics. Among the many critics and schools of criticism how, it may be asked, is one to judge? If we are really interested in any or all of the arts, we shall have observed such productions as have come our way; we shall have acquired some knowledge of the arts, and perhaps a little training in them; and we shall be in a position to make some kind of judgement of what we find to be the case, and this can be discussed. For different people may view the work differently; there may be different opinions as to what the theme is and how well it has been worked out, etc; but this is no prevention of discussion — it is an actual *condition* of discussion. And discussion will show us whether our position is tenable or not, whether it needs modifying or whether we can go on from it to make further discoveries, as one does in the learning of any subject. It is a condition of theory that propositions should be formulated, it being understood that they themselves are subject to misunderstanding — that there is always the possibility of error. Only in this way can a consistent body of theory be built up, for expressions of 'judgements' such as 'I like' or 'I feel', or even 'I think', lead to nothing but confusion.

A question asked in a letter[3] was whether 'the emotions in real life' are different from 'those we experience in response to literature and the arts'; and more particularly, 'whether we can assume any such difference if the same mental faculty is employed in both cases'; and the reply was as follows:

> I should not put the matter in terms of emotional responses; but it is perfectly possible to have aesthetic appreciation of the things and situations we encounter in ordinary life. However, ordinarily we treat things not aesthetically but in a utilitarian fashion; we are interested in them only in so far as they serve our purposes, and we ignore the characteristics of them which are irrelevant to our purposes — we consider them as means, not as they are in themselves.

In the study and practice of the arts, we learn to take up a detached or disinterested attitude — to leave aside the uses we could put things to, and to consider simply their forms. But this attitude can carry over into ordinary life. Having learnt detachment, we exercise it in everyday affairs; we find beauty in nature as well as in art. This is all the more evidently so since the materials in which the artist works (in which he finds or constructs forms) are not other than the materials of ordinary experience. The difficulty (apart from the question of utility) is that there are so many crosscurrents in ordinary life, that themes get mixed up and don't get *worked out*. At any rate, it is very much harder to see their working out than when the artist 'highlights' them or detaches them from their surroundings. But the main point is still the utilitarian (prosaic, pedestrian) character of ordinary life. The arts encourage the *effort* that is required to 'see the object as in itself it really is' (Matthew Arnold).

Of course, many take a quite utilitarian view of art itself (the famous Communist slogan 'Art is a weapon' is only an extreme form of a very common attitude), but one can learn to distinguish between an interested and a disinterested view of things other than works of art. In fact, a person cannot be thoroughly appreciating literature *unless* it sharpens his perception of human affairs.

And, it may be added, he cannot be thoroughly appreciating music and painting if he has to interpret them in terms of human emotions instead of appreciating them as structures in sound and structures in shapes.

Notes

Introduction

1 Professor Passmore's Introduction to *Studies in Empirical Philosophy*, and J. L. Mackie's 'The Philosophy of John Anderson' in *Australian Journal of Philosophy*, vol. 40, no. 3, December 1962, pp. 265–82. See also A. J. Baker, *Anderson's Social Philosophy* (Angus & Robertson, Sydney, 1979) and a review of that book by Henry Mayer (in 'The Critic', *Twenty Four Hours*, February 1980, p. 53) where he stresses the importance of Anderson's writing about aesthetics.

2 In the Archives of Fisher Library in the University of Sydney there is a holograph set of lectures given to an Honours Course in Philosophy in 1942 on Aesthetics, Ethics and Politics. In these lectures Anderson relates the central questions in these fields in an original and exciting way. Unfortunately we are unable to reproduce the lectures in this volume.

3 This is briefly described in J. Docker, *Australian Cultural Elites* (Angus & Robertson, Sydney, 1974) and A. J. Baker, *op. cit*. A personal account can be found in D. Horne, *The Education of Young Donald* (Angus & Robertson, Sydney, 1967). An examination of the summaries of addresses to the Sydney University Literary Society in the *Union Recorder* from 1930 to 1955 indicates that James McAuley, Margaret Mackie, J. L. Mackie, A. R. Walker, J. Passmore, E. Kamenka, A. J. Baker, J. W. Campbell, A. D. Hope and P. H. Partridge all addressed literary and critical questions in a manner suggestive of Anderson's.

4 For Anderson's reactions to a parallel problem in ethics, see the articles 'The Meaning of Good', 'The Nature of Ethics', 'Ethics and Advocacy' and 'The One Good' in *Studies in Empirical Philosophy*. See also Mackie's comments on this issue in the article referred to in note 1.
5 Stephen's elaboration of this view can be found in *A Portrait of the Artist as a Young Man* (Penguin, Harmondsworth, 1960), pp. 211ff.
6 In this, Anderson's sense of what artistic presentation is resembles Aristotle's account of dramatic *mimesis* in *Poetics*; particularly chapters 6 to 9 where Aristotle distinguishes between the 'universal truths' (Dorsch's translation) of poetry and the contingent truths of history.
7 Joyce, *op. cit.*, pp. 204–5.
8 These qualities are freshly displayed and defined by S. L. Goldberg in *The Classical Temper* (Chatto & Windus, London, 1961).

1 Some Questions in Aesthetics

1 In Anderson's papers there is a short, undated, holograph account of Rebecca West with respect to *The Strange Necessity*. The review was, perhaps, not published or offered for publication for fear of a possible libel suit. There is, however, a section which bears on this distinction in 'Some Questions ...'. After observing that West's talk of 'liking' *Ulysses* and her remarks about 'empathy' and 'conditioned reflexes' simply boil down to the assertion that she is *satisfied* by the work, Anderson continues:

> The utter barrenness of expressionism is well displayed — also its inherent snobbery when she argues that there must be a difference between Joyce and the pornographers because the most noted critics have found a difference.
>
> The realist comes out into the open; he says 'If you don't regard this work as beautiful you are wrong.' There you have an objective issue, which can be discussed; is the work beautiful or not? But the expressionist takes the superior line: 'If you're not able to see the beauty in this work, it is because you don't know how to aestheticise, because you are too coarse to feel your way into the subtleties of the object.' With the use of such *argumenta ad hominem* science disappears, and uppishness takes its place.

Notes

2 Anderson does not specify an edition but the quotations given here and below may be found on the indicated pages of *Literature and Revolution* (Russell & Russell, New York, 1957).
3 In *Breviario di Estetica*.

3 Classicism versus Romanticism

1 William Archer (1856–1924) was best known as a drama critic and translator of Ibsen.
2 J. M. Murry (1889–1957) was best known as a literary critic, husband of Katherine Mansfield and one-time friend of D. H. Lawrence.

4 Romanticism and Classicism

1 We omit a short note of Anderson's referring to a prior contributor to *Hermes*.
2 Anderson did not pursue the analogy any further. There is, however, a related claim in 'Classicism': 'it is not true that "the same language" is used by the learned and the vulgar … on the contrary, it is pre-eminently in *letters* that a language has its characteristic existence' (*Studies in Empirical Philosophy*, pp. 194–5).

7 The Nature of Poetry

1 Anderson makes a related point in 'Biography' (Essay 2 in this volume).
2 This is implicit in Vico's distinction between poetry, science or philosophy, and history in the *New Science*.

8 Poetry and Society

1 On Tuesday, 17 April, under the Union scheme for lunch-hour addresses, Professor John Anderson spoke on 'Poetry and Society' for the Literary Society. He remarked at the outset that the Literary Society, in its endeavour to treat literature scientifically, had had to take account of the social interpretation of literature and art generally, and in criticising that view had been led to consider in some detail the actual connections between literature and society. [From the *Union Recorder*, 7 June 1945.]
2 For a brief account of the hoax see A. N. Jeffares, 'The Ern Malley Poems' in G. Dutton (ed.), *The Literature of Australia* (Penguin,

Melbourne, 1964). The poems themselves along with introductions, commentaries and an account of the court case can be found in *Ern Malley's Poems*, with an introduction by Max Harris (Lansdowne Press, Melbourne, 1961).

3 A recent collection of Anderson's major writings on education is D. Z. Phillips (ed.), *Education and Inquiry: John Anderson* (Blackwell, Oxford, 1980).

4 In 1946 Pound was tried for treason in the United States. He was acquitted as being of unsound mind and confined for a period in a public mental hospital in Washington.

5 See 'Orage and the *New Age* Circle' (Essay 29 in this volume).

6 A similar point is made in, for example, *Aesthetic* Bk I, XVII and the conclusion to Bk II, XIX.

9 Art and Morality

1 See Anderson's review of a work on Orage in 'Orage and the *New Age* Circle' (Essay 29 in this volume).

2 For discussion of 'solidarism', see A. J. Baker, *Anderson's Social Philosophy*.

10 *Ulysses*

1 For an aesthetic way of making the distinction see 'The Comic' (Essay 6 of this volume).

2 In a manuscript note Anderson has evidenced the claim thus:

> Shaw's Peter Keegan in *John Bull's Other Island* discussed with a grasshopper whether Ireland is Hell or Purgatory; the remark of Don Juan in *Man and Superman* that 'music is the brandy of the damned' is recalled by the scene in the Ormond Hotel; while Shakespeare, in 'The Dark Lady', gives a romanticised version of the 'affirmation' in *Ulysses*.

11 The Banning of *Ulysses*

1 Anderson's point is a complex one in that 'illusions' here means both 'mistakes' of a certain kind and the readiness to be mistaken (cf. 'The Comic'). Among his papers there is a summary in point form of an address by Anderson to the Literary Society. Apparently he had promised to talk about *Love Me Sailor* but changed his mind and talked about censorship. Anderson seems to have talked about

prosecutions against writers, including Max Harris (cf. 'Poetry and Society') and remarks that this procedure is gaining ground: 'viz. proceeding against a person on account of the effects his action might possibly have, without any evidence that it *has* had such effects'. He then went on to consider both sedition and pornography. Point no. 4 reads thus:

> There is, however, this difference between the two cases: that 'treason', if committed, is a crime, whereas the act of sexual intercourse, to which 'obscene publication' might be supposed to lead, is not a crime. Thus, prosecutions for obscenity illustrate a second bad legal principle — that legislation should concern itself with people's morals. The vital point here is that people have entirely opposed views of what is moral, and it is not the function of law to impose the moral outlook of one group on another.

That contention was crucial to Anderson's social philosophy. In this context he went on to recapitulate his view of the artist, who

> in particular, is concerned to cast doubt on prevailing values; he is a heretic. That means we can never make the world safe for art, that the struggle of art against orthodoxy is a perennial one, that censorship will always recur.

13 James Joyce: *Finnegans Wake*
1 *John Bull's Other Island*.

14 *Exiles*
1 In *Honi Soit*, 20 September 1951, there appeared a brief report of an address, 'James Joyce and Freethought', which Anderson gave to the Freethought Society. In it Anderson was primarily concerned to distinguish Freethought from libertarian disbelief. He is reported to have discussed *Exiles*, and his central point qualifies the case he put forward in 1942. To quote from *Honi Soit*:

> *Exiles* is a drama of freedom. Richard Rowan is working with the notion of a life without bonds, love without bonds or a relation with a woman which would not even have the bond of love.
> While this would be an illusion and Joyce allows us to see this to some extent, he does not expose the illusion fully in the mind of Richard (and certainly not at all in the minds of the other characters).

This accounts for the fact that the play is unsatisfactory in spite of one's feeling that there is something important in it.

15 *The Applecart*
1 Cook (1855–1931) was General Secretary of the Miners Federation of Great Britain.
2 Taylor (1869–1945) was Professor of Moral Philosophy at Edinburgh University.

16 George Bernard Shaw
1 Dotheboys Hall is the school owned by a Mr Wackford Squeers in Dickens's *Nicholas Nickleby*.

18 *Emperor and Galilean*
1 *The Road to Endor* was an account of how two prisoners of war at Yozgad in Turkey won their way to freedom. It was first published in London by John Lane in 1919.
2 Mrs Anderson has observed that the ambiguity of the prophecy is more obvious in Norwegian where the same word stands for both 'empire' and 'kingdom'.

19 Kenneth Grahame
1 Anderson is probably referring to G. K. Chesterton, 'The Age of the Crusades', *A Short History of England*, Chapter VI. Chesterton there writes about 'the pressure of a general sentiment' and 'the cult of the Virgin'.
2 Mrs Anderson remarks: 'Several essays by Kenneth Grahame are to be found in the *Yellow Book*, including the unusual tale, "The Headswoman", while in a Bodley Head Monograph (1963) Eleanor Graham gives a very interesting account of Kenneth Grahame, to whom she was not related in any way. These were not used by my husband: the former because I don't think he had read them; the latter because by 1963 he was dead.'

20 Kipling

1 'D' in real life was L. C. Dunsterville. The long-suppressed biography by Lord Birkenhead, *Rudyard Kipling* (Random House, New York, 1978) tends to bear out Anderson's claims. See pp. 38–46 in particular.

21 George Meredith

1 Samuel Alexander (1859–1938) was Professor of Philosophy in the University of Manchester. Anderson heard the Gifford lectures which Alexander gave in Glasgow (1916–18), later published as *Space, Time and Deity* (Macmillan, London, 1934), in which this remark is made.

23 H. G. Wells

1 Mrs Anderson thought it would be fitting to end with a section entitled 'Prophet Wells', a holograph by Professor Anderson, found among his odd papers.

26 Feodor Dostoevsky

1 An article published in *Sozial-Demokrat*, No. 18, 16 (29) November 1910. We cannot locate the source of this translation, but readers might like to compare it with the translation on pp. 351–6 of D. Craig (ed.), *Marxists on Literature* (Penguin, Harmondsworth, 1975).

2 *The Possessed* or *Devils* (1871–2) was never dealt with as a whole by Professor Anderson. In passing he once remarked that he found in it an element of ill-nature, and that, for some years, he had been repelled by the grotesque and seemingly incredible political situation with which it was concerned. Later, he discovered that Dostoevsky had presented almost literally the position of Nechaev (who was connected with Bakunin) with its belief in 'general destruction for ultimate good'. These observations were made in a paper which was read at the Newport conference in 1941. The notes which survive are sketchy and bear on political rather than aesthetic questions. The political assassination in the book was, according to Aimée Dostoevsky, based on an actual case and Russian readers at the time were quick to recognise the originals of the various characters involved.

3 Found in the essay 'Turgenev and Dostoevsky' from *Books and Persons: being comments on a past epoch, 1908–1911* (Chatto & Windus, London, 1917).

28 The Detective Story

1 In this address, Freudian distinctions of the Id, Ego and Superego are made use of. Mrs Anderson feels that though these are not satisfactory for deeper psychological analysis, they are quite adequate for an investigation of the detective story.
2 Anderson neither gives nor tries to give any reasons or evidence to support this claim. It is an uncharacteristic paper because of Anderson's willingness to see the nature or significance of the detective story in terms of something else: a theory about 'identification' proffered in crudely Freudian terms.
3 *The Unknown Murderer* by Theodor Reik.
4 A quotation from Reik.

29 Orage and the *New Age* Circle

1 For a relatively full selection of Orage's own writings on literature see *Orage as Critic*, ed. W. Martin (Routledge, London, 1974).

30 Music and Emotion

1 This holograph differs slightly from the *Union Recorder* report of 28 July 1932. Clearly Anderson had submitted this as the summary of his address and the editor of the journal shortened it and modified its form for publication.

31 Art and Morals

1 J. A. Passmore, former Professor of Philosophy in the Research School of Social Sciences at the Australian National University, who was a student of Anderson's and who has been mentioned in earlier papers.

32 Australian Culture

1 Stephensen is perhaps best known as the author of the *Foundations of Culture in Australia* (W. J. Miles, Gordon, N.S.W., 1936) and as an advocate of Australian culture.

33 Literature and Life

1 This article is probably a summary of the address prepared by a scribe but approved by Anderson. Again the original paper has been lost.

Anderson clearly made a number of familiar points but also seemed to have broken new ground or qualified earlier arguments.

34 Literary Criticism

1 The paper has been lost and, again, the summary suggests that Anderson was articulating and facing some new questions which grew out of his earlier writing.

35 Further Questions in Aesthetics: Beauty

1 Mrs Anderson observes that this is a construction from more or less scrappy notes of lectures and discussions; from ideas jotted down on the back of envelopes or on any piece of paper that was handy when the idea occurred; and ending with a reply to a correspondent which Professor Anderson evidently thought important enough to copy and keep. There is little indication as to dates, but some of the ideas are not expressed in any of the other studies, and together they seemed to make a coherent whole. It is to be remembered that a good deal of it is tentative — 'thinking in progress' — and is meant to provide material for further discussion, for further development of a positive science of aesthetics.

2 Alexander suggests that 'the beautiful object is illusory for it does not as an external reality contain the characters it possesses for the aesthetic sense' (*Space, Time and Deity*, III, ix, D).

3 The editors have no knowledge of this correspondent. In the archives of Fisher Library at the University of Sydney there are a number of Anderson's letters to various people, as well as a set of articles on Anderson which are culled from sources as diverse as *People* and the *N.S.W. Police Gazette*.

Index

Aesop 109
Alexander, Samuel 197, 307, 321, 323
　Space, Time and Deity 321, 323
anarchism 245
Anderson, John, *Studies in Empirical
　Philosophy* xi–xxxi
Aquinas, St Thomas 303, 310
Archer, William 37, 317
Aristotle 111, 316
Arnold, Matthew xxiii, 196, 312–314
'Art and Morality' 77–88
'Art and Morals' 289–291
Art for Art's sake xxix, 8–9
'Australian Culture' 293–295
authoritarianism 77–82

Bach, J. S. 285
Bailey, H. C. 266
Baker, A. J., *Anderson's Social
　Philosophy* 315
Bakunin, Mikhail 149, 321
Baring, Maurice, *Outline of Russian
　Literature* 248
Baudelaire, Charles 9

Beesley, E. S. 52
Beethoven, Ludwig van 151, 153
　Pastoral Symphony 308
Belloc, Hilaire 129, 171
　The Four Men 171
Bennett, Arnold ix, 11, 93, 95, 210, 254,
　277
　Books and Persons 11, 175, 189, 193,
　　213, 214, 277
　Things That Have Interested Me 40
　Things That Have Interested Me (2nd
　　Series) 93
Benson, R. H. 257–262
　The Conventionalists 258
　The Necromancers 260
　None Other Gods 261
　The Sentimentalists 259
　A Winnowing 261
Bernard, C. 252
biography xxv, 31–34, 297
　'Biography' 31–34
Birkenhead, Lord, *Rudyard Kipling* 321
Borrow, George 220

Index

Bourne, G., *Memoirs of a Surrey Labourer* 171
Brahms, Johannes 136
Brawne, Fanny 183
Brennan, Christopher 293
Brougham, Lord 226
Brown, W. S. 207
Browning, Robert 10, 304
Buffon, Comte de 227
Bunyan, John
  The Pilgrim's Progress 204
Butler, Samuel 228
Byron, Lord 220, 241

Cabell, J. B., *Jurgen* 123, 175
Campbell, J. W. 315
Carritt, E. F., *Philosophies of Beauty* 15
censorship 77–84, 91, 101, 299
Cézanne, Paul ix
Chaucer, Geoffrey 184
  Canterbury Tales 68
Chesterton, G. K. xxvi, 143, 171–173, 269
  A Short History of England 320
Christie, Agatha 266–268
classic xix–xxiii, 38–40, 60, 114
classicism xxiii, xxvii–xxx, 98, 115, 214, 298
  'Classicism versus Romanticism' 37–41; *see also* romanticism
Coleridge, Samuel Taylor 220, 227
  'Kubla Khan' 51
Colum, Padraic 99, 108–110
comedy 175, 189–200
  and tragedy 59–64
'Comic, The' 59–64, 222, 305
Comte, Auguste 179
Conrad, Joseph 180
Cook, A. J. 131, 320

Crees, R. H. C., *Meredith: A Study of his Works and Personality* 190
Croce, Benedetto 12, 15, 75, 160
  Breviario di Estetica 15, 317
cummings, e e, *The Enormous Room* 202–207

Dante 95, 98, 117
  Inferno 40
De Quincey, Thomas 311
'Detective Story, The' 265–274
Dickens, Charles 39, 92, 143, 235
  Oliver Twist 235
  Nicholas Nickleby 320
Docker, J., *Australian Cultural Elites* 315
Dostoevsky, Aimée 321
  Fyodor Dostoevsky: A Study 244
Dostoevsky, Feodor viii, xxi, xxiii, 98, 118, 241–255, 268, 269, 312
  The Brothers Karamazov 244, 248, 250–254, 269
  Crime and Punishment xx, 95, 246–251, 269
  The Idiot 244, 248, 253, 261, 270
Douglas, Major 275
  'Douglasism' 277
drama 60, 238, 286
  and music 147
  of ideas 168
Dunsterville, L. C. 321
Dutton, Geoffrey 317

Eastman, Max, *Artists in Uniform* 74
Eliot, George 92
Engels, Friedrich, *Condition of the Labouring Classes in England* 153
expressionism 3, 7, 12, 15, 28, 45, 124, 156, 284, 302, 308, 316

325

Fabianism 130, 131, 145, 148
fabrication 17
Feuerbach, Ludwig 83, 85, 163
  Essence of Christianity 85
Flügel, J. C., *The Psychoanalytic Study of the Family* 55
Forster, E. M., *Aspects of the Novel* 212
France, Anatole, *Revolt of the Angels* 101
Freeman, Austen 267
Freud, Sigmund xxviii, 63, 108, 273, 278, 289, 322
  Interpretation of Dreams 111
  Wit and Its Relation to the Unconscious 195
  Totem and Taboo 251, 273

Galsworthy, John 102, 262
Gardner, Erle Stanley, *The Case of the Howling Dog* 269
Garnett, Constance 245
Gibbs, George, *The Castle Rock Mystery* 268
Gilbert, Stuart 109
Godwin, W., 220
Goethe, J. W. von 98, 118
Goldberg, S. L., *The Classical Temper* 316
Gorman, H. S. 23, 107, 124
  James Joyce: His First Forty Years 23, 93
Gould, G. 290
Graham, Eleanor 320
Grahame, Kenneth viii, 171–176, 320
  Dream Days 174
  The Golden Age 173–176
  The Lost Centaur 172
  Pagan Papers 172–174
  The Playway 174
  The Wind in the Willows 175

Graves, Robert 202
  Goodbye to All That 201
Hardy, Thomas 180
Harris, Max 72, 318
  Angry Penguins 74
Harte, Bret 294
Hastings, Beatrice 279, 280
Hegel, G. W. F. 149, 163
Heraclitus 122
historical novel, the 32
Hitler, Adolf 145
Homer xxx, 93, 98, 109, 117, 118
  Homeric material 84, 97
  The Iliad xx, xxii, 39, 41, 93, 305, 311
  The Odyssey xxii, 93, 94, 95, 311
Hope, A. D. 315
Horne, Donald, *The Education of Young Donald* 315
Huxley, Aldous 114
  on Art and Joyce 11–12
  Point Counter Point 9

Ibsen, Henrick 98, 118, 125, 131, 137, 140, 145
  Brandt 165
  The Doll's House 137
  Emperor and Galilean 10, 125, 141, 159–169, 247
  The Ghosts 137
  Peer Gynt 99, 167
idealism 3, 6, 15, 86, 138
imitation xxv, 41, 297

James, Henry 210, 211
  The Middle Years 10, 303
Jeffares, A. N. 317
Johnson, R. Brimley 222, 226
Jones, Elias, *The Road to Endor* 163

Index

Jones, Ernest, *Essays in Applied Psycho-Analysis* 6, 54
  Papers on Psycho-Analysis 54
  theory of *Hamlet* 278
Joyce, James viii, xxiii, xxviii, 18, 19, 21, 22, 68, 91–99, 101–103, 105–114, 115–119, 249, 310, 316
  Anna Livia Plurabelle 99, 108
  Chamber Music 22, 159
  Dubliners 111
  Exiles 86, 93, 98, 112, 121–127, 131, 319
  Finnegans Wake ('Work in Progress') 12, 102, 106, 115–119, 124
  poetry of 22–28
  Pomes Penyeach 22, 112, 122, 159
  A Portrait of the Artist as a Young Man xx, xx, xxviii, 93, 111, 113, 121, 159, 197, 303
  Ulysses xx, 11, 18, 40, 77, 82–88, 91–99, 105–107, 110–114, 159, 239, 265, 304, 311
  Huxley's remarks on 11
  the banning of 101–103

Kamenka, E. 315
Kant, Immanuel 81, 225, 227
Keats, John 184
  'St Agnes' Eve' 184
  'Ode to a Nightingale' 184
Kennedy, J. M. 279
Kipling, Rudyard xxvi, 16, 92, 116, 143, 179–187, 257, 261
  Actions and Reactions 183
  The Day's Work 182, 183
  A Diversity of Creatures 183, 186
  Life's Handicap 180, 182
  Stalky and Co. 185
  Traffics and Discoveries 181, 183

Lawrence, D. H. 114, 317
Lefevre, F., 'An Hour with Aldous Huxley' 9
Lenin 162, 242, 244
'Literature and Life' xxvi, 297–299
Lvovsky, Z., 'Soviet Literature' 5
Lyons, Eugene, *Assignment in Utopia* ix

McAuley, James 72, 315
MacDonald, Ramsay 131
Mackie, J. L. xiv, 315
Mackie, Margaret 315
Maeterlinck, Maurice 94
Malley, Ern 72, 74
Malloch, G. R. 266
Mansfield, Katherine 317
  Bliss 40
  'Je ne parle pas Francais' 40
Marsh, Ngaio 266
Marx, Karl 52, 130, 137, 148, 167
Mayer, Henry 315
Melville, Herman viii, xxiii, 219, 231–239, 312
  Battle Pieces 236
  Billy Budd 236, 237
  Clarel 235
  The Confidence Man 236
  Israel Potter 235
  John Mann and Other Sailors 236
  Mardi 232, 237
  Moby Dick xx, xxii, 231, 234–239, 311
  Omoo 232
  Pierre 234
  Redburn 232, 233, 237
  White Jacket 233, 237
Meredith, George xxii, 62–64, 116, 189–200, 219, 257, 258, 299
  Diana of the Crossways 191, 192
  The Egoist xxii, 193, 195, 198–200, 311

An Essay on Comedy 62, 189, 191, 194, 195, 198
'Hymn to Colour' 69
Modern Love 192, 196
Ode to the Comic Spirit 196
One of Our Conquerors 192
The Ordeal of Richard Feverel 190
The Shaving of Shagpat 189, 192, 199
The Tragic Comedians 198
Merejkowsky, *The Death of the Gods* 161
Millais, Sir John Everett, *The Cardplayers* 40
Milton, John, *Paradise Lost* 225
Monboddo, Lord 227
Moore, George, *Confessions of a Young Man* 290
Mozart, Wolfgang Amadeus ix
Mumford, Lewis 232–233, 235–237
Murry, John Middleton 40, 317
'Music and Emotion' 283–286
Mussolini, Benito 130, 145

New Age ix, 275–281
Nietzsche, Friedrich 95, 126, 137, 139, 195
nihilism 252
Nordau, Max, *Degeneration* 136
Norwood, Gilbert, *Euripides and Shaw* 20, 60

objectivism xii, 26, 195
Oellrichs, Inez, *The Man Who Didn't Answer* 268
Orage, A. R. 75, 79, 275–281, 318, 322

Panferov, F. I. 5–6, 9
  Brousski 5–6
Partridge, P. H. 290, 315

Passmore, J. A. xiv, 51, 290, 301–302, 315, 315
Peacock, Thomas Love 219–229, 233
  Crotchet Castle 33, 141, 220–222, 225, 228
  The Genius of the Thames 219
  Gryll Grange 219–221, 225–227
  Headlong Hall 219–221, 223–225
  Maid Marian 219–221, 224
  Melincourt 219–225, 227
  The Misfortunes of Elphin 220, 221, 224
  Nightmare Abbey 220, 227
  Palmyra and Other Poems 219
  Poems 222
  Sir Oran Haut-ton 220
Petronius, *Satyricon* 220
Phillips, D. Z. (ed.), *Education and Inquiry: John Anderson* 318
Plato 59
  Apology 247
  Phaedo 52
  Symposium 59
Poe, Edgar Allan 303
'Poetry and Society' 71–75
positivism 179
Pound, Ezra 74–75, 279–280, 318
pragmatism 179
presentation xix, xxi, 12, 17, 20, 27, 31, 32, 38, 53, 61, 67, 92, 116, 140, 153, 194, 200, 245–248, 257, 260, 303, 309
propagandism 114, 180, 186, 257, 276
psychoanalysis 168, 213, 299, 312
  and romanticism 51–56
Pushkin, Alexander 241, 245

Quaine, F. 9
Quarterly Review 227
Queen, Ellery 267

Randall, A. E. 278
Rank, Otto, *The Trauma of Birth* 6, 52, 56
realism xii–xxxi, 175, 179, 200, 211, 298
realist conception of poetry 69
realist position 16, 307–314, 323
Reik, Theodor 270–274
  The Unknown Murderer 322
relativism xv–xxxi, 12, 16
Renfree, Isabel 5
representation xix, xxv, xxvi, 13–17, 33, 149–154, 298
representationism 16, 28, 150, 151, 211, 308–310
Robertson, J. M., *Christianity and Mythology* 54
romantic xix–xxx, xxix, 17, 38, 40, 61, 93, 114, 138, 140, 146, 150, 174, 203, 211, 223, 236, 245, 251, 255, 298
romanticism xxiii, xxix, 17, 20, 40, 115, 124, 139, 140, 149, 159, 172, 175, 308, 310, 313
  and classicism 43–49
  and drama 61
  and dream-structure 48
  and psychoanalysis 51–56
Russell, George (A. E.) 106

Sacco and Vanzetti 210
Salinger, J. D., *The Catcher in the Rye* 278
Sarto, Andrea del 6
Sayers, Dorothy 267
  Busman's Honeymoon 269, 272
  'The Unsolved Puzzle of the Man with No Face' viii
Schopenhauer, Arthur 109
Scott, Sir Walter 32, 33
  Old Mortality 33

Selver, P. 275–281
Shakespeare xxii, 20, 37, 46, 68, 73, 98, 111, 194, 201, 237, 291, 312
  Hamlet 46, 62, 94, 106, 278, 310
  Othello 46
  'pessimism' of 73
Shaw, George Bernard 33, 93, 98, 116, 118, 129–132, 135–143, 189, 209, 214, 215, 257, 318, 320
  Androcles and the Lion 143
  The Applecart 129–132
  Arms and the Man 143
  Back to Methuselah 141, 146, 217, 254
  Candida 19, 125, 140
  The Dark Lady of the Sonnets 20, 139
  The Devil's Disciple 143
  The Doctor's Dilemma 135, 140
  Heartbreak House 143
  Major Barbara 136, 139, 140
  Man and Superman 141, 143
  Misalliance 20
  The Perfect Wagnerite 135, 145–156
  The Philanderer 141, 143
  Plays Pleasant and Unpleasant 17, 139, 143
  Pygmalion 33
  Saint Joan 136, 217
  Mrs Warren's Profession 137, 140
  Widowers' Houses 140
Shelley, Percy Bysshe xxiii, 220, 227
signified (and signifier) 47
Smollett, Tobias 235
socialism 85, 130, 145, 166, 245, 252, 277
Socrates 31–32, 52, 59, 247
solidarism 82, 137, 318
Sorel, G. 8
  La Ruine du Monde Antique 85
  Reflections on Violence 52
Southey, Robert 220

Stalin, Joseph ix, 130, 145, 166
Stephensen, P. R. 293, 294
Foundations of Culture in Australia 322
Stewart, J. 72
Stout, Rex 268
Stream 5, 9
subjectivism xii, xxx, 2, 26, 139
Swift, Jonathan 214
Sykes, W. Stanley, *The Missing Moneylender* 268

Taylor, A. E. 131, 320
Tchekov (Chekhov), Anton 124
Tennyson, Lord, 'Locksley Hall' 10
Tey, Josephine 266
Thackeray, William Makepeace 92, 235
Thamin, 'Saint Ambroise' 85
Thiers, Abbé L. 148
Tolstoi, Leo 241, 242–244, 255
tragedy 6, 17, 59–62
 tragic 169, 238, 291
Trotsky, Leon, *Literature and Revolution* 7–8
Trotskyism ix
Tukachevsky 166
Turgenev, Ivan 241
Twain, Mark 236
 Huckleberry Finn 294
 Innocents Abroad 294

utilitarian xvi, xxiv, xxix, 8, 68, 72, 116, 242, 313
utility 82
 and the consumer's view of art xxix, 87
 and master-servant relationship 82, 87
Utopianism 52

Van Dine, S. S. 268, 269
 The Benson Murder Case 268
 The 'Canary' Murder Case 268, 270
Vico, G. 68, 116, 162
 New Science 317
Virgil, *Aeneid* 39, 118
Voigt, F. A., *Combed Out* 203

Wagner, Richard 135, 136, 145–156
 Die Götterdämmerung 155
 The Ring 142, 146–156
Walker, A. R. 315
Walpole, Horace 195
Walpole, Hugh, *The Golden Scarecrow* 53–54
Ward, H. (Mrs) 193
Ward, J. 290
Warren, N., 'Letters of Ruth Draper' x
Watts-Dunton, W. T. 220
Webb, Beatrice 214
Webb, Sidney 131, 145, 214
Wells, H. G. 116, 209–217
 Ann Veronica 141, 146, 213
 Mr Blettsworthy on Rampole Island 141, 210, 213, 215
 Boon 211, 303
 Mr Britling Sees it Through 213, 215
 Christina Alberta's Father 213
 The First Men in the Moon 212
 The Food of the Gods 209, 210
 The History of Mr Polly 213
 Kipps 213
 Love and Mr Lewisham 213
 Marriage 210, 213
 Meanwhile 210
 Men Like Gods 209
 A Modern Utopia 209, 213
 The New Machiavelli 209, 213, 214
 New Worlds for Old 209, 217
 Outline of History 213

Possible Worlds 209
The Soul of a Bishop 213
The Time Machine 209
Tono Bungay 211, 213, 214
A Vision of Judgment 209, 214
West, Rebecca 316
Wilde, Oscar, *The Picture of Dorian Gray* 185, 290

Wordsworth, William xxiii, 44, 53, 92, 227, 304
 'Ode on Intimations of Immortality' 52

Yeats, W. B., 'Hosting of the Sidhe' 23

Zweig, Stefan, *The Case of Sergeant Grischa* 202

www.ingramcontent.com/pod-product-compliance
Lightning Source LLC
Chambersburg PA
CBHW062005180426
43198CB00037B/2414